THIS GREAT
STAGE

This GREAT

BY
ROBERT
BECHTOLD
HEILMAN

UNIVERSITY OF

STAGE

IMAGE
AND
STRUCTURE
IN
King Lear

WASHINGTON PRESS

OTHER BOOKS BY ROBERT BECHTOLD HEILMAN

AUTHOR

America in English Fiction 1760–1800
Magic in the Web: Action and Language in Othello

EDITOR

Understanding Drama (with Cleanth Brooks)
Modern Short Stories: A Critical Anthology
An Anthology of English Drama Before Shakespeare

TO
R. C. H.

FOREWORD

I AM grateful to the Research Council of the Louisiana
State University for a grant which permitted me to devote
most of the summer of 1945 to this study. During that summer I worked at the Harvard and Cornell libraries, and I
am glad to acknowledge the courtesies extended to me by
the staffs of those libraries. The staff of the Louisiana State
University library has been very helpful and kind; I should
especially mention the members of the Reference Depart-
ment, whom I have constantly troubled.

For their kind permission to use the quotations which ap-
pear at the head of various chapters I am indebted to the
following: Hermann Broch and the Pantheon Press for the
passages from Mr. Broch's *The Death of Virgil;* Robert Penn
Warren and Harcourt, Brace and Company for the passage
from Mr. Warren's *All the King's Men;* Professor Raymond
Short and Henry Holt and Company for the passage from
Herman Melville's *Billy Budd, Foretopman;* and Professor
Eliseo Vivas and *The Western Review* for the passage from
Professor Vivas' article, "Don Alonzo to the Road Again."

Since assembling the textual evidence on which my conclusions are based, and formulating my conclusions, I have
consulted, less with the expectation of ultimate completeness
than with the intention of doing a little more than a casual

vii

sampling, the works of various editors and critics who have contributed to our understanding of the complexities of *King Lear*. Though I have occasionally indicated disagreement, I have been mainly concerned to note the points at which my own conclusions are anticipated or paralleled or implied by the interpretations of other students. For, even at the expense of a rather bulky section of notes, I have been glad to claim all the support I could find for the different parts of my own analysis.

Besides having access to these public critical documents upon which all may draw, I have also had the advantage of expert private criticism from a number of fellow-teachers who have been good enough to read my essay in manuscript and to point out some of its shortcomings: Professors Cleanth Brooks of Yale, Leonard Dean of Tulane, Leo Kirschbaum of Wayne, Eric Voegelin of Louisiana State, and Robert Penn Warren of Minnesota. Besides receiving, from all of these readers, valuable help in numerous matters of detail, I am indebted especially to Professor Dean for suggestions with respect to general organization; to Professor Warren in my treatment of the materials in Chapters I, IV, V, and VI; and to Professor Voegelin in my treatment of the materials in Chapters I, IV, V, and X. Professor Kirschbaum I called upon primarily as a textual expert, and I found him an unflagging sentence-by-sentence critic of the whole essay—of its clarity and logic and strategy, indeed of all aspects of style and method. At his instance I have done much rewriting, and if I have not profited from his kind severity, the fault is mine. To Professors Brooks and Voegelin I owe an especial debt in that they have been not only good critics but good neighbors subject to daily call. I have called often and have learned, I hope, much. To them my debt is less the specific one of which a foreword can give a comparatively full account, than the intangible one owed to good teachers with whom personal association is a continually enriching experience.

ROBERT B. HEILMAN

Baton Rouge, Louisiana
December 15, 1947

CONTENTS

*A*nd take upon 's the mystery of things.

* * *

*W*hen we are born, we cry that we are come
*T*o this great stage of fools.

CHAPTER I

PRELIMINARIES:
CRITICAL METHOD

A POET and critic of a century ago said of the criticism of Shakespeare: "On Shakespeare so much has been said already that it might seem as if nothing were left to be said; yet it is the quality of the spirit that it will move the spirit forever." [1] A poet and critic of the present, commenting upon our continuing reinterpretation of familiar works, has spoken similarly: "A poem works immediately upon us when we are ready for it. And it may require the mediation of a great deal of critical activity by ourselves and by others before we are ready. And for the greater works we are never fully ready. That is why criticism is a never-ending process." [2] What are the greater works? Well, a recent essayist proclaims it as a mark of a "great book" that it "has the largest number of possible interpretations—not ambiguities but significances—each interpretation possessing a clarity and a force that will allow other interpretations to stand by its side without confusion." [3]

For two centuries *King Lear* has elicited a series of interpretations which, whatever their compatibility, would, by their frequency alone, establish the greatness of the play— if it were necessary to establish the greatness by such external means. Long after Goethe's time it is more than ever apparent that the "quality of the spirit" in Shakespeare's tragedies is perennially capable of moving the critical spirit. In a sense such tragedies, merely by existing, are an invitation to and a justification of fresh critical acts. Yet the individual act needs, perhaps, a kind of special introduction to the world which it enters, and that introduction might well be a statement of the specific readiness which accounts for the act—the relative and partial readiness, the readiness now, the state of the intellectual climate which encourages a new critical examination.

For the readiness is ultimately a kind of condition of the critical world: this condition makes possible certain modes of perception by means of which the individual critic operates. The methods upon which the present essay fundamentally relies will not seem strange to anyone who has some acquaintance with the techniques of poetic analysis that have come into general use during the last two decades. Recent criticism has been primarily concerned with matters of tone and with the function of central poetic devices—of irony, for instance, and the suggestive value of images and metaphor, and symbol; of the interanimation of the parts, and the sources of tension; perhaps a visitor from Nowhere, coming fresh into this critical world, would be especially struck by our concern to demonstrate that in the best poetry metaphor is not merely a prettification but rather a primary element in structure, the basic constituent in form. With the growth of our experience in such critical activities we have constantly extended our methods to wider fields.[4] To apply them to the language of drama is far from being a new adventure; yet in drama the structural problem has special complexities that require extensions and amplifications of the method. To these I shall come shortly.

The language of Shakespeare's plays has always been a stimulus to critics. Even in the eighteenth century, when bare problems of meaning at the level of reference and idiom, and somewhat narrow issues of propriety, absorbed a good share of editorial attention, some of the Shakespearians—as a glance through the Variorum will establish most easily—could on occasion sense how the poetry works. It is in Coleridge, of course, that a careful analysis of the organic quality of Shakespeare's language first begins. And today, for all of our accumulation of critical essays on this theme, it is possible that we have, for most of the dramas, not yet got very far into the close-fibered body of meanings and suggestions and effects which the language of a whole play comes at its best to be. We constantly hit upon new approaches. John Crowe Ransom, for instance, not long ago called attention to a poetic phenomenon apparently not before noticed—the creation of a particular kind of tension in Shakespeare's language by the introduction of Latinate phrases into verbal contexts predominantly Anglo-Saxon.[5]

The unique effectiveness of Shakespeare's language seems always to be present in the mind of writers who have had some direct experience of it. In discussing some other, though not unrelated, subject Montgomery Belgion sets down an obiter dictum: "For it is one peculiarity of a play by Shakespeare that its language instantly fills auditor or reader with a swarm of feelings, some distinct, many indefinite, but all of the nature of an exaltation." [6] One might wish to modify some of Mr. Belgion's terms: *instantly* needs qualification, and *exaltation* is woolly. But his direction is right; the "swarm of feelings" are indeed aroused; and they have various degrees of distinctness. Part of the subject of the present essay is the genesis of such feelings in the reader of *King Lear*, and my hope is to give some account, if only an imperfect one,[7] of the ways in which certain words and combinations of words affect the reader.

THE PROBLEM OF RECURRENCY

In *King Lear* the words do not work merely as individuals with a certain denotation and connotation; nor do they work merely in those elementary combinations which form syntactical or logical units. The problem is more than one of etymology, idiom, and parsing, and it is also more than the recording of metaphorical reverberations. For the student of *Lear* soon discovers that certain key words continue to be repeated more or less regularly throughout the play, and that such words thus become involved, naturally, in semasiological relationships which are different from those of the immediate grammatical context. Such relationships we shall have to explore—in order to account, as far as we can, both for the functioning of the bodies of related words as wholes, and for the enrichment of the single word which comes about through its being felt as a part of such an imaginative paradigm. Thus far I have employed *word* to denote any element of speech which we find in striking repetition; and I have used *word* simply as a lowest common denominator which could apply equally well to a verb or noun used with apparently complete literalness, with apparently no extension beyond the context, and to a verb or noun used in such an evidently symbolic manner that it seems scarcely to belong to a single context at all or else to have been borrowed by the context, as it were, from the play's central storehouse of meaning. For the reiterations that we discover are reiterations of families of terms, often of considerable qualitative difference, clustered about some root-idea—an idea such as sight or disease or age or sex. The problem of such reiterations is not a new one; it is perhaps known most familiarly through the term "recurrent imagery," which is regularly used by one of the most energetic investigators in the field, Caroline Spurgeon.[8] Miss Spurgeon, who defines imagery in a necessarily inclusive sense,[9] seems never fully to grasp the organic nature of the imagistic systems which she so fully describes, particularly their structural significance in the plays as wholes; [10] yet she goes far enough to give us a good start on the critical journey on which we must consider certain bodies of imagery. She speaks of the function of bodies of imagery in "raising and sustaining emotion, in providing atmosphere or emphasising a theme"; [11] symbolism in the tragedies, she says, "is closely connected with the central theme, which it supplements and illuminates, sometimes with extraordinary force, as in *Hamlet* and *King Lear*, . . . " [12] and she attributes our total response to *Macbeth* in part "to the subtle but definite and repeated action of the imagery upon our minds, of which, in our preoccupation with the main theme, we remain often largely unconscious." [13] To judge from these statements, Miss Spurgeon regards the discernible language patterns of the plays as having only a kind of auxiliary or supplementary role, being somehow outside the theme and yet pointing to it, perhaps in a choral manner. If this interpretation of her position is correct, she does not find an organic role for the

7

imagery but regards it merely as a kind of soft music in the background, helping to catalyze and amplify feelings which are to be understood as created by other means. Perhaps in drama, language must be regarded in such a way; yet in *King Lear* the evidence strongly suggests that the imagery groups are not merely theme supporters but theme carriers. When images become symbols, they become integrated into the total structure, and must be taken into account in structural analysis. But if Miss Spurgeon does not carry her study of dramatic poetry on toward such a conclusion,[14] she does considerable service in establishing the prevalence of recurrent imagery, in recognizing that it has at least an affective function, and in setting up an important critical problem.

My own concern, then, is with families of words and their functioning; it is not with the mere anthologizing of images and the classification of them by such subjects as animals, nature, food, drink, and so on; nor with the solitary image which does all its work in its own passage; nor with *all* the images in a play, but with those that are repeated and interconnected. This essay, then, has as its subject not images as such but the structure of a meaning in which images, whether the image words are used literally or figuratively, have an important role. Now in Shakespeare's language recurrency is an objective fact, not a figment of critics' enthusiasm; and this fact, simply by its presence, compels us to consider the mode of action of the words which are used recurrently. These words participate in two kinds of meaningful relationship. One is the conventional relationship to the thing denoted: *hat*, as a word, refers to a familiar kind of head apparel. If we say, "The man is wearing a grey hat," there is practically no problem of reference; the explicit

8

meaning of the statement as a grammatical unit is, for most purposes, the end of the matter. Yet to say this is not to say that the explicit meaning of the statement exhausts the possibilities of meaning in this combination of words. For the word *hat* has, or may have, several latent meanings or dormant powers of suggestion that under certain circumstances may palpably modify or amplify the express meaning of the syntactical unit. *Hat* may contain, in unresolved form, the ideas, say, of formality or decency or protectedness; that is, the word *hat* not only denotes the commonplace object but also serves, or *may* also serve, to set in motion whatever concepts may attach to *hatness*. What then arises is the question of when these powers of implication in the word are aroused and do invest a passage with something more than its literal meaning. Here we come back directly to the problem of recurrency. A recurrent word, as I have said, is found to exist in a dual relationship: one of its links is to the thing denoted, the other is to the sum total of uses of the word. All these uses constitute a community which by its very existence calls our attention to it and which, once we are aware of it,[15] sets up imaginative vibrations and thus imparts to us meanings beyond the level of explicitness. Repetition itself is a mode of meaning.[16] The trivial or accidental will not be repeated by a knowing artist, at least beyond the narrow limits of linguistic necessity; so that reiteration—whether we regard it as consciously planned or as a necessary mode of acting of the creative imagination which has not defined all its processes—invests that which is repeated with special, transliteral values. Briefly, it is the recurrency of *hat* which calls *hatness* into play, and *hatness* then is seen to have some thematic import in the work as a whole. The object named has become a symbol, and the critical task is the discovery of the structural role of the symbol. At some time or other, in some key passage, the symbolic value of the object (or status, or process) is fairly likely to receive an unequivocal statement, and it is of course such passages which are most quickly observed and critically discussed. But the way in which reiteration—of the symbolic object or of related objects or processes—extends symbolic meanings throughout the work sometimes calls for the further analysis. The symbolic significance of the blindness of Gloucester will be readily apparent to a reader of *Lear*; yet the reader may less readily perceive, throughout the play, a consistent use of the imagery of seeing and blindness which suggests that the literal meanings of seeing and not-seeing have passed over into the symbolic.

There are, of course, different types of recurrency which are empirically distinguishable. We might find, for instance, a series of references to hats, kinds of hats, hatlessness, modes of wearing hats, and along with these primarily literal, but not exclusively literal, references, a metaphorical use of hats—"His speech wore no hat," "He is high hat." It is this kind of community of words which especially characterizes the language of *Lear*, and which, therefore, furnishes us with our principal materials in structural analysis. But there is another possibility: the playwright may find it perfectly natural for his characters to make hats a direct object of inquiry or speculation, and hence to ask questions or draw conclusions about hats. "What is the hat?" "Why wear hats?" "Bareheadedness is the 'natural' state." And so on. In *Lear* we find at least one important instance of this sort of recurrency of *theme*: the subject is the nature

10

of "nature," and repeatedly characters inquire or make
statements about nature (and about a related subject,
justice). The relevant lines also form a community, but in a
different way from the group of images which become symbolic, for in these lines on nature the explicit, logical content comes closer to exhausting the total meaning; yet these
lines must be considered as a group because no single statement may be taken as a final theoretical formulation of the
issue at stake. What Edmund says about nature, and what
Lear says, are hardly likely to coincide. We can assume, of
course, that any statement of each is relevant only to its own
dramatic context, that is, the situation of the speaker. But
it seems safer to assume, as a working hypothesis, that, when
there is repeated speculation upon nature, the play is to that
extent an essay upon nature—an essay necessarily broken
up into parts which are apportioned according to, and probably modified by, dramatic necessity. It may never be possible to put together an adequate discursive statement of
what the whole play "says" about nature; but it is at least
possible to observe how the individual passages are qualified
by their contexts and by each other, and to see toward what
sort of conclusion they tend.

At this stage in the discussion, however, the sole point is
that a series of dramatic statements about one subject does
constitute a bloc of meaning which is a structural part of the
play. This bloc may be understood as one of the author's
metaphors. It is a metaphor just as a body of recurrent
images, with its burden of implications, is a metaphor. The
dramatist's basic metaphor is his plot . All of his metaphors
are valid parts of his total meaning, the search for which
must include a study of the relationships among the parts.

All the constituent metaphors must be related to the large metaphor which is the play itself.

RECURRENCY IN PRACTICE: THE PATTERN

The preceding is a relatively abstract, schematized statement of kinds of relationship which may be observed among passages in different parts of *King Lear;* how plausible it is as an account of the way in which areas of meaning are created within the play will naturally be decided by the individual reader. At best such theoretical statements, when divorced from the concrete materials of the literary work, are not likely to come off very satisfactorily. Yet it has appeared better to run the risk of seeming perhaps intangible, elusive, and uncomfortably detached from the dramatic substance now, than to risk the appearance of proceeding, throughout the analysis, without either plan or theory. Actually, of course, the theory of meaning would become apparent as the different patterns are discussed, and there is something to be said for the gradual unfolding of an interpretative scheme as the materials interpreted are presented. But the complications of the play itself make it desirable, I believe, to start by defining the boundaries and assumptions of the study. The assumptions remain to be tested by the evidence of the play itself, and obviously they can claim only provisional indulgence until the reader can inspect the poetic facts and determine what kind of poetic theory they justify.

Recurrency, as I have said, is a fact, and a fact that invites critical attention. Cleanth Brooks has already studied *Macbeth* in the light of its patterns of imagery and has shown how important the language structure is to the meaning of the play. He has not attempted to describe and account

12

for all the imagery in *Macbeth*, but, as his title, "The Naked Babe and the Cloak of Manliness," suggests, has followed through two images that are used repeatedly and shown how these images, extended into patterns of meaning, embody a good deal of what the drama has to say. They become symbols, he says, "which we must understand if we are to understand either the detailed passage or the play as a whole," and he adds, "If this be true, then more is at stake than the merit of the quoted lines taken as lines. . . . If we see how the passages are related to these symbols, and they to the tragedy as a whole, . . . we may have learned something about Shakespeare's methods—not merely of building metaphors—but of encompassing his larger meanings." [17] The important matter here is the stress which is achieved by his successive phrases, "the play as a whole," "the tragedy as a whole," "larger meanings": the key words which are repeated in various passages in a play have a reference not only to each passage but also to "larger meanings" that are integral parts of the whole meaning of the play. Mr. Brooks does not want us to forget that he is dealing not only with parts, but with a sum that the parts, though they are not arranged for formal addition, nevertheless do add up to; and it is with a statement of the sum that he concludes: "But with a flexibility which must amaze the reader, the image of the garment and the image of the babe are so used as to encompass an astonishingly large area of the total situation. And between them—the naked babe, essential humanity, humanity stripped down to the naked thing itself, and yet as various as the future—and the various garbs which humanity assumes, the robes of honor, the hypocrite's disguise, the inhuman 'manliness' with which Macbeth endeavors to cover up his essential humanity—between them, they furnish Shakespeare with his most subtle and ironically telling instruments." [18] Recurrency is aesthetically important only to the extent that it does in this fashion illuminate the general form of the play.

The subtlety and flexibility of the symbols in *Macbeth* are matched by the qualities of the symbols in *King Lear*. In fact, the special patterns of meaning in *King Lear* are so complex that it may be judicious, as a part of these preliminaries, to trace the occurrences of one family of images—images which occur relatively infrequently and yet tend to take on a symbolic significance which can be related to a central theme of the play. A passage which is apparently self-contained may turn out to contribute to and to draw from other parts of the play. For instance, there is the Fool's riddle: "Thou canst tell why one's nose stands i' th' middle on's face?" Lear of course answers "No," and the Fool explains, "Why, to keep one's eyes of either side's nose, that what a man cannot smell out, 'a may spy into" (I.v, 19–24). The Fool makes a good joke, and no one wants to ignore the fun. But in *Lear*—and indeed in Shakespeare generally—it is never good policy to dismiss a joke as merely a joke. Since the play, as we have already said, has a good deal to say about man's seeing and his blindnesss, *spy* inevitably calls our attention to the larger problem of man's sight and insight: to this problem we shall return. For the moment we should observe how smelling also becomes a kind of seeing—but not merely for the sake of the joke.[19] For if man can perceive by smelling, there is something to smell; and in view of what Lear is now learning about his daughters, the implication is that something evil-smelling is present. The Fool's joke alone would suggest this meaning; yet the meaning gains the force of a generalization about the whole world of the drama in part because of the support which it receives from other olfactory imagery in the play. At the very beginning Gloucester, referring to Edmund's birth, asks Kent, "Do you smell a fault?" (I.i, 15). Gloucester, whose capacity for distinctions is as yet unawakened, may be using his verb neutrally, as an idiom for *detect;* but here is an early suggestion of an unhealthy world. The suggestion is carried further by the Fool's epigram: "Truth's a dog must to kennel; he must be whipp'd out, when Lady the brach may stand by th' fire and stink" (I.iv, 125–26). The bad-smelling itself has come into the place of honor (and then Lear, who brought this situation about, can be called a "bitter fool" and the Fool, by contrast, a "sweet fool"—I.iv, 150 ff.). A little later the Fool varies the smell symbol: "All that follow their noses are led by their eyes but blind men, and there's not a nose among twenty but can smell him that's stinking" (II.iv, 69–71). *Stinking* is an ironic statement of Lear's loss of authority, and at the same time a comment upon the world that honors "Lady the brach" but deserts the true king; and to *smell,* as the word is used in this passage, is to see things as Lear has not seen them—realistically, with a view to one's own profit. Then there is Regan's brutal sneer at Gloucester after he has been blinded: ". . . let him smell/His way to Dover" (III.vii, 93–94). Here is an echo of the Fool's joke which makes a connection between smelling and seeing, an echo by a reversal of the original terms, ". . . what a man cannot smell out he may spy into." But there is the same secondary value. Although Regan, of course, is merely indicating contempt for blind Gloucester, her words push us on to another meaning:

15

Gloucester can smell his way because it is through the sense of smell that the rottenness of the world may best be perceived. The smell symbol became almost obsessive for Lear in Act IV, where, in his climactic mad scene, he fiercely describes the world that his kingdom has come to be: "They flatter'd me like a dog, and told me I had white hairs in my beard ere the black ones were there . . . when the thunder would not peace at my bidding; there I found 'em, there I smelt 'em out" (IV.vi, 97–104). *Smelt* is *detected*, of course, but it implies also the detection of a particular kind of world. Even more specifically, the evil smell is that of flattery; and so the passage recalls the Fool's earlier thrust "Lady the brach may stand by th' fire and stink"—Lady the brach, who is directly contrasted with the dog "truth." If there is still any doubt of the quality of that which is to be smelled, the doubt ought to be finally dispelled by the climax of Lear's ensuing twenty-five-line speech about his daughters. "Beneath is all the fiend's," he says, and he goes on to particularize: "There's hell, there's darkness, there's the sulphurous pit; burning, scalding, stench, consumption. Fie, fie, fie! pah, pah! Give me an ounce of civet, good apothecary, to sweeten my imagination" (IV.vi, 129–34). As a preceding line, "Down from the waist they are Centaurs," makes evident, it is lustfulness which Lear's words imply. But the passage is ambivalent, for, although the reader can connect Lear's words literally with the sisters' lust for Edmund, it is highly improbable that Lear has any knowledge of that triangle; so that lustfulness is actually a figure for their general corruption. That corruption is what *stench* ultimately symbolizes. And wholly just as Lear's accusation is, the lines that follow utilize the symbol in such a way as to destroy any air of the melodramatic which even the just accusation may have. When Lear finishes his long speech, Gloucester cries, "O, let me kiss that hand!" and Lear answers, "Let me wipe it first; it smells of mortality" (135–36). This may be merely an ironic comment on his own decline; but whatever the intention that may be imputed to Lear, the words still convey something of his own involvement in, and responsibility for, the total situation in which these mortals are entangled. The image pattern is a part of the expression of the tragic theme. And since to tragedy belongs the philosophic note, it is not surprising that near the end of this scene Lear comments to Gloucester:

> We came crying hither;
> Thou know'st, the first time that we smell the air
> We wawl and cry. I will preach to thee. Mark. (182–84)

Lear is milder, for a moment, and has a tone of resignation. He is not the prosecutor in these lines, but *smell* is the word that he uses to describe the world men come into. In the context it cannot be taken as merely a passive sense word. It rounds out the area of meaning with which the pattern is concerned.

The smell pattern is not an extensive one; yet plainly it exists, and we cannot dispose of the recurrent images by remarking simply that Shakespeare had an acute olfactory sense. It does not take much study of the details of the passages and their dramatic contexts for the reader to realize the symbolic import of the key words and to become aware of the role of recurrency in setting off, so to speak, the levels of meaning that extend beyond and below the local and literal. Separate passages draw together in reciprocal illu-

17

mination, and the repetition of basic words opens the consciousness to all the expressive possibilities of these words. But the reiteration is reiteration plus variation, so that the resources of the symbol are tapped in different ways according to different contextual demands. Thus the symbol, in its flexibility, becomes what Mr. Brooks calls a "telling instrument." We have seen how the instrument works; what kind of commentary on experience does it make possible? The smell pattern actually implies a good deal about Lear's world—the decay within it, its confusion of values, the terribly faulty perceptions of some of its inhabitants, and even the opportunism of those who can sense in part the state of affairs and attempt to profit from it.

This essay will attempt to trace other patterns of meaning in *King Lear* which are more pervasive than the smell pattern and which therefore go more deeply into the thematic materials of the play. But before proceeding to a preliminary description of the other patterns, we should consider another structural possibility, or rather, another kind, and a very important kind, of dramatic material which may be understood as a part of a symbolic pattern. Suppose, for instance, that in *King Lear* there were present some actual evil-smelling substance or object (such as Philoctetes' offensively infected foot in Sophocles' *Philoctetes*), and that at different times, as a part of dramatic situations, the characters were to be understood as literally experiencing various smells. Not only would these objects and these experiences invite consideration as a part of the pattern; but they would complicate and enrich the pattern, and in such an amplified pattern we could discern a close functional coalescence of *all* the constituents of drama—elements of action, experiences of characters, properties, thematic discussions, and symbolic language. Such a collaboration of all parts is perhaps the ideal situation in poetic drama; the individual drama then becomes, in the most complete sense possible, an organism. That this kind of organic relationship among diverse parts does exist is strongly implied by observations that have already been made of the ways in which certain plays "work." The theory of drama as an integration of all the expressive devices available to the dramatist is given very useful support by some of the *aperçus* of Miss Spurgeon, who, in spite of her disinclination to grapple with structure, at times cannot help sensing the confluence of diverse poetic and dramatic impulses in the final effect of a play. She finds, for example, that the dominant impression made by *The Tempest* comes "not through any one single group of images which fall easily under one heading, but rather through the action itself and the background, reinforced by a number of images taken from many groups. . . ." [20] If this description does not go as far as it might, it at least does distinguish three different strands in the dramatic fabric: action, background, and images. Again, Cleanth Brooks observes that in *Macbeth* the symbolism of infancy involves references to infancy "on a number of levels. The babe appears sometimes as a character, such as Macduff's child; sometimes as a symbol, like the crowned babe and the bloody babe which are raised by the witches on the occasion of Macbeth's visit to them; sometimes, in a metaphor. . . ." [21] All kinds of references, the number of which "can hardly be accidental," can be combined to form one area of meaning. [22]

THE SIGHT PATTERN IN OEDIPUS REX

That the combination of such different elements as action, character, and images is not only a fruitful but even a necessary technique of expressing meaning in drama may be surmised from the fact that it is not limited to Shakespeare or even to English drama. It is used by at least one classical tragedy, Sophocles' *Oedipus*. The climactic action in the play is Oedipus' blinding himself; but the blinding is not merely an expiatory injury selected by chance; instead Oedipus justifies the "horror of darkness" [23] that enfolds him by developing at length the theme, "Why was I to see, when sight could show me nothing sweet?" Much more important, however, than his own understanding of his blindness, is the fact that it has been prepared for throughout the play by a series of references to seeing which make a running commentary upon man's sight and his blindness generally. At the level of action itself the theme receives a statement in the presence of Teiresias, the blind seer, and in the tension between him and Oedipus: the blind man sees, but Oedipus the shrewd solver of riddles does not. How ironic it is then, that, when Creon, referring to the death of Laius, uses the phrase "dark things," Oedipus boasts, "I will . . . once more make dark things plain." He is to do that in a way which he does not anticipate.

Part of his first sentence spoken to Teiresias has a special meaning for us ". . . thou feelest, though thou canst not see. . . ." The first evidence of how well the blind Teiresias does perceive is his comment to Oedipus, " . . . I see that thou . . . openest not thy lips in season . . ." and his explanation, "Thou . . . seest not that to which thou thyself art wedded. . . ." The shallowness of Oedipus' view of things appears in his angry taunt, " . . . thou art maimed in ear, and in wit, and in eye"; and the irony of their relative situations is the real substance of his next attacks: "Night, endless night hath thee in her keeping, so that thou canst never hurt me, or any man who sees the sun," and " . . . a tricky quack, who hath eyes only for his gains, but in his art is blind!" Teiresias then brings the whole problem of seeing out into the open: "And I tell thee—since thou hast taunted me even with blindness—that thou hast sight, yet seest not in what misery thou art. . . . And thou . . . [wilt have] darkness then on the eyes that now see true." Oedipus refers scornfully to the seer's "dark words," and Teiresias fittingly retorts, "Nay, art thou not most skilled to unravel dark speech?" And he prophetically describes what Oedipus is to be, "A blind man, he who now hath sight. . . ." In the midst of these passionate accusations the Chorus modestly admit that they do not have "clear vision"; Creon asks whether Oedipus' charge against him was made "with steady eyes"; he insists, " . . . where I lack light, 'tis my wont to be silent." Thus we are never allowed to forget the issue: what kind of men do see? Jocasta, conveying far more than she intends, says that the god will "easily bring [everything necessary] to light"; and in a minute Oedipus is compelled to admit, "Dread misgivings have I that the seer can see." Then Jocasta, wanting to reassure Oedipus and head off his growing insight, gives the theme a new twist by taking on what is really a deliberate blindness: why, she asks, should man fear, man "who hath clear foresight of nothing"? By denial she paradoxically asserts a theme of the play—that a man may see all, if he will but look properly.

The sight pattern now begins to point directly toward the climax. " . . . 'tis sweet to see the face of parents," Oedipus remarks, almost nostalgically, in words even more heavily loaded with irony than most; and later he insists that he must not "fail to bring my birth to light." Then at last everything comes to light, and Oedipus exclaims, "Then light, may I now look my last on thee—" The chorus summarizes: "Time the all-seeing hath found thee out . . . and through thee darkness hath fallen upon mine eyes." The citation of this series of passages should be more effective than any argument in establishing the symbolic level of meanings in the tragedy; but, almost as if to offer a final evidence of what he is doing, Sophocles makes Oedipus, at the time he strikes the golden brooches into his eyes, address the following words to his eyes: "No more shall ye behold such horrors as I was suffering and working! long enough have ye looked on those whom ye ought never to have seen, *failed in knowledge* of those whom I yearned to know—henceforth ye shall be dark!"

The italicized words define the symbols: seeing is knowing, sight is insight; and the problem concerns the ways in which man sees, or fails to see, the truths that are available to him. The self-confident, keen-eyed reasoner fails; he does not go beyond limited truths of fact. The blind seer who must be led about has the long vision; he inherits a tradition, and sees the inescapable truths that lie beneath all present situations.

This is not the place, however, to attempt a complete formulation of what is being said in a very complex drama.[24] But Sophocles' method—or at least that aspect of his method which has been presented in this section—is plain: he combines, into a body of symbolic meaning, actions of characters, qualities of characters, direct references to qualities of characters, and images and metaphors. Language harmonizes with plot in such a way as to set loose a great suggestive force and make possible an imaginative experience which extends way beyond logical, literal, and immediate meanings. The critical reader can hardly fail to be struck by the resemblances between what Sophocles does in *Oedipus* and what Shakespeare does in *King Lear*. That resemblance is something more than an accident: what it tells us is that this description of the working of the two plays may in effect be a schematic account of the structural procedures necessary to the most concentrated poetic drama. The tendency of totally independent poetic imaginations to explore comparable situations in identical, or at least comparable, ways leads to the suspicion that a certain complex of raw materials may always, as it were, exact from the artist a certain kind of aesthetic strategy. At any rate, whatever the speculative limits to such a discussion, the fact is that Sophocles and Shakespeare present some amazing similarities in detail. Oedipus says to his eyes, " . . . long enough have ye . . . failed in knowledge. . . ." Gloucester says, "I stumbled when I saw." Oedipus says, of his daughters, "Ah, could I but touch them with my hands, I should think that they were with me, even as when I had sight." Gloucester says, addressing Edgar, whom he supposes to be absent, "Might I but live to see thee in my touch,/I'ld say I had eyes again!"

The likenesses, as well as the poetics that they may imply, will become more apparent in time. For the moment we have been primarily concerned with observing how a pattern works in a classical drama. This brief analysis should prepare the way for, and in some sense lend support to, the tracing out of the complex system of patterns in *King Lear*.

THE PATTERNS IN KING LEAR

I am using the word *pattern* to denote a combination or system of poetic and dramatic elements which can be shown to work together in encompassing a body of meaning that has a place in the over-all structure of the play. Although our main business will be the examination of recurrent imagery and recurrent statements on certain themes, we need for the moment to focus our attention on the larger and more conspicuous elements of the drama which not only provide the most obvious means of identifying the patterns but also actually serve as organizing centers for the patterns. From what has already been said of Oedipus and Gloucester it is evident that one of the important dramatic facts in the play is the *blindness* of Gloucester: in addition to carrying out its function in the plot and in the system of symbols, it also serves to focus a considerable body of language concerned with sight and blindness. Other such powerful components in the drama are the violence of the storm—*disorder in nature;* the *nakedness* of Edgar, which so affects Lear that he tries to tear off his own clothes; and, most impressive of all, the coming together of different kinds of real or apparent *mental disorder*—the Fool's wit and irrelevance, Edgar's assumed idiocy, and especially Lear's real madness. It is a familiar fact that these components of the drama are very active on the symbolic level; the storm, we all know, figures forth vividly the mental and moral disorder of the world. Madness is more than a pathological condition which is to be viewed clinically, and nakedness is more than a cliché state

24

designed to entrap lovers of the pathetic. The symbolic situations react upon each other; Shakespeare's utilization of their interaction appears overtly in Gloucester's line, " 'Tis the time's plague when madmen lead the blind" (IV.i, 46). Their appropriateness, boldness, and uncompromisingness would alone account for some of the effectiveness of such symbolic instruments. But the nakedness, the storm, the blindness, and the madness do not become symbols merely on the spur of the moment or function as symbols only for the duration of a scene; they are prepared for, and they are followed up; their strength and their impact are in part dependent upon their relationship to the organic bodies of language such as we have already seen exemplified in the smell pattern in *King Lear* and the sight-and-blindness pattern in *Oedipus*. That is, the blindness, etc., not only provide a focus for the patterns but themselves draw upon the bodies of language which join them to form the patterns. The dramatic and poetic elements are reciprocally illuminating and animating; they are interdependent in the manner of the parts of an organism; together they form rich and stimulating patterns of meaning.

The blinding of Gloucester might well be gratuitous melodrama but for its being imbedded in a field of meanings centered in the concept of *seeing:* references, whether literal or figurative, to the act of seeing, to things seen (sights), to the conditions of seeing (darkness and light), and to the means of seeing (eyes) persist throughout the play. This sight pattern relentlessly brings into play the problem of seeing, and what is always implied is that the problem is one of insight, of the values which determine how one sees.

Edgar's nakedness dominates the area of meanings which

is outlined by the *clothes* imagery of the play. There is a whole set of variations upon the multivalued theme of nakedness, dress, and the special kind of dress which is disguise—a symbolic range extending from innocence (which may also be defenselessness) at one extreme to plotted concealment at another extreme, from candor to an ornamented covering up of thought, and including the ambivalence of clothes that may be defense or encumbrance or pretense.

An old cliché for violence of storms and such phenomena, "convulsions of nature," points toward the role of the storm. It is obviously a symbol of subversion and perversion, of a turning upside down of the nature of things, of human unnaturalness. Now throughout the play there are, also, numerous uses of the word *nature*, in a variety of senses: taken together, these constitute a continuing inquiry into nature—into human nature and natural order. *Nature* is often used figuratively, but at the same time this pattern, much more than the sight and clothing patterns, relies upon a series of statements whose content is mainly logical. At the same time the inquiry is supported and greatly extended by the voluminous animal imagery of the play, nearly all of it used as a means of commenting upon human beings, upon their nature and their status in the world; and by the use of sex, in both dramatic and verbal form, as a means of seeking further definition of the human being. The insistence of these patterns of expression amounts really to a series of implied questions: What is man's nature? What is nature? What in the nature of things may man depend upon? From considerations of what is natural and unnatural it is only a step to the problem of justice, to which the play returns repeatedly; and images of age and injury and values amplify still further the inquiry into right and wrong with which this whole group of meaning patterns is concerned.

Finally there are the Fool, the supposedly mad Edgar, and the mad Lear, through whom almost all is said that could be said of the ways in which a sensitive mind may come to grips with a distraught world. Yet here again there is more. Before actual or feigned derangement appears, there are many lines about *madness* and about the capacity of man's wits. Other lines comment directly or indirectly upon, or imply the nature of, *reason*. There is a constant echo of reason and madness; what we find, when we put all the materials together, is a questioning of the nature and sufficiency of the rational man. What is reason? What is folly? What is wisdom? In what kind of thinking about experience is man's salvation? Finally, when salvation becomes the problem, the gods remind us of their presence; that is to say, they come into the consciousness of the characters in *Lear*. Because references to them also recur, the gods likewise have a place in the total meaning, and the critical issue is the determination of that place.

THE RELATIONSHIP OF THE PATTERNS

In general I shall discuss the patterns in the order in which they are tentatively described in the preceding section. That order may be arbitrary, and yet the sequence is one into which the different problems of meaning seem naturally to fall. The sight pattern has Gloucester as its chief figure, and since he is in a secondary tragic role, his symbolic world is a quite logical starting place from which to work toward the heart of the drama. The implications of the sight pattern do of course carry quite far, but they are not

27

ultimately as encompassing as the implications of the same pattern in *Oedipus*. The question of man's seeing, we soon find, is complemented by the question of the obstacles to sight, of the resistance offered to his vision by that which is to be seen: hence the clothes pattern, with its complex ramifications, comes next into view, and focuses for us what the play has to say, or intimate, about appearance and reality. Thus we have moved into the realm of metaphysics, a realm in which the play is speculatively very active. We find constant endeavors to define the nature of man, the relationship of man and nature, and the nature of nature: these efforts belong to the nature pattern. But man makes conflicting definitions, and these definitions spring out of quite different ways of thinking about his universe. When, then, we make the logical step from formulations of reality to the kinds of thought which these formulations represent, we move from the nature pattern to the madness pattern. And we find ourselves at the organic center of the play.

For the evidence will indicate, I believe, that *King Lear* is finally a play about the ways of looking at and assessing the world of human experience. In *Lear* Shakespeare gives dramatic form to a vast range of value judgments that the student of the play must take into account. But these judgments tend to resolve themselves into a formal dichotomy which determines the essential conflict of the play: we see, ultimately, the shrewd, sharp-thinking, worldly people (Goneril, Regan, Edmund) balanced against a set of apparently helpless incompetents (Edgar, the Fool, Lear). Yet the former stop at a superficial understanding of things, and the latter come to profound insights. Shakespeare's paradox makes *King Lear*, indeed, a reminder of one of the characteristic modes of literary functioning—the denial of the apparently true in order to assert the really true, and the assertion of the really true by means of an imaginative shock which may itself provide considerable initial difficulty. The mad Lear is in one sense the man of letters: [25] his imagination is wholly alert, and, whatever the disorder present, he has the searching and synthesizing insight of the poet. He may not seem quite safe. But the good poet never is. And the entirely safe man is never the good poet.

The examination of the patterns should lead to some statement of the theme, or to such an approximation of it as is possible to expository prose. But a statement of theme is not a mere abstraction from the full dramatic texture; it must include also an account of the *tone* which is at the heart of the author's interpretation of his materials. A study of the different areas of meaning in *King Lear* will lead gradually to the realization that Shakespeare's tone is authentically tragic: it springs both from a recognition of man's capacity for bringing catastrophe upon himself and from the ability to assert the endurance of the values by which the catastrophe may be defined and understood. So far as I know, no one has ever called *King Lear* sentimental; what is important to recognize is that the play also avoids the other extreme—cynicism. Shakespeare is concerned with evil, as the writer of tragedy must be; and he gives a dramatic definition of a specific kind of evil. He is concerned with it as a private, inner reality and as a public force, and he is uncompromising in his record of its destructiveness to those whom it possesses, in whole or in part, and even to innocent bystanders. But a whole awareness of evil does not mean a denial of good or of man's ability to make distinctions or of the possibility

29

of his achieving a certain quality of life. That he can ultimately learn, through representative suffering, is one of the
fundamental intimations of the patterns in *Lear*.[26]

But before we can venture conclusions we need to see how
the patterns work within themselves and how they influence
each other. I have so far described them as if they were
separable entities; they can, it is true, be felt as distinct organisms; but in the dramatic body they are interwoven in
very complex ways, and it is probably impossible to trace all
their interactions. Yet they always influence each other. The
manner of their co-operation, and the result of it, are very
well described by words applied by R. P. Blackmur to another work: "We see how it is that the stress and tensions between the symbols interanimate the words beyond any force
of narrative or allegory and give the whole poem 'expressive integration' and a kind of absolute momentum of its
own." [27]

THE TRAGIC STRUCTURE

The preceding sections have emphasized sufficiently, I
hope, the necessity of analyzing in detail, even at the risk of
tediousness, the very elaborate imagery of *King Lear*. In
this imagery is contained the fullest statement of this tragic
theme. But to speak of the tragic theme is to imply a definition of tragedy. In the best sense, I suppose, that definition
can come only at the end, as an extension of what we have
seen one tragedy to be. But since the progressive consideration of the symbolic patterns must always rest in part upon
certain assumptions about the tragic form, those assumptions should be made explicit at the start.

The Aristotelian definition of the tragic hero as the good

man who by some error or frailty comes to disaster is the basis for many statements which this essay will make about tragic quality. This definition itself implies other characteristics that identify the tragic form and distinguish it from the nontragic. If the tragic hero is good but is capable of error, it follows that there is not unity in his personality; the disparate elements cannot be imagined to exist peacefully side by side, but must clash and produce what we now call inner conflict. In tragedy this is fundamental, just as melodrama and certain types of comedy are characterized by conflicts between relatively "whole" people (the good and the bad). This is not to say that in tragedy there is not open conflict, physical and mental, for it is obvious that some of the best of all tragedies have a great deal of overt conflict between characters on different sides; but it is to say that the winning of this outer conflict is not identical with the statement of the tragic theme, and indeed that this outer melee may exist only as a secondary part of the turmoil which follows inevitably when moral principles are at stake. At its best the outer clash is symbolic of the movement of universal issues and is at the same time an objectification of the war within the protagonist. In tragedy the private, the public, and the universal are at one.

That disaster follows from the hero's tragic flaw implies that the world is a moral organism in which events are morally meaningful. Tragedy is concerned, not with evil fortune that may lead to cynicism or despair, but with evil that is understandable in terms of human character; a literary work that tells of destructive mischances may have its own excellence and validity, but its cosmos is a quite different one from that of tragedy. Tragedy records, eventually, victory rather than defeat; it asserts the authority of the spiritual scheme of things to which man, because of his flaw, does violence; and it presents man as understanding his deviation, undergoing a spiritual rehabilitation, recovering the insights by which he may endure. The suffering in tragedy is not an end, but a product and a means; through it comes wisdom, and, if not redemption, at least a renewed grasp upon the laws of redemption. The Eumenides exist only because man's soul is not corrupt.

This is the kind of tragic structure exhibited in *King Lear*. In its fullness the structure can be set forth only by means of the patterns of imagery, which realize everything that is happening, and in a sense what has to happen, in the tragic process. But taking the play simply at the level of plot, and attempting to treat it for the moment as if it were written merely in a logical prose, we can discern partial outlines of tragic form which can be set down provisionally, to be amplified or corrected by the evidences of the symbolic language.

Most of the action is organized with Lear and Gloucester as centers, and what happens in the play is to be seen as proceeding from them and as having a certain impact upon them. Lear and Gloucester evince certain faults of understanding, and the justification for having them both in the play is that these flaws complement each other, and thus, presented jointly, become a movingly inclusive dramatization of man's liability to error.[28] Lear imposes certain mistakes upon the world; the world—most conspicuously as it acts through Edmund—imposes certain mistakes upon Gloucester. The men are the active and passive forms of that moral frailty by which man may fall into very serious trouble. But their frailties, which have both moral and intellectual aspects, need more precise definition; and giving this definition is one of the functions of the poetry.

The relationship between the mistakes of Lear and Gloucester and the retribution which comes to them is clear even at the plot level: [29] Lear puts into power the daughters who, trespassing on the small autonomy he had retained for himself, use that power, in effect, to destroy him; and Gloucester, deluded by Edmund, is really betrayed twice by him—first in his being persuaded to unjust action against Edgar, and then directly, in that Edmund discloses Gloucester's intention to support Lear and thus brings about the blinding. But the big question still awaits an answer: what is the meaning of the actions of Lear and Gloucester? From what mental habits, or from what human tendencies, do their errors spring? The easiest way out is to suppose that all they do is make mistakes in identity. But it is obvious that a mistake in identity is of itself a pretty trivial starting point for such tragic actions as make up the body of *King Lear*. The fact is that these mistakes do illustrate certain qualities of mind which we must seek out; and for the definition of those qualities we must rely upon the patterns of imagery.

In the latter part of the play Lear is reunited with Cordelia, and Gloucester with Edgar, just as in Act I the old men were enjoying close pseudo intimacies, respectively, with Goneril and Regan and with Edmund. It is, I think, not pushing the evidence too far to say that from the plot alone we may conclude that the change in associates has symbolic value. The reunion with the better children takes place after Lear and Gloucester have undergone a great deal of enlightenment; it may be read, then, as a kind of sign that there has taken place the achievement or recovery of insight which marks the experience of the tragic protagonist, just as the banishing of these children showed their fathers at their most obtuse. Thus Edgar and Cordelia symbolize a side of each of their parents, that side in which there lies the potentiality of salvation. But Edgar combats Edmund; Cordelia is on the opposite side from the sisters—those who once had paternal confidence. By now the implication must be quite unmistakable: the children, like the Good and Evil Angels in Marlowe's *Faustus, represent the different elements which are in conflict in the fathers.* This is not true in a closely restrictive allegorical fashion, as we shall see; but it contains enough truth to indicate, together with what has already been said about the symbolic relationship between Lear and Gloucester, the essential tightness of structure of a play which has in it an unusual number of actions and characters. We see good and evil in conflict in the world, but by the structure we are reminded that the conflict is an emanation of that in the individual soul. Lear must recognize evil, must resolve his conflict—a conflict externalized in his attitudes to Goneril and Regan and to Cordelia. By the fact of relationship the outer and the inner evil become one, the two struggles are united. The children are not children for nothing; to be the father of Goneril is to create a symbol of the evil brought forth from oneself. The discerning reader of the play will hardly feel that he has done all his duty by hating Goneril.

Gloucester's initial gullibility is reproduced in Edgar, as is his capacity, which appears later, for loyal and kindly service; Gloucester's shallow foxiness as a detective grows, when "freed" in Edmund, into a deep and mature wiliness.

Gloucester's proscribing Edgar and giving authority to Edmund is to turn a part of himself loose in the world; one element is freed from the restraint imposed by the rest of the personality. In Gloucester and Lear we see that personality is an equilibrium of potentially antagonistic forces; evil is ready at all times to escape from the spiritual whole; autonomy is its end, and any disturbance of tensions may set it on its way. In investing Goneril and Regan with power, Lear gives rein to a part of himself which becomes the whole being of Goneril and Regan [30]—a part which I am going to call, tentatively and imperfectly, the spirit of calculation. This is simply a clue to the interpretation; the justification must rest upon the study of text and symbol which is to follow.

In some respects the relationship between Lear and Cordelia submits easily to definition: Cordelia is the side of Lear capable of tenderness, love, and insight. Yet in Cordelia is the best evidence that, as I have already said, the children do not become mere allegorical equivalents for isolated parental qualities. For if Cordelia is chiefly the part of Lear which makes him capable of redemption, she also embodies some of his proneness to error. I say "some of" because Lear makes, as we shall see, a whole series of desperate mistakes, in most of which Cordelia conspicuously does not share. He, for instance, misestimates the protestations of Goneril and Regan, as she does not. But Lear's abdication represents a flaw which *is* echoed in Cordelia. For the abdication is a kind of refusal of responsibility, a withdrawal from a necessary involvement in the world of action, and the effect of it is to turn the kingdom over to Goneril and Regan. Likewise Cordelia's rejection of Lear's distribution scheme —her nonjurancy, so to speak—is a withdrawal from the immediate world of action, and it leaves the world of action entirely to her sisters. Perhaps her motive is entirely honorable, and there is for her no practical way of mediating between two claims each with its own kind of validity; in that case her situation is roughly analogous to Antigone's. But perhaps in her refusal we are to see something of spiritual pride (of which Lear accuses her in I.i, 131), "some little faulty admixture of pride and sullenness;" as Coleridge puts it.[31] In either case Cordelia becomes a tragic actor, a secondary one, it is true, but still one whose decision involves her in the tragic consequences, and not merely a pathetic victim.[32] In both her withdrawal and Lear's there is a rather narrow self-protection, an attempted elusion of the fettering of circumstance—an escape which may at times be the right moral goal but which is not a moral absolute: the immaculateness of nonparticipation must be balanced against action which may bespot the actor but is yet a responsibility.[33]

The intention of the present section, however, is not to state the themes but to describe the general tragic structure and thus to outline the problems which a study of the imagery can illuminate. I have already spoken of the coincidence, in tragedy, of the public and private conflicts, and of the necessity that the tragic experience be representative. *King Lear* illustrates how these attributes are guaranteed through the use, standard in Greek and Elizabethan practice, of characters "in high place" and of intrafamily complications. Rulers were public figures; their tragedies became representative; ennoblement through suffering was a general and meaningful, not a shut-off private experience by which many suffered but few were ennobled. Yet in the public plot melodrama is just around the corner: our view of public life always inclines to the melodramatic, for we look for heroes and villains whom we can understand simply. We tend to identify evil with certain figures or groups, and if we can injure or destroy them, we cause the good to triumph. We look for Gonerils and Regans and Edmunds and turn all our wrath upon them; we forget the Goneril and Regan and Edmund that are within us all. The public event may obscure the private reality, the private reality in terms of which the experience is universal. But the ultimate identity of public and private is exactly figured forth in the symbolism of kinship: the family mediates between the soul of man and the community to which he belongs. It is at once a public fact and a projection of the soul; through it the representatively public and representatively private are seen to be one. By being the father of Goneril and Cordelia, Lear includes both of them within himself; we cannot then idly hate Goneril as evil but we must recognize the genesis of evil and hence modify our sympathetic identification with Lear so that it includes a sensitiveness to the spiritual trouble within him. Thus we move from melodrama,[34] which represents the externalized conflict as reality, to tragedy, in which the externalized conflict corresponds to the war within the soul and is indeed begotten by the war within the soul—whether the begetting is an affirmation and an imposition of error or a Gloucester-like acquiescence in worldly imperfections.

Chapter I has defined the kind of patterns of meaning to be found in *King Lear*, briefly exhibited several such patterns in action, and offered a preliminary description of the patterns in the play which are to be examined, and of their collaboration; it has also set down the basic assumptions about the structure of tragedy which this essay will make use of, and, with the plot, in the most restricted sense of the word, as material, has offered a limited, tentative account of the general structure of *King Lear*. This last undertaking has given us little more than a skeleton of the play. If we are to seize upon the absolute, organic identity of the play, this action skeleton must be joined with the flesh and blood of the poetic-dramatic patterns.

. . . *for thou wert better dead than living and blind.*

Chorus in Sophocles' *Oedipus*

*   *   *

For the truth of the eye was not in sweet blandishments, no, only through its own tears it came to seeing, only by sorrow it came to perception, only when filled with its own tears to the tears of the world, truth-filled by the obliterating moisture of all existence.

Hermann Broch, *The Death of Virgil*

CHAPTER II

I STUMBLED WHEN I SAW

THE SIGHT PATTERN

GLOUCESTER's blindness is by no means a chance product of bitter vengefulness, interchangeable with any other punitive mutilation that might have satisfied his tormentors. Like that of Oedipus, it is wholly in harmony with the aesthetic and moral context; it is the center of a whole family of cross references. Its ironic relationship to Gloucester's own defect of insight is clear enough. But that relationship is not merely left to inference; it is carefully established by the sight pattern, which not only tells us a good deal about Gloucester but is used to help qualify all the main characters in the play.

Gloucester's tragic flaw is a special kind of lack of insight. Gloucester is not a stupid man, but he is a man who does not ask enough questions, who takes evidence at its face value, who confounds appearance and substance. He is the man of the world, the sophisticate, as we might say, who has the naïveté ironically inseparable from the type.[1] His whole history is consistent. Long before the time of the play he enjoyed an adulterous liaison of which Edmund was the fruit —a liaison which indicated that he viewed sex morality entirely as a man of the world. His unperceptive worldliness is the opening note of the play: in the first few lines he talks to Kent with jaunty wit about his escapade with Edmund's mother—even, it appears, within earshot of Edmund. Gloucester does not take the trouble to go beneath the surface, he falls in with whatever is going on about him: this is his way of avoiding responsibility. When Edmund makes a specious case against Edgar (I.ii), Gloucester falls right in with Edmund's plans; he shows what we come to recognize as his characteristic suggestibility, and he dodges the responsibility of finding out what lies behind the superficial evidence. Lear's strange conduct and what he supposes to be that of Edgar elicit from him little more than startled exclamations; he wants to charge these distresses up to the "late eclipses in the sun and moon" (I.ii, 112) [2]—a convenient way of evading moral inquiry (very significantly, this astrological habit of mind is shared by no one else in the play). *Eclipses*, at the same time, is one of the hints of the *darkness* in which the now sound-eyed Gloucester is regularly operating. The light in which he sees things lights up only the surface of the world. It is quite consistent that he is inclined to get on with the new political regime: he plainly has his doubts about the way in which things are going, but that a principle is involved, a principle on which he should take a stand, simply does not occur to him. He falls in again. He regrets Cornwall's stocking Lear's follower, Kent (II.ii, 147 ff.); but he himself contributes to the infuriation of Lear by his efforts to "fix it up" between him and Cornwall. "You know the fiery quality of the Duke," he tells Lear (II.iv, 93), and, more maddeningly for Lear, "I would have all well betwixt you" (II.iv, 121). Gloucester hopes that he can "do busi-

ness with" Cornwall; despite his genuine discomfort, he inclines toward the status quo. The *de facto*, the immediate,
the circumscribing world hypnotize him: he cannot question. Yet Gloucester is not unalterably a band-wagon man;
he can rise to become a tragic figure, and finally, shocked
into a new alertness, he undertakes the commitment to Lear
which is his ruin in the practical world whose creature he has
been, but at the same time the salvation of his soul. But his
spiritual awakening is very subtly managed; there is a fine
stroke in the ambiguity of the terms in which Gloucester tells
Edmund that he intends to aid Lear (III.iii). There is no
doubt whatever that he pities Lear and realizes—note his
phrase, "this unnatural dealing" (III.iii, 1)—at last that
more is involved than political bad taste. But it is also true
that he has been abused and mistreated by the usurpers, and
that he says, "These injuries the King now bears will be re-
venged home; there's part of a power already footed; we
must incline to the King" (III.iii, 11–13). He is waking up
to the moral state of affairs, but in his consciousness there is
also some hint that to be pro-Lear may be a good thing; and
he is at least in part maneuvering toward the comfortable
stream of history. Gloucester does not consciously seek evil,
or deliberately hunt for feather beds; it is simply that he is
tragically slow in seeing what is implied in the situations in
which he finds himself.

His being blinded, then, is an ironic completion of his
career (III.vii). The symbolic reverberations of the scene
are virtually unmistakable; yet Shakespeare does not leave
the perception of them to chance. In fact, almost as if intent
upon making us see them,[3] Shakespeare continues with this

material which is fresh in our minds and devotes the very
next scene (IV.i) to Gloucester. When the Old Man says,
"You cannot see your way" (IV.i, 17), Gloucester replies:

> I have no way and therefore want no eyes;
> I stumbled when I saw. (18–19)

Thus the symbolism becomes explicit: Gloucester here
summarizes his whole career. With eyes he did not see, but
now, blind, he has come a long way—far enough even to see
into himself. He is beginning to master the eternal human
problem. And he goes on:

> Ah, dear son Edgar,
>
> . . . .
>
> Might I but live to see thee in my touch,
> I'ld say I had eyes again! (21–24)

Though he can now only touch Edgar, he *sees* him—that is,
the truth about him—as he did not see him before. And seeing Edgar is itself a symbol of understanding, so that, if Edgar were again restored to him, he could feel that he had
eyes—that is, the power for which eyes are a symbol. Thus
all the evidence of drama and language points to the conclusion that Gloucester's *hamartia* is, as we have said,
failure to see essential things. Furthermore, it seems clear,
this failure is meant to be evidenced in the original adultery
which Coleridge [4] regards as Gloucester's originating moral
misdeed. Near the end the philosophical Edgar, speaking
of Gloucester, says to Edmund, "The dark and vicious place
where thee he got/Cost him his eyes" (V.iii, 172–73). A
reader sensitive to the symbolic pattern can hardly read
dark as a mere rhetorical flourish or didactic cliché, especially when it is juxtaposed with "Cost him his eyes"; the

place was *dark* because years before, Gloucester was exhibiting a characteristic failure to see what his deed involved. The unity of his career as it is symbolized in the
sight pattern, is further supported by the bitter lines of
Gloucester near the end of the scene quoted above (IV.i),
when he is making his arrangements to be guided by "Tom":

> Let the superfluous and lust-dieted man,
> That slaves your ordinance, that will not see
> Because he does not feel, feel your pow'r quickly.[5]
> (IV.i, 68–70)

At first glance we may take Gloucester's word to be an in-
voking of divine wrath against common types of evildoer.
Actually, however, Gloucester is describing himself: he was
"lust-dieted" and he "slaved" (i.e., contemned) divine
ordinance; he would not see because he did not feel; and he
has now felt—the repetition of the verb points to his sharpened sensibility—divine power. He understands himself
wholly: the blind man has come to insight.

The irony of Gloucester's final condition is exactly paralleled by the irony of his earlier actions as a man with good
eyes. Just when he most fails to see where he is going, he
feels, like Oedipus, most shrewd and observant. The sight
pattern points the issues for us. While he is being made to
see things as Edmund wishes Gloucester feels that he is detecting the truth: "Let's see," he demands of Edmund three
times (I.ii, 35, 45)—and he does not see. Again, ". . . if
it be nothing, I shall not need spectacles" (35–36). Spectacles are a symbol of what he does need: Shakespeare hits
upon the characteristic human frailty by which the denial
of a deficiency actually announces the deficiency. It is al-

together logical, then, that Edmund's next move against Edgar takes place *at night* (II.i) : the physical darkness betokens Gloucester's failure to see into what is going on. The actors in the nocturnal setting, indeed, represent more than one phase of a human plight: Gloucester victimizes and Edgar is victimized—he flees at night—because of the same kind of unseeingness.[6] It is a meaningful, not merely a rhetorical, irony when Edmund calls, "Light, ho, here!/ . . . Torches, torches! . . ." (33–34) : those who want light least can call for it most loudly. Then Gloucester enters—how? ". . . with torches" (38)—the agent of light, but a kind of light—a physical reality like his eyes—that does him no good; it is inner illumination that he needs. It is at the end of this scene, finally, that Regan and Cornwall come to Gloucester's castle. They come, then, at night, a fact which we might easily pay no attention to if Shakespeare did not twice remind us of it. Edmund tells Edgar that Cornwall is coming, "now, i' th' night" (26) ; and then Regan's words add emphasis, "out of season, threading dark-ey'd night"—a phrase full of suggestion of things not seen and things not meant to be seen. Regan's thus coming into the sight pattern nicely amplifies the moral context: Regan joins Edmund among those who utilize the dark. These must always have a Gloucester—the not-seeing, or, better, the late-seeing.

For gradually Gloucester comes to see—in practical terms, too late. The first glimmerings come to him in III.iii, when he tells Edmund of his decision to aid Lear. But even now, as we have seen, his motives are not altogether clear, and he is still in the dark about Edmund. In giving practical form to the allegiance to Lear upon which he has resolved,

Gloucester again acts in the darkness of the night. In III.iv he hunts up Lear in the stormy night, just as he hunted for Edgar at night in II.i. This time he finds what he is looking for, and at the same time, so to speak, finds himself. The scene of his arrival on the heath is full of imaginative connections with other scenes. Just before Gloucester enters, the Fool says: "Now a little fire in a wild field were like an old lecher's heart—a small spark, all the rest on's body cold. Look, here comes a walking fire" (III.iv, 116–19). Since the play has opened with an account of Gloucester's lechery, it seems more than an accident that the Fool is given this particular simile just at the moment of Gloucester's entrance; we can hardly avoid reading it as a direct announcement of Gloucester. In another sense, too, the Fool's language is appropriate: Gloucester's heart has up until now been indeed but a "small spark," and, on the field of Lear's desolate situation, Gloucester's help is hardly more than "a little fire." Just at the moment when the Fool announces "a walking fire," Gloucester enters, significantly, "with a torch" (120). It is the only other time the play mentions lights. This time we feel that the torch is not ironic but symbolizes the first dim stage of enlightenment: Gloucester is no longer blindly confident as he travels the way of the world, and he exhibits a growing sympathy with Lear and a moderation of his attitude to Edgar, whom he once called villain repeatedly (II.i, 79 ff.) but of whom he now speaks in regret rather then anger (III.iv, 171 ff.). As I have said, he finds himself. In III.vi he warns Lear of the plot against his life. Just when Gloucester is at last taking a stand which can have very serious consequences, whether or not he can foresee them entirely, Edmund's plot against him matures. The very first threat against him is Goneril's "Pluck out his eyes" (III.vii, 5)—the eyes which have given Gloucester so limited a perception as to make him partially adjust himself to Goneril's own regime. He is arrested; then follows the "trial" scene; and his eyes are put out. He is deprived of the organs which he once used so superficially. Yet this happens just as he is at last coming to real insight.

The fifty lines of dialogue which accompany the gouging out of Gloucester's eyes are full of verbal commentary upon what is happening and its meaning. Cornwall is brutally direct: "Upon these eyes of thine I'll set my foot"(68). There is a minor tension between the horrifyingly fierce wit of Regan, "One side will mock another. Th' other too!"(71) and the dying sally of the Servant who has attacked Cornwall and has been stabbed from the rear by Regan, "My lord, you have one eye left/To see some mischief on him" (81–82)— which is at once a reminder of Gloucester's torture and yet the proffering of such comfort as may come from a slender hope of requital for the torturer. Repeatedly Cornwall betrays a mad passion to cut off the seeing process (68, 72), especially at the moment when, fatally wounded, he puts out Gloucester's second eye. "Lest it see more, prevent it" (83). Each remark of his picks up a *see* from the preceding speaker: he is frenzied by the thought, which hardly takes clear form in his mind, of what Gloucester has seen.

Cornwall's ferocity here is in excellent contrast with his bathetically considerate dismissal, a little earlier, of Edmund, who is almost equally callous. Even this dismissal is done in terms of the sight imagery. It is just after Goneril has called "Pluck out his eyes" that Cornwall speaks thus to

Edmund, "The revenges we are bound to take upon your traitorous father are not fit for your beholding" (7–8). Such considerateness sets off, also, the real, costly compassion which Gloucester has for Lear: and this is the heart of the scene—the growing insight of Gloucester. Gloucester is defensive at first, perhaps a little uncertain; but at last he recognizes the moment of decision. Questioned, he answers Regan, "Because I would not see thy cruel nails/Pluck out his poor old eyes; . . ." (56–57), his words ironically anticipating his own fate. He even becomes consciously prophetic, "But I shall see/The winged vengeance overtake such children" (65–66). The former peacemaker, once a little in awe of Gloucester, has thrown off his old character. Then Gloucester, "dark and comfortless" (85) as in the earlier night scenes, begs Edmund—who is physically absent now as he was spiritually deficient before, and whose physical absence Gloucester cannot see just as before he could not detect his spiritual shortcoming—to "enkindle all the sparks of nature" (86) to avenge him: Edmund is to be both a fire and a light. Instead, Gloucester ironically receives from Regan his climactic enlightenment: it was Edmund who "made the overture" (89) of Gloucester's treason, that is, laid it open to the eyes of Goneril and Regan. Yet the real climax comes in Gloucester's answer. Gloucester does not dwell on Edmund's treachery; in fact, he does not refer to Edmund at this moment or ever again. From now on, he is concerned about his own dreadful mistake and the wrong he has done Edgar. His words are,

O my follies! then Edgar was abus'd.
Kind gods, forgive me that, and prosper him! (91–92)

Gloucester has leapt immediately to the truth about Edgar, as he might have done when Edmund first made his accusation. Then, he avoided the hard work of consulting Edgar's life—the true image of his character. Now, in his act of inference we see that his imagination—long dulled, or perhaps never active—is at work: insight comes to him. He whom Cornwall calls an "eyeless villain" (96) sees at last.

The blinding of Gloucester is at once an act of vengeance by the tyrants, an expiatory suffering by Gloucester,[7] and an ironic commentary upon human experience. In this final character it transcends the concocted irony which at first glance the coincidence of Gloucester's coming to insight and his being blinded might be mistaken for. The irony is not a put-up effect but is inseparable from a profound writer's attitude to his materials. "Out, vile jelly!/Where is thy lustre now?" (83–84)—Cornwall's words of triumph imply, as the speeches of Shakespeare's villains often do, more than he suspects. What Cornwall does not know is that Gloucester now sees better than he has ever seen; perhaps the final guarantee of his insight is his loss of outward sight. The vile jelly, the material seeing, had but caught reflections from the outer surfaces of life; as long as these were available to him, the seeing Gloucester was spiritually blind. The sisters and Cornwall cut him off from this outer world, which, as we know, circumscribed his vision; hence their fury is self-defeating, for they give him what their general conduct has already prepared him for—inward vision. His physical and material loss is spiritual gain: he who would find his life must lose it.

This is a basic paradox of the play. It is one of a series of paradoxes which, developed by the patterns, are the main structural determinants of *King Lear*. To have eyes, and to see not, is to be at the mercy of evil, and thus to aid evil. Not to see is not to understand: the sight pattern prepares us for the study of evil that finds its main treatment in the madness pattern.

EDGAR AS TUTOR

It still remains for blind Gloucester to see one spiritual truth—that he must "bear/Affliction till it do cry out itself/ 'Enough, enough,' . . ." (IV.vi, 75–77). To this realization he is brought by Edgar, whose insight into his father enables him to defeat Gloucester's suicide—and the despair which makes Gloucester attempt suicide (IV.vi). Gloucester, indeed, provides a test for the kind of sight which his sons exhibit.[8] Shortly before the battle, for instance, Regan tells us all in one breath about a double errand of Edmund. Since the blind Gloucester evokes too much popular compassion, Edmund has gone

> In pity of his misery, to dispatch
> His nighted life; moreover, to descry
> The strength o' th' enemy. (IV.v, 12–14)

Edmund has a purely practical vision which is a logical extension of his father's worldliness: [9] he sees that a blind man is dangerous to his side—the *pity* represents the only moment of hypocrisy in Regan since the opening scene—and goes with equal dispassionateness to kill him and to reconnoiter the enemy. He is the same coolly rational person that he was at the beginning of the play; we have a further hint at the nature of the evil with which the play is concerned.

In the scene of Gloucester's attempted suicide Edgar performs an ultimate act of love—protecting his father against himself, normally a function performed by parent for child. At the same time he sees a practical problem with a new skill.[10] Now the special significance of this scene lies in its being an almost exact duplicate of II.ii, in which Edmund tricks his father into believing that Edgar is plotting against him. Thus we have another of the play's structural echoes, a reciprocal enlightenment by two related parts. The two scenes show two different kinds of practical insight at work. In each scene a son deceives a blind father: Edmund an emotionally and morally blind father, for his own profit; Edgar, a physically blind father, in the interest of that father's spiritual self-mastery. The parallelism enters into the details. Whereas Edgar really protects his father against himself, Edmund *pretends* to do just that! ". . . if you violently proceed against him, mistaking his purpose, it would make a great gap in your own honour . . ." (I.ii, 89–92). Each son lets Gloucester believe that he is having his own way and controlling the situation. Even Gloucester's credulity appears with a certain consistency, a consistency which, as we shall see later, sheds light on Gloucester's position with respect to religion: in the first scene, he attributes troubles to eclipses; in the latter, his salvation to supernatural forces. But the nicest tie of all is in the radical opinion which Edmund attributes to Edgar, that "fathers declining, the father should be as ward to the son, and the son manage his revenue" (I.ii, 77–79). That is exactly the situation in Act IV: Gloucester has declined and is ward to Edgar. Edmund's practical insight enabled him to fool Gloucester completely: in the midst of apparently bright light, Gloucester was in real darkness. But now Edgar's insight has brought Gloucester out of the darkness of despair; his later dark world is illuminated by the light of love. The basic paradox of sight is amplified.

Blindness, then, is treated from two sides; on one side the blind person is an agent who brings on his own tragic catastrophe; on the other, he is the object of good or evil conduct by others who, as they mould him, exhibit their own way of looking at life. Each pattern points to the problem of values.

THE SIGHT PATTERN: LEAR

Gloucester, we have seen, is imposed upon, whereas Lear imposes; and this relationship we should keep clear. But what one imposes on other people is also a reflection of one's insight—insight into the implications of what one does, and into those upon whom one imposes something. Lear's problem, then, we might also expect to be underlined by the sight pattern,[11] and it is; and the applicability of the same poetic terms to both protagonists is one evidence of thematic kinship between them and thus of the unity of the play.

Lear, of course, is treated primarily in terms of the understanding, and the paradox of his wisdom is that it is concomitant with madness—a stroke of genius that raises the whole problem of the uses and limits of rationalism. But the madness pattern is enriched by the support of the sight pattern, which exhibits Lear as progressing, not from a blind sight to a seeing blindness, like Gloucester, but from an unwillingness to see, through a period of gradual anguished enlightenment, to a final passionate struggle to see. Early in the play Lear, blinded by anger, orders Kent, "Out of my sight!" (I.i, 159); there is more than chance in these words, for

Kent picks them up immediately with, "See better, Lear, and let me still remain/The true blank of thine eye" (160–61). Kent sees what is involved; Lear does not. His vision called in question, Lear swears, ironically, by Apollo—the god of light; and Kent retorts, ". . . by Apollo, . . ./Thou swear'st thy gods in vain" (162–63); both invoke the power of light, and Kent obeys only on an oath by Jupiter, the overriding absolute (181). Now, in another example of Shakespeare's regular use of parallelism of scenes, this episode is replayed, as it were, with variations, late in the play, where the effect combines irony and pathos: at the end of the play, Lear can hardly recognize Kent physically, as before he could not "see" Kent's moral quality and ordered him out of his sight. "Mine eyes are not o' th' best," he says, and "This' a dull sight" and "I'll see that straight" (V.iii, 279, 282, 287). Kent cannot comfort and aid Lear now just as, though he was willing enough, he could not give him needed help at the beginning. Suitably Kent comments, "All's cheerless, dark, and deadly" (290). The meaning of Lear's words extends far beyond the immediate context; they call into play again the paradox of experience embodied in Gloucester's history: he who is sure of his sight needs to question it, but he with a sense of "dull sight" in the world may see sharply within.

For if Lear is not clear about physical identities, he is now fairly straight about moral identities: he comes both to recognize Cordelia and to know what she stands for. The treatment of the Lear-Cordelia relationship forges a still more powerful sight link between first and final scenes. In Act I Lear says,

> . . . for we
> Have no such daughter, nor shall ever see
> That face of hers again. (I.i, 265–67)

He is, as we have said, banishing a part of himself, determining to be blind. But, as Lear is bitterly enlightened, the face becomes a symbol of the sole value worth having, and Lear not only comes to want to see that face again but at the end passionately studies it, searching for a sign of life. "Lend me a looking-glass," he cries (V.iii, 261); it is to be for him a mirror of physical life, and a mirror of the life of the spirit. His words also recall the joke of the Fool, "For there was never yet fair woman but she made mouths in a glass" (III.ii, 35–36). But this fair woman, far from looking at herself, can make no kind of sign for others to see. Just before he dies, Lear strains frantically, possibly convinced that he does see life: [12]

> Do you see this? Look on her, look, her lips!
> Look there, look there! (V.iii, 310–11)

The frenzied searching of the face which he had once said he would never see again is a symbol of how his seeing, and the impulses that direct his seeing, have improved. Once he tossed light away; now, in the darkness of Act V, he seeks— and perhaps finds, for a moment—the illuminating love which came to Gloucester in his blindness. "Look up," Edgar says (312), but the time for looking has given way to sightless death.[13]

Between these opening and closing scenes there is, in Lear's experience, an unremitting stress upon darkness, a stress which permits us to feel still further the effects of the

sight pattern. Always we are reminded of the tragic failure
to see the truth in time—the failure of those who had the
power of sight but did not use it. "So out went the candle, and
we were left darkling," says the Fool in apparent jest [14] (I.
iv, 237); yet *darkling* is rich in overtones. It is at this time
in the play that—with Shakespeare's usual irony—Lear is
beginning to regain his lost vision. In a few seconds he asks,
of himself,

> Where are his eyes?
> Either his notion weakens, his discernings
> Are lethargied— (247–49);

his words are almost the equivalent of Gloucester's "I stumbled when I saw." "Alack, the night comes on," Gloucester
says (II.iv, 303)—the night which is the penalty for blindness, even though a little light is now coming through to the
blind. Lear swears, "Darkness and devils" (I.iv, 273), and
Edgar carries the hint a bit further with remarks on the
"prince of darkness" (III.iv, 148; vi, 7–8). In a distraught
world even casual phrases reflect the kind of ill it suffers
from, for it is the darkness, the failure to see, that is diabolical.[15] Lear asks where his eyes have been; then he swears, as
it were, by the very blindness that is the source of the evil.
These words are spoken in the storm and dark night—it is
notable how much important action takes place in the dark
night [16]—and then Lear falls gradually into mental darkness. Yet this darkness, instead of being a merciful blotting
out of evil sights, brings with it paradoxically a new intensity of imaginative illumination. Like Gloucester, Lear sees
better when normal faculties are gone. A terrible darkness
and a terrible light coincide. Shakespeare makes this point

explicitly in terms of the sight imagery: he has the physician tell Cordelia that his medicine "Will close the eye of anguish" (IV.iv, 15). Sleeping will cut off a burning vision—yet help restore a normal sight which cannot discern much less than anguish. Still, after this protracted dark night,[17] it is peculiarly right that almost the first words of Lear, after his restorative sleep, are, "Fair daylight?" (IV. vii, 52). At one level, of course, the words convey incredulity and sense of relief. But his inquiry opens a group of lines which symbolize the change in his power of seeing. He continues:

> I should e'en die with pity,
> To see another thus. I know not what to say.
> I will not swear these are my hands. Let's see,
>
> . . . .
>
> *Cor.*   O, look upon me, sir,
> And hold your hands in benediction o'er me. (53–58)

He can see compassionately; he can inquire—"Let's see"—instead of insisting upon his own correctness with proud obstinacy (we recall that Gloucester, when he said, "Let's see," was being gulled, and Edgar used the same words when he was skillfully managing a situation); and he can look upon Cordelia, whom once he wanted never to see again. Of what she stands for, he will not lose sight again; yet in seeing her he will have to go through a final agony.

LEAR'S DAUGHTERS

What must man see? How shall he see? Shakespeare constantly labored at the question, and in a sense he came early to a specific problem of modern civilization, which from his time to ours has been casting old insights overboard and looking for replacements. At times the problem phrases itself for Shakespeare as the problem of innocence, to which he devoted himself more than once. Innocence—not seeing enough—may itself be a gateway to evil. Othello and Desdemona are the primary innocents. Gloucester and Edgar act on a different plane, of course, yet a little more of the serpent in either would have been practically useful to both. But in Shakespeare there is an unfailing use of counterpoint: there is always the glance at the other extreme. If failure to see is dangerous, seeing too well may be fatal: the lost souls in *King Lear* are those who see too well. Goneril and Regan have freed themselves of the old insights and learned to look sharply at the immediate world; they see nothing of spirit, but they miss few of the close facts of experience. There may therefore be more content than we normally assume in the hyperbolic assurance made to Lear by the sharp-eyed Goneril—she who later shrieks, as her sentence upon Gloucester, "Pluck out his eyes!"—that she loves him "dearer than eyesight" (I.i, 57)—the words which actually introduce the sight pattern in the play. What kind of eyesight that is is exactly defined by a subsequent phrase applied by Cordelia to her sisters, "still-soliciting eye" (234), and by Goneril's own words to Regan, "You see how full of changes his age is. The observation we have made of it hath not been little" [18] (291–92). That is, they see what the situation is and know how to manage it; indeed, they see things only too clearly. But the deficiencies of their shrewd kind of observation are not left merely to inference: Shakespeare points directly at them in Albany's "How far your eyes may pierce I cannot tell" (I.iv, 368) and in the Fool's ditty, "Fathers that wear rags/Do make their children blind" (II.iv, 48–49). Even these casual lines call our attention to a myopia that has spread ironically through a society. Yet the sisters' deficiency of sight is a very special case, for it is they who especially practice a realistic looking at things; here is one first suggestion of a counterpoint to the paradox of the blinded Gloucester who has insight—namely, the paradox of blindness in those who see too well.

To say that one's way of seeing things is an index of character is a truism; yet the truism lights up with poetic energy when it becomes identified with the patterns in *King Lear*.[19] When he comes to understand her (she "Look'd black upon me," he says—II.iv, 162), Lear curses Goneril thus: "You nimble lightnings, dart your blinding flames/Into her scornful eyes!" (II.iv, 167–68). This packed speech not only places Goneril more clearly in the system of meanings of the play (her "scornful eyes" symbolize her view of the moral values assumed by Lear and the others), but also sets up a double irony: it is not she who is blinded (she is already *blind*), but Gloucester who is blinded by her, and not she, but Lear himself, who is exposed to the lightning.[20] The irony takes a new tack a few lines later when Lear, speaking to Regan of Goneril, compares the sisters: "Her eyes are fierce; but thine/Do comfort and not burn" (II.iv, 175–76). But these fierce eyes, which Lear will soon find that Regan shares, do not look ahead: they do not sense retribution. In the imaginary trial scene in the farmhouse, Edgar says, "Look, where he stands and glares! Want'st thou eyes at trial, madam?" (III.vi, 25–26) that is, can you not see the foul fiend? A minute later Lear reinvokes the original symbol for his inevitable recantation of trust in Regan's kindness: her "warp'd looks proclaim/What store her heart is made on" [21] (III. vi, 56–57).

What comes of scornful and fierce eyes and warped looks?
The distortion of experience which they bring to the minds
behind them must ultimately incapacitate those minds. It is
beautifully ironic that just when Albany has emerged from
what we may assume to be a difficult conflict of loyalties and
has come to see Goneril as she is, Goneril should sneer at
him as a man "Who hast not in thy brows an eye discern-
ing/Thine honour from thy suffering" (IV.ii, 52–53). We
recognize the human pattern: Goneril wants Albany to be
blind, for it is to her convenience that he do not see many
things: yet the reassuring conviction that he is blind—which
takes the paradoxical form of an accusation—serves for the
first time to dull her practical sight: she does not detect in
him a moral ally of the opposing forces. Or to put it another
way: the great difficulty of true perception appears in the
clear-sighted evil person's inability to recognize goodness in
another; from such a failure may come insuperable danger.
In fact, Goneril and her sister have got caught in a complex
of self-betrayals, chief of which is their passion for Edmund:
at the end all they can see is each other. The sight pattern
demonstrates that his new turn is a logical continuation of
the path they have already traveled. Regan suspects Goneril: "She gave strange eliads and most speaking looks/To
noble Edmund" (IV.v, 25–26): the hard, realistic eye engages in love play. When Regan intimates that she may
marry Edmund, Goneril retorts, "That eye that told you so
look'd but asquint" (V.iii, 72). Without knowing it Goneril, who often phrases keen truths, actually summarizes, in
this speech which comes close to the end, what the play has
been saying about Regan and herself. One kind of eyesight
was very dear to them; yet those who trust only to the outer

eye and deny the inner find themselves, at the end, looking asquint.[22]

Shakespeare has found in sight a flexibly responding symbol for the problems which arise in connection with the point of view from which man judges the meaning of experience. He enriches his commentary on the problems by another use of his symbolic pattern, which heightens the contrast between the sisters and Cordelia. They look hard, scornful, fierce. But as early as Act I Cordelia can say she leaves "with wash'd eyes" (I.i, 271)—in tears, perhaps, but also cleansed of any mote that might deflect her clear view of her sisters.[23] Later her eyes are wet with tears; the tears which denote sympathy are themselves a way of looking at experience. Gloucester condemns the man who "will not see/Because he does not feel"; shortly after his speech, Cordelia exemplifies the human being who sees because she does feel (IV.iii, 20). She feels compassion and cries; the tears come from the eyes; feeling and seeing are identified. Lear urges her not to cry (IV.vii, 71; V.iii, 23); and he constantly fights his own tears (II.iv, 280 ff.; IV.vi, 199–201). For a king, tears would be a surrender, a way of seeing failure, giving comfort to the point of view of those in control. With dry eyes he will observe what he missed before. And in resisting one impulse to cry he makes a self-criticism that has a double value: he threatens to "pluck out," if they weep again, his "old fond eyes" (I.iv, 323–24). As it turns out, it is not his eyes that are plucked out, but Gloucester's—because he did not finally surrender, but did show compassion to a public enemy. But the eyes which are "fond" because they would weep [24] have already been "fond" in another way: we are reminded again of Lear's original blindness.

CHORUS

By a full and varied use of all the functions of men's eyes Shakespeare has achieved a rich, multivalued symbolic expression of man's moral make-up. Kent, whose detachment and courage are set forth in the sight imagery,[25] uses a proverbial saying for a comment on Lear's ironic fate.

> Good King, that must approve the common saw,
> Thou out of heaven's benediction com'st
> To the warm sun! (II.ii, 167–69)

The king's experience, that is, burns him; but the sun is light, also, and Lear, by suffering, receives illumination. Lear at first not only sees Cordelia in the wrong light, but encourages Burgundy to do likewise; the terms in which Cordelia and France comment upon Burgundy's view of Cordelia indicate that he is looking at her from the wrong point of view: his "regards" are "Aloof from th' entire point"[26] (I.i, 243). That is, his seeing is directed by the wrong values—a matter which other patterns to which we shall come make much of. This line, then, and that of Kent's have a choral value; and the aptness of the symbol appears in its ability to be used chorally.[27]

An effective chorus is never a flat statement which comes up with a two-plus-two-equals-four about the figures on the stage. It needs to be integral with the design, and wholly unselfconscious, and for that reason it comes best as a speech which belongs primarily to its own dramatic context but which, by its identification with the pattern of which the reader has become aware, transcends the context and becomes an imaginative commentary upon the whole world of the drama. When the Gentleman speaks of "impetuous blasts, with eyeless rage" (III.i, 8), surely his words "eyeless rage" suggest the essence of various actions—primarily the unseeing passion of Lear, but also that of Gloucester, and that of Cornwall to come, and of the sisters still later: rages which are retribution and which call forth further retribution. When Edgar tells Gloucester that he can no longer look down the supposed cliff lest "the deficient sight/Topple down headlong" (IV.vi, 23–24), we can only think of the "deficient sight" that causes disaster throughout the play, and of those whom it has indeed toppled down headlong. When the Fool wittily exclaims, "All that follow their noses are led by their eyes but blind men . . ." [28] (II.iv, 68–70), the very fact that he makes his statement as a general truth strengthens the reminder that in the world of the play there are few that follow their eyes, or that have eyes to follow. Lear and Gloucester are blind to the meaning of those phenomena which betoken the presence of evil; Edmund, Goneril, and Regan to the existence of moral barriers to the consummation of their ambitions. But the blind man cannot be tricked by his eyes; whereas those who pride themselves on clear sight may be misled both by the world they seem to control and by the appearance of well-being within themselves. And after so much rage, so many reversals, so much agony, so much searching for truth, it is fitting for Edgar to close by saying, "We that are young/Shall never see so much. . . ." An epoch has passed; the next stage in the cycle will be quieter and less searching.

What the sight pattern never lets us forget is the importance of man's way of looking at the world: the problem is not, "How shall the world be saved?" but "How shall the world be seen?" And since seeing implies understanding, the sight pattern brings us at least to the threshold of the larger question, "How shall the world be understood?" That question is the special material of the madness pattern, in which Lear dominates. The sight and madness patterns work together creatively: they build up a reservoir of unformulated but powerful impressions which, when channeled by such a summary line as Gloucester's " 'Tis the time's plague, when madmen lead the blind" (IV.i, 46), release through it immense poetic force.

. . the Vestural tissue, namely, of woolen or other cloth; which Man's Soul wears as its outmost wrappage and overall; . . . In all speculations they have tacitly figured man as a Clothed Animal; *whereas he is by nature a* Naked Animal; *and only in certain circumstances, by purpose and device, masks himself in* Clothes.

* * *

Happy he who can look through the Clothes of a Man . . . into the Man himself. . . .

* * *

Thus in this one pregnant subject of CLOTHES, rightly understood, is included all that men have thought, dreamed, done, and been. . . .

Carlyle, Sartor Resartus

CHAPTER III

POOR NAKED WRETCHES AND PROUD ARRAY

THE CLOTHES PATTERN

T H E   P R O B L E M of *seeing* human experience accurately is not one which Shakespeare oversimplifies or reduces to a formula. In fact, the whole content of the sight pattern is resolved into the Sophoclean paradox that the blind may see better than the proudly keen-eyed. But the play also attacks the problem of seeing and understanding from another direction: it presents elaborately the obstacles which interpose between human sight and its objects. We are made fully aware that man faces obdurate materials, efforts to deceive, and his own tendency to reconstruct the objective world according to his own preconceptions. It is at least comprehensible that Lear mistakes the moral identity of Goneril, Regan, Cordelia, and Kent, and subsequently fails to suspect that his new follower is Kent: and that Gloucester likewise confuses the nature of his two sons and later does not recognize the helper of his blindness. These errors may be fatal or merely pathetic; but we are not invited merely to condemn or to sympathize. Instead we are compelled to enter fully into perceptual experiences of distracting difficulty and hence to feel— if not to follow out to metaphysical conclusions—oppressive problems of personal identity. When Edgar soliloquizes, "Edgar I nothing am" (II.iii, 21), the lines embody a good deal of the pathos of exile. But the effects are more poignant when Lear for the first time runs into a double problem of identity in a world where all has seemed secure.[1] He asks Goneril, "Are you our daughter?" (I.iv, 238), and he continues more sharply, "Your name, fair gentlewoman?" [2] (257). But his most anguished questions are addressed to himself:

> Doth any here know me? This is not Lear.
> Doth Lear walk thus? speak thus? Where are his eyes?
> . . . .
> Who is it that can tell me who I am? [3] (I.iv, 246–50)

What the play gets into, then, is some preliminary speculation about appearance and reality. In this speculation, the disguises are the larger dramatic components of the ideological structure; it is impossible *not* to regard them as something more than necessities imposed upon the characters by circumstance. There are two kinds of disguise in the play— the psychological and the physical; the psychological disguises, except Edgar's, conceal unscrupulous intentions; the physical are protective. Thus there is an ironic correspondence among all the disguised people: they cannot manage by being candidly themselves: *appearances* rule, or seem to rule, the world. Yet that kinship only heightens the moral distinction between acquisitiveness and survival. In dealing with Edmund, Goneril, and Regan, Shakespeare is actually making a sardonic comment on what we today know as "success," as "winning friends and influencing people." But if pretense and hypocrisy are base, it does not follow that can-

did integrity has an easy road in an actual world. Cordelia
and Kent suffer in their society because they are not disguised, not tempered to the prevailing winds; the Fool must
cover his grasp of reality with irrelevancies; Edgar must
undertake a complete negation of real personality; Kent
must disguise himself even from his patron. In such a world
Lear must ask what *reality* is, and he can deal with an apparently insoluble question only by departing, to all intents and
purposes, from the world of reality.

Initially the play appears to commit itself to the cynical
view that only appearances count in the world. As a whole,
however, the drama disposes of this early hypothesis: appearance comes eventually to be understood, and properly
valued. The first two lines of the last speech in the play, indeed, are more than rough-cut didacticism: they apply specifically to the theme which we are here discussing. The
speaker, Edgar, says,

> The weight of this sad time we must obey,
> Speak what we feel, not what we ought to say. (V.iii, 323–24)

Here, finally, all appearances are dissolved. In the meantime, however, they have strongly influenced the action.
Throughout the play there is a systematic commentary upon
appearances that are misread, upon the difficulties of per-
ceiving the world truly, upon the failure—which may itself
be a spiritual affirmation—to put up a good appearance,
upon, that is, naïveté, defenselessness, innocence. This commentary appears especially in the *clothes pattern*, as components of which we find, on the one hand, larger dramatic
elements such as the clothing and nakedness of characters,
and, on the other, the recurrent imagery of clothes.

In the center of this pattern is Edgar. Since his disguise has both psychological and physical aspects, Edgar has a place in different structural elements in the play. As a pretended lunatic he helps develop the madness pattern; as a disguised person he is the most conspicuous figure in the clothes pattern. His disguise, of course, is virtual nakedness, and it illustrates how inevitably the literal and commonplace goes over into the symbolic. This nakedness is at one level simply a technical propriety in the Bedlam beggar; but by its particular inadequacy to a cold and stormy night—the language of III.iv never permits us to forget the cold—it becomes a symbol of that defenselessness in the world which Edgar [3] has already shown and indeed of the situation of innocent people generally, unprotected by worldliness or pretense [4] in a world swept by the storms of ambition and other uncontrolled emotions. But Edgar's nakedness is also a defense, and in terms of the play the innocent have always a defense, if not against immediate enemies, at least against ultimate corruption. The naked wretches may ultimately have a better protection than those who are proudly arrayed in what the world values. To strip oneself may be folly; but nakedness may be an aid to understanding. The clothes pattern, like the sight pattern, contains its paradoxes,[5] and thus it is woven into the main fabric of meaning. In *King Lear* deprivation is often the way to gain.

LEAR

The clothes pattern makes a running commentary on the intellectual and moral problems that arise in Lear's kingdom. Edgar is driven to a nakedness that is a symbol of his defenselessness and yet itself a kind of defense. Lear finally tries to tear off his clothes to be like Edgar. But the impact upon us of that apparently deranged impulse becomes very much stronger when we are made to realize, by the language of earlier scenes, that in effect some of Lear's main actions have pointed toward the clothes-tearing scene as a climax. At the very start Lear says,

> Since now we will *divest* us both of rule,
> Interest of territory, cares of state, (I.i, 50–51)

but this *undressing* for easy sleep is also a removal of armor against the arrows of fortune; Lear himself points up the situation a minute later when he tells Goneril and Regan and their husbands,

> I do *invest* you jointly with my power,
> Pre-eminence and all the large effects
> That troop with majesty. (132–34)

Lear naïvely makes an exception: "Only we shall retain/The name and all th' additions to a king" (137–38). He would retain prerogatives without responsibility, immunity without safeguards, warmth without clothes. He forgets that there are no naked kings [6] (it is just a few lines later that Kent calls him mad), and he is not yet aware in what sense he can, as he has said, "unburthen'd crawl toward death" (I.i, 42). His own words symbolize a basic mistake which initiates the whole train of tragic consequences. His withdrawal from the world of action is not only the removal of a burden; it is likewise the removal of a necessary protection.[7] He cannot be "unburthen'd" unless he is willing to be unqualifiedly unburdened. Although ideally it ought not to be so, in fact abdication means the poorhouse. The paradoxical interdependence of security and responsibility Lear does not realize; he oversimplifies the situation; some hard learning lies before him.[8] Oswald gives the first lesson by his insolence in I.iv; then a brilliant teacher, the Fool, begins to bring home to him the fact that he has lost the apparel of royalty. The Fool jeers, ". . . when thou gav'st them the rod and put'st down thine own breeches,

> Then they for sudden joy did weep" (I.iv, 189–91);

this is excellent: not only does it help develop the children-parents theme, but it tells us that Lear has actually reduced himself to the status of a child. The Fool exclaims, ". . . I can tell why a snail has a house. . . . Why, to put's head in; not to give it away to his daughters, and leave his horns without a case" (I.v, 30–33). To take off his crown was to lose his house. Lear's change of garb echoes in another song of the Fool's:

> Fathers that wear rags
> Do make their children blind (II.iv, 48–49) —

lines in which—an illustration of the regular coalescence of patterns in the play—both the sight and clothing symbols are at work. Lear—told that he is a child, houseless, ragged —begins to see what has happened. When Regan suggests that Lear try to make it up with Goneril, he ironically rehearses a speech for himself as suppliant: "On my knees I beg/That you'll vouchsafe me raiment, bed and food" (II. iv, 157–58)—*raiment,* a symbol of all that he has given up and can neither get back by asking nor even ask for. So when Lear runs in the storm "unbonneted" (III.i, 14), "bareheaded" (III.ii, 60; cf. III.vii, 59), his unprotectedness is more than physical and more than an accident or device of staging. There is a special ironic pertinence in the fact that it is his *head* which is bare, for thus the experience is unmistakably connected both with his own initial decision and act and also with the madness that is to overtake him: he has specifically bared his head by giving away his crown, saying to his "beloved sons," "This coronet part betwixt you" (I.i, 141). Shakespeare seems to be consciously using the crown in his development of theme; the scepter, for instance, would not be nearly so well adapted to the symbolic structure. Now the Fool never lets Lear forget his bareheadedness or the source of it, and his repeated reference to it is a way of letting us see that it is more than a casual device for making suffering concrete. The Fool offers Lear his "coxcomb" and makes jokes about it (I.iv, 106 ff.), and finally advises him to "beg another of thy daughters" (121); then he suggests that he will break an egg and give Lear "the two crowns of the egg" to replace the two halves of the crown he gave away (171); and his bitterest comment follows Lear's first bout with the storm: "He that has a house to put's head in has a good head-piece.

> The cod-piece that will house
> Before the head has any,
> The head and he shall louse. . . . (III.ii, 27–29)

The head is bare of its crown; the torture is in part the result of bad headwork; and at the same time bareheadedness suggests the unprotected sensitive mind which will soon give way. The storm beats about Lear's head in the same way in which emotional and intellectual storms batter at his mind. In the context the efforts of Kent and Gloucester to bring Lear to shelter become more than a one-dimensional kindness; the men are trying to reduce the effect of what he has let himself in for; and their efforts are exactly comparable to Edgar's later services to Gloucester.

But if by giving up the clothes of kingship Lear has laid himself open to the buffets of the world, he has at the same time become capable of wider feelings, and wider perceptions. With the Fool's pity-by-derision is contrasted a direct expression of pity by Lear himself. The scene is on the heath, before a hovel; and Lear has told the Fool to go in first. Lear says,

> You houseless poverty—
> . . . .
> Poor naked wretches, wheresoe'er you are,
> That bide the pelting of this pitiless storm,
> How shall your houseless heads and unfed sides,
> Your loop'd and window'd raggedness, defend you
> From seasons such as these? Oh, I have ta'en
> Too little care of this! Take physic, pomp;
> Expose thyself to feel what wretches feel. . . .
> (III.iv, 26–34)

Naked, houseless (especially conspicuous in its combination with *heads*), *raggedness*, and *expose* continue the clothes pattern and gain strength from it: they must not do all their work at the moment but can call upon habits of response, and upon associations, which their fellows have helped establish. By the same token, if the passage is at one level a statement of compassion for the materially underprivileged —and the significance of Lear's new pity, which all critics have observed, is by no means to be ignored—it is also, in the symbolic context, a recognition of the fate of the innocent in the world, the unprotected with whom Lear is now iden-

tified. If "I have ta'en too little care" gives voice to a characteristic indifference of royalty, it also suggests Lear's
specific failing: his unawareness of the realities of the suffering encountered by the defenseless, his selfish passion
for verbal luxuries within his own apparently impregnable
stronghold, has played a part in undermining his own position. His passionate loathing of his daughters is complicated
by the gradual realization of his own responsibility in the
situation. Thus in the clothes pattern we find an implied commentary upon the tragic flaw.

Edgar ("poor Tom") appears a few seconds later, and
for some time the stories of Edgar and Lear are almost fused,
especially by means of the clothes pattern. When Lear,
speaking as if Edgar had been brought to his present pass by
daughters, asks, "Would'st thou give 'em all?" (III.iv, 67),
the Fool wonderfully interjects, "Nay, he reserv'd a blan-
ket, else we had all been sham'd" (68), ironically applying
a standard of modesty that, when high matters of justice are
at stake, is petty and irrelevant. He suggests, too, the ironic
disparity between Lear and Edgar: the former has literally
more clothes yet is now more seriously exposed in an inimical world. Edgar tells of his sinful past and moralizes, and
from all his words the clothes imagery, although it does not
have a primary position, is never absent. He says that he
"wore gloves in my cap" (III.iv, 88), and he exhorts: "set
not thy sweet heart on proud array" (84), "Let not the
creaking of shoes nor the rustling of silks betray thy poor
heart to women" (97–98), and "Keep . . . thy hand out
of placket . . ." (100). The ironic unnecessariness of such
injunctions is a way of emphasizing the defenselessness of
this pair who now have nothing in common with the bold and

worldly young man Edgar describes; at the same time we cannot help thinking that Lear, if he was not precisely a victim of the rustling of silks, did most certainly betray his poor heart to women, and that above all he did not intelligently enough devote himself to proud array—to the complex of privilege and responsibility implied by the purple. The imaginary young Tom and the actual Lear had both misconceived proud array, taking it as immunity to the ills that flesh is heir to.

Then Lear, still contemplating Edgar's "uncover'd body" (106), makes the speech which is the climax of the pattern so far, is, actually, the goal of most of what has gone before. Concluding that Edgar owes nothing to worm, beast, or sheep for clothes, Lear reasons, "Ha! here's three on's are sophisticated! Thou art the thing itself; unaccommodated man is no more but such a poor, bare, forked animal as thou art. Off, off, you lendings! come, unbutton here" (111–14). His effort to tear off his clothes is an ironic conclusion to the sequence begun in Act I, when Lear said that he would *divest* himself of rule, land, and cares. Then he acted in hope of a quiet old age; now he acts in bitter disillusionment in which, even though his mind is giving way, he carries to a mercilessly logical extreme his fierce sense of the appropriate, a sense which others have brutally violated. Tearing off clothes may be, clinically, a symptom of delirium; [9] but the scientifically accurate contributes perfectly to the symbolic pattern: in Lear's situation, nakedness alone is meaningful and clothes are a "sophistication." Edgar is right; he is at one with nature; unaccommodated in the essentials of royal life, Lear finds his remnants of "proud array" a mockery. After all this symbolic sloughing off of the externals of life by one who has undergone agonizing deprivations, "poor Tom's" tireless pitter-patter about his past echoes on—apparently aimless, but with its occasional thrusts into the heart of the present. For once, he tells us, he "had three suits to his back, six shirts to his body" (141–42). Lear, too, before his divestiture, had suits enough. Thus, by the aid of the pattern, pseudo-mad irrelevancies actually contribute to the imaginative richness of the play.

So the Lear who is in effect naked wants to be naked in fact; the passion for a harmonizing of inner and outer belongs to his bitter enlightenment. But his mind wanders; it is not yet ready for the fanatic concentration on a single theme that it is capable of in IV.vi, where the mad Lear gives his climactic description of the world. Yet there is an obsession with clothes that can show itself in word or deed; Shakespeare does not allow us to forget the problem of covering— whether it be for protection or literally for *decency*, that is, fittingness. From the impulse to strip down to nature Lear ironically goes on, the next time we see him, to criticize Edgar's meager garb as "Persian" (III.vi, 83–86)—contrary to "nature," perhaps?—and then, by the time of his next appearance (to Edgar and Gloucester, in the country near Dover), to put on from nature a "fantastic" garb of, in the stage directions added by different editors, "wild flowers" or "weeds" (IV.vi, 79). The immediate link with the earlier episode of Lear's stripping himself is twofold: it is Edgar, once naked, who promptly comments, "The safer sense will ne'er accommodate/His master thus" (81–82); and his very use of *accommodate* at once reminds us that Lear is still, in his own earlier words to Edgar, "unaccommodated man." Cordelia has already described Lear as

Crown'd with rank fumiter and furrow weeds,
With hardocks, hemlock, nettles, cuckoo flow'rs,
Darnell, and all the idle weeds that grow
In our sustaining corn (IV.iv, 3–6) —

plants long ago identified as "bitter, biting, poisonous, pungent, lurid, and distracting" and as emblematic of madness.[10] In Lear then is still the powerful urgency toward the appropriate, toward a correspondence of inner and outer; Cordelia's term "idle weeds," which is probably to be read as a pun, points the irony of his state, and at the same time faintly suggests the moral situation of the kingdom as a whole. It is as if some underlying sanity in Lear had driven him to a parody of himself as king, to an expression of his discovery, through his attempted exercise of prerogatives after his abdication, that all he possessed was a parody of kingship. His nakedness is covered by mock adornments. The whole sequence of experiences is emphasized by Cordelia's use of the word *crown'd*—incidentally the only authentic textual evidence of Lear's attire. For in Act I Lear took off a crown; in Act III he was bareheaded; and now he has a mock crown. Yet it is important to recognize that in this incongruity there is nothing of the ludicrous; nor is there a jeer or an easy bid for pity. In one sense, Lear has his crown of thorns—a symbol of the anguish which is the heart of the redemptive experience.[11] In another sense, he is on the way to restoration of a kind, at least to such a one as he can have—to recovery, in part, of mental balance, to a reunion with Cordelia, a realization of his own spiritual potentialities. And, considered in the immediate context, he is on the way to his final brilliant court scene in the fields near Dover (IV.iv, V.iii). I say "court scene" because there his royal quality, his personal force, and his imaginative vigor are the dominating center of all events. If not a king in fact, he is a king by nature—in this natural scene, and with a crown from nature, a crown that is a flimsy likeness of the symbol of earthly kingship, an image of grief and failure, and yet somehow an insigne of what has been kept—and of something gained.

TURNS OF FORTUNE'S WHEEL

In the clothes pattern we find regularly a symbolic echo of changes in circumstance. There is a hint of this in Lear's irony-laden remark to Edgar: ". . . I do not like the fashion of your garments: you will say they are Persian attire; but let them be changed" (III.vi, 84–86). Now actually the "Persian," that is, "luxurious," Edgar is on the point of giving up the nakedness which Lear has so ironically misconceived. But before Edgar is clothed, his nakedness is to be used for one more important point. After being blinded, Gloucester wanders on the heath and meets Edgar, "poor mad Tom," whom he proposes to use as guide. Almost the first thing Gloucester recalls from the meetings of the preceding night—the night of the storm—is that Tom is naked, and he says to the Old Man, ". . . bring some covering for this naked soul" (IV.i, 44). Thus through the clothes pattern we see that Gloucester, like Lear, is growing in charity, and at the same time that Gloucester is evincing what is tantamount to an ironic reversal of attitude to the Edgar whom he had stripped of privilege. Edgar, of course, he does not yet know, but Gloucester's act is directed *toward someone who reminds him of Edgar.* Of seeing "Tom" in the storm he says,

> My son
> Came then into my mind, and yet my mind
> Was then scarce friends with him. I have heard more since.
>   (IV.i, 33–35)

When we next see the pair, that is, on the way to Dover cliffs, Edgar is dressed (IV.vi). The end of Edgar's nakedness coincides exactly with his dual change of status with regard to his father: he is now Gloucester's guardian, and Gloucester knows the truth about him. Both as a man upon whom are thrust the responsibilities of protector and as a son who knows that he has regained his father's love,[12] he gains strength and defenses; he is no longer the unprotected wanderer. He is no longer the unloved outlander, so to speak, the Theban, the Athenian, the Persian that Lear had taken him for; spiritually he is again at home in his native country, in his own home. At the same time this meaning of clothes—the recovery of a personal status from which he had been an outcast—is richly intertwined with another meaning discussed at the beginning of this chapter,[13] that which arises from the problem of identity. Gloucester thinks his companion has changed, both in voice and in manner of speech. Edgar insists: "You're much deceiv'd. In nothing am I chang'd/But in my garments" (IV.vi, 9–10). Again the ironic note: once before, Edgar had not been changed, though Gloucester had thought so—and had been "deceived"; and, more widely, much that has been looked upon by both Gloucester and Lear as human change has been but in the garments, in the external semblance of people. But if Edgar has remained the same, the front which he has had to present to the world has had to change, and the clothes commentary emphasizes one more of these changes. In Act V Edgar appears to Albany disguised (V.i, after 37), and then, for the fight with Edmund, not only disguised but armed (V.iii, after 118); and after fatally wounding Edmund he reveals himself (V. iii, 169)—the first time he has appeared as himself since II.i. His dress has accurately mirrored every change from innocence in flight to competence in affairs.[14] But there is one other complication: Edgar tells how his identification of himself has caused Gloucester's death (V.iii, 192 ff.): for the second time Gloucester, upon the removal of a son's disguise, has seen too much. The removal of Edmund's psychological disguise brought the double shock of recognizing the nature of Edmund and the injustice to Edgar. These recognition scenes are ironically linked. The recognition of what Edmund is and of what Edmund has caused him to do to Edgar brings Gloucester to despair, and he seeks death; Edgar saves him from death-by-despair, and then, in revealing himself to Gloucester, paves the way for his death—a death-by-ecstasy. Edgar blames himself for having maintained his disguise. Disguise, then, is complexly treated: it may be necessary to saving life, but it can also be instrumental in death.

The clothes pattern continues its enriching commentary upon Lear on into his two climactic scenes in the latter part of the play. At the end of his passionate reason-in-madness speech Lear cries, "Pull off my boots; harder, harder, so" (IV.vi, 177). In one sense the words are an ironic resumption of the orders which were once his wont—appropriate to the powerful, commanding personality which Lear has exhibited throughout the scene; in another they tie up, as we shall see, with the first-act lines on his "retirement" from the kingship; finally they suggest the end of a journey and rest.

Lear's wanderings are over, indeed, and, when next we see him, he is in his restorative sleep. "Is he arrayed?" asks Cordelia—a question which, in the context we have been describing, is more than factual. What is Lear's state? Is he naked against the buffeting of a stormy world? Is he still in his wild garb? The Gentleman answers, "Ay, madam; in the heaviness of sleep/We put fresh garments on him" (IV.vii, 20–22). Lear gets a fresh start. The symbolism continues when Lear cannot identify "these garments" (or "where I did lodge last night") (67–68), just as he cannot tell generally what has happened and is happening to him. In the new clothes we see his return to something like normal understanding, and in the strangeness of his clothes to him, his failure to recognize, after distortions have become the regular thing, a normal world. From his early proud array to the present, his clothes, the outer surface or covering which he should present to the world, have been a problem to him. But such comforts as he now comes into are too late to save him, and, as Lear goes down, we see in the clothes pattern, precisely as we have found it in the sight pattern, a synthesizing comment on his career. Just before the final "look, look" with which he calls attention to Cordelia's face, he says, "Pray you, undo this button. Thank you, sir" (V. iii, 309)—an indication, presumably, of the physical distress which is death's messenger. But these unobtrusive words extend imaginatively way beyond the bare physiological fact which at the realistic level they denote: they are a means of pulling together a whole series of lines into an embracing system of meaning. Lear makes his last royal command, a very mild one, yet it takes us into the heart of the tragedy. For his words take us back to the *divest* of Act I,

when he was preparing casually for retirement, for ease before the final sleep; to the frantic *unbutton here* of Act III,
when he was attempting to make physical fact conform to the
spiritual unprotectedness which he had brought about by his
earlier disrobing; and to thé *pull off my boots* of Act IV,
when the fiercest travel in the hard world was over; and they
tell us of a final freeing from clothes that can be followed
by no new agony. Lear gives up prerogative and protection,
throws away clothes which have no meaning, prepares to rest
after a long struggle, and finally, a consequence of all that
has gone before, gives up life. The king's only safe divest-
ment is death.

So we see Lear repeatedly taking off what in a practical,
normal situation he should be keeping on—and, at the same
time, undergoing losses that finally include life. Yet
these losses are not spiritual; indeed, they accompany an
adjustment of values. If we see the movement of Lear from
well-accoutered king to half-clad fugitive, from putting off
of cares to giving up of life, we also observe his progress
from eyeless rage to seeing beneath the surfaces that deceived him. Once a victim of angry pride, he says to Cordelia, in his next-to-last speech to her, "I'll kneel down/And
ask of thee forgiveness" (V.iii, 10–11).

Not that we should ignore losses in the world. In fact, we
tend to think primarily, if not exclusively, of the fact that he
who does not clothe himself properly against a hard world is
lost. Yet there is another side to the picture: he with too thick
a sheathe in the workaday world is morally lost.

LEAR'S DAUGHTERS

The play constantly asks that we consider the front that characters present to the world and the relationship between that front and their moral quality. Not only the disguises, but the imagery raises the subject. Speaking of Oswald, Kent expresses anger "That such a slave as this should wear a sword,/Who wears no honesty" (II.ii, 78–79). In contrast with the physically naked, the relatively well-heeled Oswald is naked morally.[15] Only a few lines later—an ironic juxtaposition—Cornwall accuses Kent of putting on a false surface—just as Kent has accused Oswald of having a dishonest exterior: the two sets of lines make an interesting counterpoint within the scene. Cornwall says of Kent, who, having verbally cut Oswald to pieces, defends his own "plain" speech:

> This is some fellow
> Who, having been prais'd for bluntness, doth affect
> A saucy roughness, and constrains the garb
> Quite from his nature. (II.ii, 101–104)

Cornwall is wrong; plainness is Kent's regular garb. It is not a good shield in the practical world,[16] but it is an index of a saving spiritual quality. But Cornwall's words unite with Kent's words on Oswald to form a miniature word drama characteristic of the play: it briefly presents for us the whole problem of appearance and reality—and of what kind of appearance or dress really saves the human being.

Like Lear, Cordelia at the start seems to be divesting herself of an essential protective covering: she astonishes France by being able to "dismantle/So many folds of favor"

(I.i, 220–21). In one sense, the figure describes what, as we have seen, Cordelia herself has done. But Lear, uncrowned, unbonneted, beaten by the storm, has come to insight; he blames himself for Cordelia's fate. Kent tells of Lear's "sovereign shame" for "his own unkindness,/That stripp'd her from his benediction . . ." [17] (IV.iii, 44–45). At this time in the play, when the clothes pattern has been fully developed, *stripp'd* has special force.

But if Cordelia has opened herself to misfortune, she penetrates with assurance the disguise in which her sisters appear to have wooed fortune successfully:

Time shall unfold what plighted [enfolded] cunning hides;
Who cover faults, at last shame them derides. (I.i, 283–84)

Here is the other side of the case: in contrast with those who are stripped but save their souls we must see those who have thick clothes in the world but of whose souls there is no evidence. Ironically, even in the world these latter are not finally safe. But time is slow to unfold, and three acts, full of injury and suffering, must pass before the garments of the worldly begin to wear thin and betray the wearer. Things are at last going badly for the sisters when Albany, picking up Cordelia's word from Act I, can cry to Goneril, "Thou changed and self-cover'd thing, for shame" (IV.ii, 62) ; and it is appropriately Albany who closes the record of Goneril and Regan with exactly the right words, "Cover their faces" [18] (V.iii, 242). The dead must be covered, of course; but beneath this conventional meaning there lurks an ironic commentary prepared for by the clothes imagery—the final covering of the self-covered, the final removal from sight of those who had kept their true selves from Lear's sight. Time

85

unfolds, and death covers at last. And the line is "Cover their *faces*" [19]—the hard looks and scornful eyes; clothing and sight patterns come together.

CHORUS

In the record which Albany closes there is one earlier entry, a speech by Lear to Regan, which in itself is powerful enough but which, when it is read in the light of the pattern, takes on the resonant force of a choral statement about human experience. In a minute Lear is to plunge bareheaded into the storm, and there to join the naked Edgar. He is delivering a passionate invective against his daughters.

> If only to go warm were gorgeous,
> Why, nature needs not what thou gorgeous wear'st
> Which scarcely keeps thee warm. (II.iv, 271–73)

Lear almost foreshadows his own effort, in Act III, to strip down to nature by this accusation that his daughter is out of harmony with nature. She wears more than she needs, but to him she applies the canon of necessity. She strips him as he had stripped Cordelia from his favor. She is overdressed, but she will not allow him a satisfactory equipage. She shows us proud array at its worst—irresponsible, selfish. Ironically, what she wears does not keep her warm; Lear now recognizes her essential coldness. Yet she is the very antithesis of the poor naked wretches of whom Lear will soon think more, and among whom he will be. For the poor naked wretches of the play, the victims of the world, will survive in spirit. The gorgeous are doomed. In proud array, Lear failed; uncrowned, half-naked, he is saved. This is a central paradox of the play.

In interpreting the play, we must place beside the vast implications of *seeing* and *not seeing* the equally extensive ones of *taking off* and *putting on*. Human beings may with ironically good intentions remove the coverings which constitute or symbolize their defense against experience; or they may be stripped of them; or they may resort to nakedness. Human beings may likewise put on new coverings, as a defense in a disordered world, or as a disguise of real intentions that must not appear openly until evil ends have been achieved or until the danger from evil forces is lessened. Some men do not see clearly enough; some see too clearly; some are not adequately clad; and some are overdressed. Further, fate does not let some dress as they will, and others cannot see the character behind the dress. The images and symbols give us an inordinately complex world. But we may say, in general, that upon the quality of his seeing and upon the quality of his dress depends man's fate in the world. The play, however, goes on to a subject beyond man's fate in the world—man's moral and spiritual fate. In that realm, paradoxically, blindness and nakedness may have their values, for they do not exclude the possibility, respectively, of man's having insight, and immunity to worldly corruption. The blind are not misled by their eyes, nor the naked by their proud array.

We are rational; but we are animal too.
Cowper

*　*　*

. . . a woman without heart . . . who lived in a strange loveless oscillation between calculation and instinct.
Robert Penn Warren, *All the King's Men*

CHAPTER IV

THE BREACH IN NATURE

HUMAN NATURE

T H E C L O T H E S S Y M B O L I S M of the play leads inevitably to another problem. For the clothes symbolism, as we have seen, introduces questions about the relationship of appearance and reality, speculations about the character behind the disguise and the quality in need of protection. What is the nature of the reality behind the appearance, the nature of man who wears his defenses or presents his disguises or appears in appalling nakedness? What is the nature of man, and what is the nature of nature? If the blind see, and the naked survive, are there comparable paradoxes in the heart of man and in the universe which he inhabits? Insofar as it suggests answers to such questions, the play develops what we may call *the nature theme*. I say that the play "suggests answers" because it is concerned, of course, not with making a formal philosophic statement but with presenting the quality of experience. But various characters do make formal statements that help develop the nature theme; certain actions likewise constitute statements of the theme; and finally the imagery itself is thematically important.

The patterns of language in the play, as we have seen, gain some of their strength from the fact that they work in concert with certain events, certain larger dramatic facts and situations, which they both prepare for and amplify. The imagery of sight is an ally of the actual blindness of Gloucester; that of clothes collaborates with the nakedness of Edgar, which Lear emulates, and with the wide use of disguise in the play. Similarly the inquiry into the nature of man and his world finds its physical counterpart in the terrific storm of Act III; the storm is terrible, something out of nature, as all critical comments indicate; the characters' awareness of its violence and unnaturalness is paralleled by their incredulous commentary upon the unnaturalness of the human conduct throughout the play. There are convulsions of nature on two levels.[1]

The storm, of course, is most easily thought of in its relation, in Lear's words, to "the tempest in my mind" (III.iv, 12); his madness is another convulsion of nature. Coleridge, whose description of the parallel is well known, says that "the howlings of convulsed nature would seem converted into the voice of conscious humanity."[2] There is a moral convulsion as well as a physical and a mental. The storm and madness are tremendously real, but we are never allowed to forget the moral disorder of which they are both symbols. Lear himself keeps reflecting upon the moral *cause* of his mental turmoil, and it is this which he tends to identify with the peltings of the physical storm. "In such a night/To shut me out! Pour on; I will endure," he says (III.iv, 17–18). That is, daughters and tempest both *pour on,* and both he will *endure.* Earlier there is a still more explicit passage. Rain, wind, thunder, fire are not his daughters, he says; they are not unkind; they owe him no allegiance; he is their slave. But yet, he says paradoxically,

. . . I call you servile ministers,
That will with two pernicious daughters join
Your high-engender'd battles 'gainst a head
So old and white as this. O! O! 'tis foul! (III.ii, 21–24)

In the storm, then, we see human nature torn loose from all law and order, and, in its orgiastic quality, the moral derangement of the human agents.[3] So the question arises: what is the human nature which is capable of such derangement? And which is, conversely, capable of enduring such evils? How account for the whole scheme of things here presented?

The way in which the play comments upon such problems is extraordinarily complex: there are no easy and simple answers, but a multitude of philosophical implications are made by the poetic and dramatic structure. Several premises lie behind the words and events which are the immediate materials of the play. One is that there is an order, a system, a realizable core of meaning in the universe; the other is that that order is able to be catastrophically disrupted. The tragic world is a kind of chaos: the disorder within the soul is projected into the larger world. Yet the tragedy as a whole affirms the pre-eminence of order; the paradox of tragedy is that order comes out of a world wracked by disorder, that chaos proves order.[4] There cannot be a breach in nature unless there is a nature.

But the breach absorbs the primary attention of tragedy.[5] If as a whole the play asserts man's ability to achieve salvation—it is virtually a commonplace that the experiences of Lear and Gloucester are purgatorial—*King Lear* constantly points out man's liability to damnation. Human nature is ambivalent; it operates on two levels; one represents its proper order, and action on the other level clashes with that order. The clash produces the breach which *King Lear* is tirelessly intent upon defining.

One of the chief means of definition is the animal imagery, of which there is a profusion.[6] Only by a constant recourse to it do the characters seem capable of setting forth the quality of the life amidst which they find themselves; animality is what they observe behind the surface, behind the coverings and the disguises. In the same way the play makes use of the facts and the imagery of sex to show the descent of man, who has high spiritual potentialities, into animal will and appetite. By implication man may regard himself in two ways: as moving by discipline toward spirit, or by undisciplined desire toward the animal. In *King Lear* the former is almost taken for granted as the course of human nature; but the occurrence of the latter is documented without modification, and recorded with horror.

What we are told by the language which we shall examine in this chapter is that the animal often takes over in man who has extraordinary intelligence, that is, is gifted in a particularly human way. There is a paradoxical union of generically opposed qualities.[7] The combination is fertile, productive; it generates immense force; like a storm, it is a wrench in the order of things; and like a storm, it sweeps all before it and seems irresistible. Yet it fails—another paradox. The clear-seeing are blind, ultimately; the gorgeous are unprotected; those of animal strength and sharp mind, though they may destroy much, do not conquer.

But before we can follow Shakespeare's paradox further, we need to see how the nature theme is presented by the animal and sex imagery.

THE ANIMAL IN MAN

Much of the animal imagery is employed, as I have suggested, to emphasize the ferocity and bestiality into which human beings can fall. More than a dozen times the imagery is thus used to categorize Goneril and Regan. Their actions speak for themselves, of course; but the figures used, aside from heightening the characterization, serve to indicate that other dramatis personae can qualify the sisters only by metaphors from the animal kingdom.

The first definition of the daughters' character by this means sets the tone for the whole. It is the Fool's couplet:

> The hedge-sparrow fed the cuckoo so long,
> That it had it head bit off by it young. (I.iv, 235–36)

Goneril and Regan mercilessly injure him who has fed and enriched them; the figure tells us, besides, that things are upside down, that natural order is violated.[8] Shortly afterward Lear first turns upon them a stream of metaphors that will flow on even in his madness. Goneril's ingratitude, he says, is more hideous "Than the sea-monster" (I.iv, 283). He calls her "Detested kite!" (I.iv, 284), and Regan, he assures Goneril, will "flay thy wolvish visage" (I.iv, 330). "To have a thankless child," he generalizes, is "sharper than serpent's tooth" (I.iv, 310–11). The Fool's final line in this scene is appropriate:

> A fox, when one has caught her,
> And such a daughter,
> Should sure to the slaughter. . . . (340–42)

In the next act Lear continues of Goneril: ". . . she hath tied/Sharp-tooth'd unkindness, like a vulture, here!" (II.

93

iv, 136–37); and again, "struck me with her tongue,/Most serpent-like, . . ." (II.iv, 162–63). When Lear understands that Regan is not different from Goneril, he speaks of "Those pelican daughters" (III.iv, 77), and in his madness he addresses them, as if they were present, as "you she-foxes" (III.vi, 24).

But from here on his violence, though it does not disappear, has less recourse to this kind of denunciatory imagery. In fact, in the midst of the fierce indictments of the trial scene, Lear has one line of exceptional mildness, antici-patory of the manner he is to have when he awakes in the presence of Cordelia: "The little dogs and all,/Tray, Blanch, and Sweetheart, see, they bark at me" (III.vi, 65–66); thereupon Edgar, as Mad Tom, proceeds to scare off the imaginary dogs—of which he names various species—by an exorcizing chant. Hazlitt comments that Lear now sees every creature in league against him.[9] Yet it seems also possible that Lear may be stating the problem of his daughters in a different way, momentarily reverting, in a change of mood and rhythm characteristic of madness, to his incredulity at the situation: the friendly house dogs—they are identified as such by their names—are unbelievably turning upon him. But once they have turned, they must simply be regarded as other curs; and it happens that in his final castigating use of animal imagery, Lear's words pick up the dog imagery. In pretending to chase away "Tray, Blanch, and Sweetheart," Edgar calls, "Avaunt, you curs!" (III.vi, 68). An act later we find this dialogue,

> *Lear.* . . . Thou hast seen a farmer's dog bark at a beggar?
> *Glou.* Ay, sir.
> *Lear.* And the creature run from the cur? There thou mightst

behold the great image of authority; a dog's obeyed in office.
(IV.vi, 159–63)

This is a part of the very fine reason-in-madness speech, so
that it comments generally upon evil in the political world:
the human being who holds office has authority over other
human beings, even though he has become subhuman or
animal. This is precisely the situation of Goneril and Regan.
In the meantime, the description of the sisters by means of
the dog imagery has been continued by Kent and Gloucester.
The former calls them "dog-hearted daughters" (IV.iii,
47), and Gloucester, during the inquisition which precedes
his blinding, says of himself, "I am tied to th' stake, and I
must stand the course" (III.vii, 54)—that is, he is like a
bear being attacked by a relay of dogs. The dog imagery is
very effective: in other comparisons the daughters are called
ungrateful, treacherous, and ferocious, but in the dog imagery their commonplace selfishness, plus their fawning
upon Lear in Act I, is set forth. Too, this imagery shows the
domestic world in moral turmoil along with the political
world.

In the latter half of the play other characters besides Lear
find it increasingly necessary to use animal imagery to describe Goneril and Regan. In the blinding scene, Gloucester
refers to their "boarish fangs" (III.vii, 58). Goneril evokes
from Albany a whole series of such terms. "Tigers, not
daughters," he exclaims (IV.ii, 40), and he adds that Lear's
"reverence even the head-lugg'd bear would lick" (42). If
heaven, he continues, do not quickly

> . . . tame these vile offences
It will come

Humanity must perforce prey on itself,
Like monsters of the deep. (47–50)

"Be-monster not thy feature," he tells Goneril (63), and near the end of the play he calls her "This gilded serpent" (V.iii, 84) and her deeds, "Most monstrous!" (159). The body of meaning built up by this series of terms gains force from the fact that even a "Third Servant" contributes to it: if Regan, he says after the blinding of Gloucester, lives long and dies a natural death, "Women will all turn monsters" (III.vii, 102). And there is, finally, a neat rounding-out of the scheme [10] in Edmund's description of the sisters: "Each jealous of the other, as the stung/Are of the adder" (V.i, 56–57). His own vanity, and his insight into them, contribute to an ironic ratification of all that has been said of them. Each of them has become, to the other, the destroying animal she is to other characters. For the second time the imagery has shown Goneril and Regan using against each other the qualities that have been felt by the victims of both of them. They turned their hard looks against each other (the sight pattern); now they have become serpents to each other.[11]

A few times "good" characters are described in terms of animal imagery: Gloucester calls Edgar a "monster" (I.ii, 102) and "worse than brutish" (I.ii, 82); Cornwall calls Kent "beastly knave" (II.ii, 75); Regan calls Gloucester an "ingrateful fox" (III.vii, 27) and the Servant who defends Gloucester "dog" (74). In these passages it is the speakers who are characterized: it is one index of the art of the play that such metaphors are as a class used ambivalently. A still more meaningful complication appears in two other passages. Astonished by Lear's early attitude to Cordelia, France says

96

> Sure, her offence
> Must be of such unnatural degree
> That monsters it. . . . (I.i, 221–23)

For France, of course, this is merely a way of commenting upon the irrationality of Lear's whole proceeding with his daughter; since France's term, although Cordelia has some responsibility for the total situation, is too strong to be applicable to her, the term tends actually to make Lear into the monster. Now this passage is yoked with another considerably later in the play, in which Kent says of Lear that "these things"—his taking away Cordelia's rights and giving them to her sisters—

> . . . sting
> His mind so venomously that burning shame
> Detains him from Cordelia. (IV.iii, 47–49)

Sting, venomously, and the suggestion of fever in the phrase *burning shame* describe Lear's past deeds as if they were poisonous serpents: in other words, Lear himself cannot be wholly distinguished from the outright evil characters of the play; just as the sight pattern stressed Lear's blindness, so it now appears that there has been something of the animal, of the monster, in him too. The link between France's lines in Act I and Kent's in Act IV is reinforced by the fact that each passage juxtaposes the animal imagery and the clothes imagery, already quoted, which describes Cordelia's being stripped of "favour" and "blessing." [12] The two examples of collaborating imagery—which, as we begin to see more and more, is a stylistic mark of the play—explain a deprivation as a product of man's yielding to the animal element in him. The irony of it is, of course, that Lear is taking something away not only from Cordelia but from himself. But whatever the outcome, the fact is the responsibility of Lear: the animal imagery, like the sight and clothes imagery, helps realize Lear's tragic flaw. Since the animal imagery is used primarily to characterize his daughters, what I have contended earlier finds some corroboration in the animal pattern—that it is not for nothing that Lear is the father of Goneril.

Two examples of animal imagery of different tone, both occurring late in the play, contribute to the system of paradox of *King Lear*. Speaking to Edmund of Albany, Goneril refers to "the cowish terror of his spirit" (IV. ii, 12); primarily, of course, her words characterize herself, but perhaps they also tell us something of Albany, who, although he is certainly not cowardly and has become very dependable, does appear to have been sluggish.[13] An act later, after they are made prisoners, Lear says to Cordelia, "Come, let's away to prison./We two alone will sing like birds i' th' cage" (V. iii, 8–9). Conquered, imprisoned, these two, as birds in a cage, seem to have come to very little—and even that they do not retain long. Yet they have come to insight: that is their victory. In that sense the cowish man, and the birds in the cage survive, while ruthless and powerful animals go down —just as the blind see and the poor naked wretches find salvation. In such paradoxes the play speaks.

SEX

The immediate function of the animal imagery is making evil concrete. What is said in terms of the imagery is that the nature of man is explicable only if we consider him closely related to a lower order of creation. Man's nature partakes of animal nature, and the animal in him can easily be called forth. The elaboration of this insight into human reality, an insight which never rests at an abstract level but is presented with concrete dramatic force, appears in several other passages which, since they are not limited to the description of specific characters, have a summary function. In one of his mad speeches Edgar describes himself as "hog in sloth, fox in stealth, wolf in greediness, dog in madness, lion in prey" (III.iv, 95–96). If we can read *madness* as *wrath* and *prey* as *covetousness*, and consider that he mentions *pride* and *lust* literally (87, 88, 92), Edgar has six of the Seven Deadly Sins, not to mention other vices on the side. Not only is such a catalogue a useful auxiliary way of stressing the sense of evil that permeates the play, but it also—even in Edgar's incoherent speech—ties in with and supports the animal imagery of the rest of the play: man in his sins is animal-like. Further, in speaking of his vices Edgar especially stresses lust: his speech refers at least four times to his alleged sexual misdeeds, which also receive later mention (IV.i, 59 ff.). It is hardly an accident that Shakespeare has Edgar accent sex in his pseudo confessional, for Edgar's speech works very effectively with other parts of the play which identify animality and lustfulness. Lear has a strong speech entirely on the subject:

> What was thy cause?
> Adultery?
> Thou shalt not die; die for adultery? No.
> The wren goes to't, and the small gilded fly
> Does lecher in my sight.
> Let copulation thrive . . .
>
> .   .   .   .

Behold yond simp'ring dame,
. . . .
The fitchew, nor the soiled horse, goes to't
With a more riotous appetite. (IV.vi, 111–25)

The ironic exculpation of the adulterer serves to stress the
fact that undisciplined sexuality is animal, and these climactic remarks of Lear's strengthen the language pattern
which emphasizes the subhuman ingredient in mankind. The
complex view of man set forth by the play is epitomized in
Lear's brilliant continuation of the lines quoted above:

> Down from the waist they are Centaurs
> Though women all above;
> But to the girdle do the gods inherit,
> Beneath is all the fiend's. (126–29)

Man is equally capable of salvation or damnation. The Centaur is exactly the right image here, for it admits the possibility of high intellectual and spiritual attainment and yet connotes primarily the proneness to violence and disorder which
the play exhibits throughout. It exhibits man as a rational
animal.

In its embodiment of sexual license, also, the Centaur figure is especially effective as a sharp focusing of the sex
motif that constantly appears in the play. Indeed, sex is used
almost exclusively as a symbol of evil, of the animality that
is continually put before us as a definition of vicious conduct. The language of sex, then as now, may be used to denote evil entirely unrelated to sex. In this play it happens, of
course, that Lear's adultery speech has a literal as well as
metaphorical value; it applies to conduct of his daughters
which is itself another metaphor for the animal evil in them.

Now in the development of the sex motif there is one highly ironic circumstance which is worth noting: the first reference to sex which is accompanied by words of moral disapproval is Goneril's.[14] Indignantly she tells Lear that his retainers, "so disorder'd, so debosh'd, and bold" have made the court look

> . . . like a riotous inn. Epicurism and lust
> Make it more like a tavern or a brothel
> Than a grac'd palace. (I.iv, 265–67)

We must assume, I think, that some recollection of this speech, and of the scene of which it is a part, motivates the following lines of Lear in the already-quoted adultery speech in IV.vi—lines in which he recalls both the retainers of which Goneril went on to deprive him and especially her affectation of offended decency:

> To't, luxury, pell-mell! for I lack soldiers.
> Behold yond simp'ring dame,
> Whose face between her forks presageth snow,
> That minces virtue and does shake the head
> To hear of pleasure's name. (IV.vi, 119–23)

How could one who appeared so sensitive go on to the monstrous filial conduct which Lear has observed? Lear's word drama about sex is an excellent metaphor for the general corruption of his daughters.

In the meantime the play has presented fully the sexual passion of the sisters for Edmund, from its inception until the sisterly alliance breaks down in sexual rivalry. Edgar speaks of Goneril and Edmund as "murderous lechers" (IV. vi, 282); Regan bluntly asks Edmund how far his relations with Goneril have gone (V.i, 10 ff.); to Regan, Albany makes the bitterly ironic speech which ends "If you will marry, make your loves to me;/My lady is bespoke" (V.iii, 88–89); and Edmund, fatally wounded, pronounces his own ironic requiescat on the triangle: ". . . all three/Now marry in an instant" [15] (V.iii, 228–29). This characterization of the sisters by the sex theme is aided by at least one careful contrast of them with Cordelia. Asking her father to make clear the cause of her disgrace, Cordelia insists that

> It is no vicious blot, murder or foulness,
> No unchaste action, or dishonour'd step. . . . (I.i, 230–31)

Without the thematic context, *unchaste* might be merely part of a general catalogue; as it is, the word helps underline the sisters' animality.

At one time or another nearly all the characters contribute to the heavy atmosphere of sexual vice. At the very beginning of the play Gloucester jokes about the adulterous begetting of Edmund (I.i, 8 ff.). Edmund harps upon his illegitimacy, sneers at the legal begetting of children, prays equivocally,[16] "Now, gods, stand up for bastards!" (I.ii, 22) and then engages in conduct which is a frame of reference for the pejorative use of *bastard* as a metaphor. We cross the sight pattern again: Gloucester castigates himself as the "lust-dieted man,/. . . that will not see/Because he does not feel" (IV.i, 68–70), and Edgar tells Edmund, "The dark and vicious place where thee he got/Cost him his eyes" (V.iii, 172–73). But the sharpest echo of Gloucester's past is in several lines of Lear's adultery speech;

> Let copulation thrive; for Gloucester's bastard son
> Was kinder to his father than my daughters
> Got 'tween the lawful sheets. (IV.vi, 116–18)

102

The tone of bitterness created by the passage is sharpened by the reader's awareness of the ironic impact of these words upon Gloucester, who hears them: here his past once again recoils upon his consciousness. The reader recognizes, too, that Lear's sardonic justification of adultery almost repeats Edmund's cynical defense of illegitimacy (I.ii, 11–15).

Lear uses the sex pattern as well as the animal pattern in expressing his feelings about his daughters. "Degenerate bastard!" he calls Goneril (I.iv, 275), and his first curse against her is, "Into her womb convey sterility" (I.iv, 300). He tells Regan that if she were not glad to see him "I would divorce me from thy mother's tomb,/Sepulchring an adultress" (II.iv, 133–34). When he sees the storm as punishing secret wrongdoings, he cries, "Hide thee, . . ./. . . thou simular man of virtue/That art incestuous" (III.ii, 53–55). Thus, as in other language patterns, there is created an atmosphere in which even apparently casual words of the Fool have a choral significance: "This is a brave night to cool a courtesan" (III.ii, 79);

> Leave thy drink and thy whore,
> And keep in-a-door,
> And thou shalt have more
> Than two tens to a score (I.iv, 137–40);

in the "Prophecy" often regarded as spurious, "No heretics burn'd, but wenches' suitors" and "And bawds and whores do churches build" (III.ii, 84 and 90); ". . . a little fire in a wild field were like an old lecher's heart" (III.iv, 117–18); and "He's mad that trusts in the tameness of a wolf, a horse's health, a boy's love, or a whore's oath" (III.vi, 20–21). The most inclusive comment by the Fool is in the final

103

couplet of a song already mentioned in connection with the themes of sight and clothes:

> Fortune, that arrant whore
> Ne'er turns the key to th' poor. (II.iv, 52–53)

This accumulation of sexual terms used pejoratively and of sardonic comments upon sexuality is too impressive to be an accident; it is more impressive still when taken in conjunction with the fact that the play says almost nothing of chaste love between the sexes, and that we are shown almost nothing, for instance, of the France-Cordelia relationship. The sex motif, as it is developed in *King Lear,* suggests a corruption of creative energies—a suggestion which coheres exactly with that made by the main lines of dramatic movement, for we follow the careers of certain characters of tremendous energy—Goneril, Regan, and Edmund are the chief—who use their energy corruptly. Here is another approach to the underlying paradox of the play: under certain circumstances human beings undergo a kind of liberation that enables them to plunge vigorously and masterfully into the world and apparently to gain possession of all things valued in the world—yet their unchecked energizing has in it the seeds of their destruction. Likewise sex is used consistently to support the impact of the animal imagery: the whole mass of sex and animal references functions as part of an effort to define, to find a rationale for, human conduct which falls below the norms of everyday experience. What we have is a powerful statement of the animal in man, not a statement that the animal always triumphs, but an insistent reminder that the animal is always there to be dealt with. The animal energies of man may corrupt the human potentiality. To paraphrase the analysis of man in terms of the play's clothes symbolism, man is often a wolf in sheep's clothing; and what the sight symbol tells us, among other things, is that man often fails to recognize the presence of the wolf. Lear's angry cry of "Centaurs" is more than mad raving; what the play says is that man is both man and beast [17]—a creature of humane reason and of lustful violence.

The play's ultimate refinement of statement, to which we come later, is that man is wholly evil when reason and animality work together.

THE CONDITION OF MAN

The animal imagery thus far considered, together with its auxiliary, the dramatic and verbal treatment of sex, has constituted part of the effort to define man as an active being, a moral agent. One of the aspects of the complexity of the play is that it also considers man, if not wholly as passive, at least as recipient, as object, as possessor of certain qualities and occupant of a certain status, which the play also defines. Shakespeare uses the animal imagery to describe the condition of man as well as the character of man—especially the condition of man as he is treated by man.[18] As it is set forth by the animal imagery, man's estate is not a pretty thing. ". . . if I were your father's dog,/You should not use me so" (II.ii, 143–44), Kent tells Regan; Kent's state is more humiliating and contemptible than that of dogs. And after Regan has had Kent put into the stocks, the Fool describes him thus: "Horses are tied by the head, dogs and bears by th' neck, monkeys by th' loins, and men by th' legs" (II.iv, 9–10). Edgar takes

105

> . . . the basest and most poorest shape
> That ever penury in contempt of man
> Brought near to beast. (II.iii, 7–9)

So it is consistent that he should tell how he has eaten revolting food: "the swimming frog, the toad, the tadpole, the wall-newt . . . cow-dung . . . the old rat and the ditchdog . . . mice and rats and such small deer" (III.iv, 134–44). Hence he is not acting a part when he says later that he had had "t'assume a semblance/That very dogs disdain'd" (V.iii, 187–88).

It is Lear, naturally, whose situation is most fully described by these imagistic means. Rather than return to Goneril he will "be a comrade with the wolf and owl—/Necessity's sharp pinch" [19] (II.iv, 213–14)—a figure doubly ironic because he is shortly to be out in the wild like an animal and because he has so far depended on daughters whom the play does frequently compare with the wild animals which he mentions as a bitter alternative. The passage is picked up and amplified, too, by the Gentleman's description of Lear in the storm:

> This night, wherein the cub-drawn bear would couch,
> The lion and the belly-pinched wolf
> Keep their fur dry, unbonneted he runs. . . . (III.i, 12–14)

Gloucester tells Regan that she could not have refused asylum even "If wolves had at thy gate howl'd that stern time" (III.vii, 63); this is echoed by Cordelia's

> Mine enemy's dog,
> Though he had bit me, should have stood that night
> Against my fire; and wast thou fain, poor father,
> To hovel thee with swine. . . . (IV.vii, 36–39)

"They flatter'd me like a dog," Lear rages (IV.vi, 97–98);
later he says that whoever parts him and Cordelia will "fire
us hence like foxes" (V.iii, 23). After all this, it is fitting
that, just before his death, Lear should cry, over Cordelia's
dead body, "Why should a dog, a horse, a rat, have life,/And
thou no breath at all?" (V.iii, 306–307) Animals live on,
but the finest human beings die: Lear's despairing words—
in a speech where the animal, clothes, and sight imagery
work side by side—give a powerful thrust to the movement
of the animal imagery, of which they are the final example
in the play.

THE CONDITION OF MAN: CHORUS

What this series of passages says is that man, in the misery inflicted by his fellows, is often less well off than an animal. The primary point of the animal imagery is not that the
miserableness which man experiences is deserved or unde-
served, for the subject of the pattern is not justice; all we are
told is that man's fate can be fittingly described by references to the animal world. So far these references, whatever
their transcendent suggestive value, have functioned chiefly
as a means of expressing the feelings of a moment or the
quality of a specific situation. There are also, however, a few
passages which in themselves grope toward generalizations
and therefore have a larger philosophical ingredient than
those already quoted. These passages are a kind of chorus
—a chorus such as we have already seen in the sight and
clothing patterns. For instance, after he has virtually called
Lear a fool and been threatened with the whip, the Fool says,
"Truth's a dog must to kennel; he must be whipp'd out,
when Lady, the brach, may stand by th' fire and stink" (I.

iv, 124–26). The Fool here represents Truth, of course—as do Cordelia and Kent—and "Lady, the brach" inevitably suggests Regan and Goneril. Yet, taken in conjunction with the events of the play so far, the speech becomes more than a comment on characters in the play: it is a philosophic statement about experience, not to be taken as dogmatic and final, perhaps, but at the very least becoming a hypothesis which the drama as a whole may reject or confirm. At the moment Truth seems at a painful distance from the hearth.

But however far its implications go, this speech of the Fool's seems casual compared with two of Lear's at the moments of intense feeling. When Regan and Goneril have cut off his attendants, he protests against their stress on *need*. "Allow not nature more than nature needs,/Man's life is cheap as beast's" (II.iv, 269–70). Human life is distinguished from the bestial by its having more than bare necessity (". . . nature needs not what thou gorgeous wear'st," Lear points out to Regan in passing). Yet there are human beings in the play who scarcely have what is necessary, and to Lear it appears that he is being deprived of a necessity. And essentially he is right. For the real significance of Lear's followers is this: they are not a literal "need" but a symbol of something that he as an aged king has earned, and, beyond that, of the gratuity in excess of need, the dignity, the honor, which distinguish human kind from the animal.[20] Lear's language and reasoning establish a direct connection between this vehement expostulation with his daughters, which occurs just before Lear's plunge into the storm, and the later scene during the storm in which Lear tries to emulate Edgar's nakedness and in which he also philosophizes about clothes. This stripping scene in the storm derives its power

from the fusion of several lines of development: we see the
suffering of Lear and Edgar directly, but in addition to that
we feel the poetry of the clothing pattern and of the animal
pattern and of the nature theme (the storm), all brought together in tight nexus. Besides being fused here in one intense
speech—the "Off, off, you lendings" speech—the animal
and clothes symbols mark this speech as a logical extension
of Lear's ideas at the time he denounced Goneril and Regan
and plunged into the stormy night. Having no longer the
superfluities which distinguish man from beast, he will have
no more pretense but will follow through the implications of
his state with relentless logic. If man's life is indeed "cheap
as beast's" (II.iv, 270), surely it is the naked Edgar who is
in tune with the universe. "Consider him well," says Lear,
as if he were objectively examining a phenomenon. "Thou
ow'st the worm no silk, the beast no hide, the sheep no wool,
the cat no perfume. Ha? here's three on's are sophisticated."
His intensity increases, and he rises passionately, yet in his
terms logically, to his climax: "Thou art the thing itself;
unaccommodated man is no more but such a poor, bare,
forked animal as thou art. Off, off, you lendings! come, unbutton here" (III.iv, 107–14). This passage is additionally
linked with that in II.iv by the economic figures: *superfluous, need, cheap* (II.iv), and *owest, lendings* here. It is a
suitable way of expressing the conviction that for him to
wear clothes, which animals do not wear, is to take something from animals—obviously an illogical step: since man
is an animal, it is "sophisticated." In a world which is full of
sophistication, Lear will make a radical return to nature.
Such a return, it seems to him now, is the only logical thing
to do. Man, as animal, is "unaccommodated"—Edgar with

clothes, Lear with followers; without all the perquisites of humanity, it is impossible for Lear not to want to go all the way toward the beast. His attempt to act upon his decision gives the final twist to the passage, which is the climax of the scene, and which serves to focus all the animal imagery which is used to define the condition of man.

It remains for Gloucester to carry a step further the philosophic implications of the animal imagery which we have been treating. After he has been blinded, he tells the Old Man who first guides him of a poor creature he saw, someone like "mad Tom," "which made me think a man a worm" (IV.i, 33). That man is a worm is virtually the same point of view which we have seen Lear expressing in the storm. But Gloucester had half recognized Tom as Edgar, whose true nature he now knows; so his reflections carry him on to a still more sardonic aphorism:

> My son
> Came then into my mind, and yet my mind
> Was then scarce friends with him. I have heard more since.
> As flies to wanton boys, are we to th' gods;
> They kill us for their sport. (IV.i, 33–37)

This is the end: if man is animal, he can ultimately be only victim, and if he is merely a victim, there is no need for continuing existence. In his second speech after the one just quoted Gloucester makes clear that he is going to Dover: he has already decided to commit suicide by leaping from the cliff.

Gloucester has fallen into the sin of despair (various critics, especially Knight, have stressed the Christian background of the tragedies). It is worth pointing out here that

110

this is a completely logical outcome for Gloucester, for it is consistent with his essential passivity, his tending to fall in with whatever forces are brought to bear upon him. His despair is right, for the worldly man is one who, by accepting the custom of the time, despairs of the good. The man who always gives in finally gives up: suicide is his final adjustment.

But Gloucester's despair the play as a whole repudiates, and repudiates in two ways. Though various critics have taken Gloucester's "As flies to wanton boys, we are to the gods" as the thematic center of the play, Chambers has successfully shown that the line is to be read simply as an expression of Gloucester's mood.[21] What the reader already knows is that Gloucester is in the care of, and has the love of, his son Edgar; Edgar and his love for his father have both survived, so that the main cause for Gloucester's despair no longer exists. But the play also repudiates Gloucester's despair by making Gloucester himself repudiate it; and this repudiation is brought about in the hard way—as a matter of principle, not as the easy result of a happy family reunion. The method which Shakespeare has Edgar use is a daring one —so daring, indeed, that Edgar, when he seems to be helping his father to fulfill his intention of committing suicide by leaping from Dover cliff, must reassure the audience: "Why I do trifle thus with his despair/Is done to cure it" (IV.vi, 33–34). Gloucester is "saved," and so lessoned, and he states his new credo—to "bear affliction." But the pressure is not relaxed; the battle goes badly; Gloucester again is ready to give up. Again, however, he can assent to Edgar's moral prescription: "Men must endure/Their going hence, even as their coming hither" (V.ii, 9–10).

111

But this chapter is on the nature of man as it is defined by the animal imagery, and the relationship of Gloucester's despair and attempted suicide to that definition should by now be clear. The play never denies that man is an animal, and that he is capable of falling back wholly into the animal; in fact, man's animality is asserted again and again. The animal imagery and the sex imagery tell us repeatedly how the human being may betray himself. But the play also reaffirms man's specifically human quality, his moral quality, one of the evidences of which is his will to endure. The man who imposes a discipline upon himself asserts his humanity.[22] For a time the human being who relies upon the human may seem to be the victim of the man who has joined his intelligence to animal unrestraint, and as victim man may fall into a state which seems to ally him with the animals. Man may reduce man to an animal state: the play continually shows this to be true. But the play does not reduce man to the status of a fly tortured by boyish, irresponsible, cruel gods. Torture is not the end, as torture by gods would have to be. Gloucester triumphs over his torture. After repeated disaster he can assert, "And that's true too" to Edgar's "Ripeness is all" (V.ii, 11). For man may ripen into fullness of being, which means, among other things, that one part of him does not rule all the rest and that one moment's mood does not close off all the perspectives available to him.

This is what the patterns say about the nature of man. But man belongs to a universe; there are principles which operate both within him and outside him. From the nature of man it is a necessary step to the nature of nature.

Now that law which, as it is laid up in the bosom of God, they call eternal, receiveth, according unto the different kinds of things which are subject unto it, different and sundry kinds of names. That part of it which ordereth natural agents we call usually Nature's law; . . . For what good or evil is there under the sun, what action correspondent or repugnant unto the law which God hath imposed upon his creatures, but in or upon it God doth work according to the law which Himself hath eternally purposed to keep, that is to say, the first law eternal? . . . See we not plainly that obedience of creatures unto the law of Nature is the stay of the whole world? . . . If here it be demanded what that is which keepeth nature in obedience to her own law, we must have recourse to that higher law whereof we have already spoken, . . . Who the guide of nature but only the God of nature? . . . The axioms of that law, therefore, whereby natural agents are guided, have their use in the moral, yea, even in the spiritual actions of men, and consequently in all laws belonging unto men howsoever.

Richard Hooker, *The Laws of Ecclesiastical Polity*

* * *

Oedipus. The gods, their own heralds, bring me the tidings, with no failure in the signs appointed of old.

Theseus. What sayest thou are the signs of these things, old man?

Oedipus. The thunder, peal on peal,—the lightning, flash on flash, hurled from the unconquered hand.

Sophocles, *Oedipus at Colonus* (Jebb's translation)

CHAPTER V

HEAR, NATURE, HEAR

THE NATURE OF NATURE

K I N G L E A R presents a twofold view of nature, or, perhaps more accurately, shows men holding two contradictory
views of nature. The characters in the play say a good deal
about nature; but the characters differ morally, and their
differences extend into their philosophies of nature. All the
characters who think about nature at all claim the aegis of
nature; some ignore the subject entirely, but no one is willing to be an enemy of nature. So *nature* has different meanings in the usage of different moral agents. To most of the
characters in the play, nature is a fundamental principle of
order; it is the *lex naturalis,* the divinely ordained cosmic
scheme; it implies a distinction between good and evil, and
the operation of an eternal justice. On the other hand, nature
is understood simply as vital force, the physical drive and
the impulses of the individual, the totality of unfettered and
uncriticized urgencies. The two senses compete with each
other; thus they set up a special tension; and this tension
qualifies the total dramatic statement.[1]

The two "natures" of the play are roughly analogous to
the two potentialities of human nature implied by the evidence which we examined in Chapter IV: man's ability to

achieve salvation, and his liability to damnation. As presented by the animal and sex imagery, man moves toward self-destruction—toward an animality that cancels his humanity, toward appetite which denies spirit. On the other hand the play asserts the reality and the persistence of the human; it asserts that man can realize his humanity. Man can move toward spirit—by endurance, by discipline, by love, by insight; thus he achieves the order of humanity.

The animal imagery which sets forth the ruthlessness and predatoriness of various dramatis personae is not used of all the characters; the bestiality of some is in contrast with the humanity of others. The storm suggests, on one level, the victory of a nature hostile to humanity; yet the storm is regularly regarded as a convulsion of nature—a disorder which interferes with but does not destroy an essential order which still *is*. There is chaos in the world; but tragedy sees chaos in perspective; it measures chaos by order. Chaos is irreparable only when it is mistaken for order; when it is felt as disorder, there is still hope. Tragedy recounts disorder and reaffirms the hope.

Lear and Edmund both address nature as a deity. But they conceive of this deity quite differently, and the services for which they pray imply differently functioning deities. In seeing how the play treats their antithetical concepts, we can draw also upon the frequent use of such terms as *natural* and *unnatural* by various characters. One thing is certain: that Shakespeare will not merely make the psychological observation that people of different beliefs use the same term of approval to dignify their contrasting codes. As a first-rate poet he will not stop at a comment upon the relativistic hazards met by a profoundly important term in the world of general speech.

LAW AND ORDER

Of the various meanings with which *nature* is used, not all are philosophically significant. At times it refers neutrally to character,[2] or to physical being and life.[3] But when Edmund says, of his betrayal of Gloucester to Cornwall, that "nature thus gives way to loyalty" (III.v, 4–5) and that his loyalty and his "blood" are in conflict (III. v, 23), *nature* means a characteristic to be expected of men generally, the emotional responses evoked by family ties; [4] and, regardless of what Edmund's tone is, a moral implication has come into the field of meaning. Likewise the phrase "oppressed nature," which is used several times,[5] and Lear's phrase "more than nature needs" (II.iv, 269; cf. 272) imply a normal state of affairs to which suffering or excess are contrary. In an extension of this usage several passages direct our attention to the placing of excessive pressures upon the normal ability of human life to deal with antagonistic forces. Lear tells Kent, who has objected to the treatment of the three daughters, that his interference "nor our nature nor our place can bear" (I.i, 174). But this brief opposition by Kent is nothing compared with what Lear must still bear, and, in another of the innumerable ironic reminders of earlier incidents, Shakespeare leaves it to Kent to point the unendurable. Of the storm he says, "Man's nature cannot carry/ Th' affliction nor the fear" (III.ii, 48–49), and "The tyranny of the open night's too rough/For nature to endure" [6] (III.iv, 2–3). Now the storm, we have seen, is a symbol of

117

the emotional stresses to which Lear is subject—as Kent puts it, his "unnatural and bemadding sorrow" (III.i, 38). The effect of these stresses, upon a human being of normal capacities and sensitivities, is constantly registered by the language of the nature pattern. Soon aware of his misunderstanding of Cordelia, Lear says that her "most small fault" "wrench'd my frame of nature/From the fix'd place" (I. iv, 288–91). Under the Fool's lashing he exclaims, "I will forget my nature" (I.v, 35), that is, lose control, go mad.[7] And after he has gone mad, Gloucester apostrophizes, "O ruin'd piece of nature!" (IV.vi, 137).

By now it should be clear that if, at which might be called a scientific level of usage, *nature* simply denotes qualities, without reference to goodness or badness, or, more frequently, *being* at the physical level, there is also bound up in the word a suggestion of norm, of wholeness, of a desirable and permanent order of things. That is, *nature* is not merely any given state of affairs in life, but a regular disposition, an informing principle with which, indeed, any given state of affairs may not be in harmony. Naturally we associate human life and *enduring:* that which it seems impossible to endure, then, runs counter to the nature of things. Thus wellness is the state of nature; and the treatment which Lear receives from others, and his sorrow and madness, are a "ruining" of nature, a "breach in nature." They are abnormal. They run counter to what is felt as a dominant order in the universe [8]—an impression which, in its impact upon us, is greatly strengthened by the imagery of physical suffering which Miss Spurgeon has observed.[9]

There is, then, a normal, ordered functioning of the physical world which is *nature*. But this fact is only preliminary to a more important issue, namely that, in the metaphorical usage of this play, *nature* comes also to mean a normal, ordered functioning of the *moral* world, a final principle to which all moral phenomena are to be referred. If on the surface there is moral chaos, beneath there is a "nature," an eternal fitness of things, with which the chaos is inconsistent and to which it does violence. Many characters rely on this principle of order; they understand in terms of it; and they judge phenomena by it, as their language constantly shows. Gloucester does this in the crudest possible way when he sets up a causal relationship between astronomical phenomena and moral conduct: what is wrong in the human world is traceable to irregularities in a "nature" which he oversimplifies by reducing it to the world of physics.

These late eclipses in the sun and moon portend no good to us; though the wisdom of nature can reason it thus and thus, yet nature finds itself scourg'd by the sequent effects; love cools, friendship falls off, brothers divide: . . . and the bond crack'd 'twixt son and father . . . the King falls from the bias of nature; there's father against child. We have seen the best of our time. Machinations, hollowness, treachery and all ruinous disorders follow us disquietly to our graves. . . . And the noble and true-hearted Kent banish'd! his offence, honesty! 'Tis strange. (I.ii, 112–27)

The king, we should observe, falls from the bias of *nature;* what follows us is *disorders;* and it is *nature* which is scourged. Violence is done to more than the physical world; some essential, universal normalcy has been broken in upon.

It must be said for Gloucester that if he is superstitious, he can at least recognize moral disorder; if he has a naïve concept of cause, he at least does not confuse cause and effect. In contrast with him is the rationalist Edmund, who with sneering common sense debunks Gloucester's superstitiousness. But Edmund cures a logical headache by decapitation: in his attack on astrology (I.ii, 129 ff.) he throws out not only superstition but also the accompanying moral sensitivity. The specific contrast between father and son persists as Edmund echoes, with enjoyment of the irony, the words in which Gloucester defines the evil of which he believes Edgar to be guilty, as running counter to "nature." "Unnatural, . . . villain" Gloucester calls Edgar (I.ii, 81), and Edmund, as if seriously, repeats to Edgar Gloucester's prediction of "unnaturalness between the child and the parent" (I.ii, 157). Gloucester refers to the treatment of Lear as "this unnatural dealing" (III.iii, 1–2), and Edmund repeats solemnly, "Most savage and unnatural!" (III. iii, 7). In one scene Edmund, telling Gloucester about Edgar, initiates the use of the term ("unnatural purpose," II. i, 52) and is rewarded for his actions against Edgar by Gloucester's stamp of approval, "loyal and natural boy" [10] (II.i, 86). The echoes do more than establish an ironic tone; they help create a conception of a "nature" or moral norm which provides the perspective for the human conduct in the play. The very fact that Edmund can make use of this conception, although he does not believe in it, shows how powerful it is.

The idea of an absolute order in terms of which man may be judged is amplified in the lines of other characters. ". . . Nature disclaims in thee," Kent assures Oswald (II. ii, 59). Albany says to Goneril,

> Cannot be border'd certain in itself;
> That nature which contemns it origin

She that herself will sliver and disbranch
From her material sap, perforce must wither
And come to deadly use. . . . (IV.ii, 32–36)

These lines, in which *wither* is a reminder of Lear's earlier prayer that she may become sterile (I.iv, 300), point to evil as a separation from nature. A little later Albany calls Goneril "degenerate" (IV.ii, 43). Even minor characters, as we have seen elsewhere, help develop the language patterns: a Gentleman says that Lear has one daughter "Who redeems nature from the general curse/Which twain have brought her to" (IV.vi, 210–11).

But it is Lear who must face, for longest time and in most unmitigated fashion, the convulsions of nature, physical and moral, and in whose language, therefore, there is the greatest evidence of effort to understand the forces which beat him down. Shakespeare skillfully makes Lear show his change of attitude to his daughters in terms of nature just as we have seen him show this change in terms of sight and clothing. With regard to the division of territory Lear says he proposes to extend largest bounty "Where nature doth with merit challenge" (I.i, 54), that is, where natural strength of affection shows its deserts. The competitive speeches over, Lear decides that it is Cordelia "whom nature is asham'd/Almost t'acknowledge hers" (I.i, 215–16), and this remark is followed up by France's comment that indeed Cordelia's offense "Must be of such unnatural degree/That monsters it" (I.i, 222). Only three scenes later he calls Goneril "Degenerate bastard!" (I.iv, 275). For a while he thinks that Regan knows the "offices of nature" (II.iv, 181) better than Goneril, to whom he says directly that she is

> . . . a disease that's in my flesh,
> Which I must needs call mine; thou art a boil,
> A plague sore, an embossed carbuncle
> In my corrupted blood. (II.iv, 225–28)

"Corrupted blood" is another reminder of Lear's tragic complicity, which finds recurrent expression in the different patterns: disease means receptivity to disease,[11] and if Lear suffers from an infection, it is because he is in some way hospitable to that infection. But his illusions about Regan do not last long, and he addresses both daughters as "unnatural hags" (II.iv, 281). Then he calls upon the thunder: "Crack nature's moulds, all germens spill at once/That make ingrateful man!" (III.ii, 8–9); that is, the machinery that made man should be destroyed [12] because, when man is ungrateful, he is acting in a way contrary to that in which he is supposed to act—contrary to nature, to the *lex naturalis*. Of Edgar as Poor Tom, Lear says, ". . . nothing could have subdu'd nature/To such a lowness but his unkind daughters" (III.iv, 72–73). The unkind, that is, unnatural, daughters have completely reduced nature; Edgar appears to have lost normal humanity.

It is relatively early in the play, however, that Lear states most powerfully his conception of Goneril's conduct as a violation of nature. The first part of his curse upon her (I.iv, 297–311) is that she shall be sterile, shall have a "derogate," i. e., a "denatured" body: his desire to have her cut off from the functions radically identified with woman "in nature" is an ironically apt reflection of her cutting herself off from nature, from fundamental humanity ("sliver and disbranch/From her material sap," as Albany says later—IV. ii, 34–35). The alternative curse is that she shall have an ungrateful child ("sharper than a serpent's tooth"), the meaning of which, with reference to general principles, is explicitly stated by Lear in the phrase "a thwart disnatured torment to her." But most significant of all is that this curse is also a prayer: [13] it is addressed, in the first line, to Nature herself, "Hear, Nature, hear; dear goddess hear!" Nature is clearly conceived of as being not merely the totality of the physical universe, but as a regulative principle, a restorer of moral equilibrium. At this point we might almost, by means of the nature passages alone, read the tragedy as consisting in the reassertion of a natural principle of justice, comparable to the divine justice which is an essential ingredient in Marlowe's *Faustus.*

So much for one meaning given to *nature* in *King Lear:* nature is the order which makes the universe meaningful. What is really implied by the passages I have cited is the Christian principle of *lex naturalis;* the paganism of the play is on the surface. But religion is a subject to which we come later. In the meantime, nature is the right order of things. In that sense the term *nature* is used, with one exception, by every character who uses it at all. The exception is Edmund.

EDMUND'S NATURE

Lear prays, "Hear, Nature, hear"; Edmund uses the same name in addressing his divinity: "Thou, Nature, art my goddess; to thy law/My services are bound" (I.ii, 1–2). He then elaborates the famous apology for bastards which ends "Now, gods, stand up for bastards" (1–22). It is clear from the start that Lear and Edmund are thinking of different kinds of deity: Lear, impassioned, cut by a terrible sense of injustice, calls instinctively upon powers of retribution to punish the unjust; Edmund, comparatively calm—not that he is not feeling resentful and injured; but he is in complete control of all his logical faculties—*reasons* against the order of the world by which he is the loser, and he sets forth, and asks aid for, his plot to inflict injustice upon Edgar. Shakespeare, then, is not oversimplifying the subject of nature but is bringing into dramatic focus another conception of nature which usage has made available.[14] The question is, however, whether he stops with a presentation of the complexities of definition—which is in itself no minor literary task—or whether all the evidence of the play has the effect of making, in dramatic form, a judgment upon the problem of conflicting usages.

Edmund attacks "the plague of custom" and "the curiosity of nations" (3, 4) and against the rules for man and society which come from such sources he sets the virtues of nature, as they appear in the "natural" son. Why do they call us "base," he asks,

> Who, in the lusty stealth of nature, take
> More composition and fierce quality
> Than doth, within a dull, stale, tired bed,
> Go to th' creating a whole tribe of fops
> Got 'tween asleep and wake? (11–15)

Nature, then, is vital force, the individual will, sexual vigor. Whereas he elsewhere with mocking expediency repeats the *unnatural* which Gloucester applies to evil deeds, here Edmund says that nature, rather than being a norm, a necessary standard by which man is judged, is whatever forces or undisciplined impulses make a man act in a given way; it is the human and physical status quo, without reference to

moral quality. "Whatever is, is nature" is Edmund's naturalism. Edmund glorifies it in opposition to traditional
order, the order of society and civilization, which he wishes
to dismiss as foolish convention—"the plague of custom."
Edmund asserts his will against the order of the whole—the
order implied by *nature* as it is used by practically every
other character.

Shakespeare introduces another complication by the contrast between Edmund and Gloucester in this scene. Gloucester also stands for the order of the whole: he sees a relationship between all parts of the cosmos, as appears in his as-
trologism ("These late eclipses in the sun and moon portend
no good to us"—I.ii, 112–13). But this position—which is
obviously related to that of Lear—has a defect which Shakespeare, giving Edmund's rationalism its full deserts, permits Edmund to point out. Edmund sneers at the theory
that we are "villains on necessity; fools by heavenly compulsion" (132–33): what he places his finger upon is Gloucester's failure to give the individual will its due. Through
his words we see that Gloucester is rationalizing and, as I
have already pointed out, evading responsibility. On the
other hand, again, Gloucester has a full sense of what is taking place in the world of humanity; he assents to astrology—
"Though the wisdom of nature can reason it thus and thus"
(113–14)—and yet is sensitive to the fact that another
problem remains: "Yet nature finds itself scourg'd by the
sequent effects" (114–15). He is still concerned about
humanity: he is not entirely superstitious and superficial.

In view of the fact that he permits Edmund a very solid
rightness in his critique of Gloucester, what does Shakespeare do with him and his "nature" in the play as a whole?

In the first place he suggests the weakness of Edmund's position by revealing him as an *ad hoc* metaphysician: he wishes to equate "nature" with "unsanctioned sexual intercourse," and his "more composition and fierce quality" is strictly question-begging.[15] Edmund, however, is elaborating a defense not only for an irrevocable past but also for a future which he is voluntarily determining: he speaks, as if to Edgar, "I must have your land," and he expects that he shall "to th' [or, top the] legitimate" (16, 21). Now, the announcement of his plan follows immediately upon his exposition of Nature, and it is connected with the statement of his nature theory by the word *then*—precisely as if his scheme followed as a logical projection of the theory into action. The passage is a brilliant self-revelation. In his rationalization, in his seeking a "scientific" authorization for the rapacity he *wants* to engage in, Edmund reveals his Nature as something wholly different from Lear's retributive principle (his Nature is *nemesis*, really)—as, indeed, being much like what a later poet called "nature red in tooth and claw." [16]

Edmund's Nature is one which is, within limits, of tremendous efficacy. The disruption of order and the turning loose of the individual will generate enormous force. But the play presents that force as eventually finding its boundaries. On the one hand, Lear's Nature does reassert itself: the evil are punished, and those who are redeemable find salvation. Lear's Nature conquers Edmund's Nature. The "natural boy" meets nemesis. What is more, there is some evidence that Edmund recants. "The wheel is come full circle," he says at the end (V.iii, 174). The wheel is the wheel of fortune, of course, and yet in the context it becomes also a symbol of the order which Edmund had revolted against but which has again assumed authority over him.[17] Then Edmund seeks to do one good deed: he endeavors to recall his writ for the execution of Lear and Cordelia. And in what terms does he announce his intention to do "some good"? He will act, he says, "Despite of mine own nature" (V.iii, 244). By implication he repudiates his own theory—the theory of the man begotten by "stealth of nature" and therefore naturally licensed to take what custom does not allow him; for here he is attempting to give, or at least to give back what he has taken. Whatever the situation of the stars, he said earlier, "I should have been that I am" (I.ii, 143–44); but here he revolts against the implied inevitability of character and acts in a way contrary to the "that I am" in which he has believed.

Goneril and Regan are not at all concerned about the problem of nature. Edmund is at least concerned with first principles, and his interest, which is in contrast with their indifference, indicates the possibility of his acquiescing in a better set of first principles than those which he first enunciates to justify his projected self-aggrandizement. But whether or not his deeds and words at the end can be construed as the equivalent of a formal recantation of his theory of nature, the fact is that the play as a whole proceeds on the assumption that nature is a principle of order—a principle subject to violation and apparently conquerable by chaos, and yet ultimately able to reassert itself as the order of the whole and to bring into conformity with it that other "nature" of Edmund's, the individual impulse and will.[18]

What *King Lear* says about the nature of Nature parallels what it says about the nature of man (Chapter IV): it presents a twofold view of each subject. Man may give way to the animal, or he may realize his humanity; nature may be viewed as uncriticized motive, or as a total order that it is perilous to violate. Impulse, desire, appetite—if these are the sole reality, they lead man to the animal; but by the acceptance of order as the final reality, man becomes human. That is his ripeness.

INQUIRIES

Such formulations are made by the total play as metaphor and are of course not to be sought within the texture of the play. Various characters, indeed, speak philosophically at times; Edgar, whose maturing is remarkable both in his ability to act and in his intellectual mastery of experience, generalizes with a good deal of depth: "The worst is not/So long as we can say 'This is the worst' " (IV.i, 27–28); "Ripeness is all" (V.ii, 11); "The gods are just, and of our pleasant vices/Make instruments to plague us" (V. iii, 170–71). Other characters are reflective; in fact, there is a constant interplay of action and reflection. In one sense, all the experiences of the major characters are a testing of ideas of theirs, and by and large their initial ideas do not hold up very well; we can see the gradual disappearance of the programmatic certainties which, at the start, various persons of the drama rather brightly held. Lear, in particular, has had to emend and rephrase his initial theories of life. But he is so beaten about by the tumultuous world that, although he has come, as we shall see, to some remarkable insights, he cannot finally resolve his sense of life's meaning into aphoristic finalities. An intellectual like Dr. Faustus, even in his final despair, can repeat the formal propositions that describe a world in which salvation and damnation are cardinal facts. But Lear is an imaginative man rather than an intellectual, and he cannot forge orderly paradigms of wisdom. At death he is, as other evidence from his language will show later, what might be called "orthodox." In the latter part of the play he appears, however, not as a master of the rules but as an inquirer and learner. When he is studying the naked Edgar he asks, "Is man no more than this?" (III.iv, 106–107). To his auditors in the farmhouse he poses the question, "Is there any cause in nature that makes these hard hearts?" (III.vi, 81–82) Such inquiries pave the way for his announcement, after they have been taken prisoner at the end, of the future which he and Cordelia will share: we will, he says, "Take upon's the mystery of things,/ As if we were God's spies" (V.iii, 16–17). For Lear, as well as for seekers of pat formulae, many questions remain unanswered: only the ancient metaphors for experience remain.

And the ability to use those metaphors is evidence of how far Lear has gone toward salvation. Indeed, the Christian transvaluation of the values of Lear's historically pagan world becomes, in this speech of Lear's to Cordelia, quite explicit. Lear is repentant and asks forgiveness (V.iii, 10–11); he will pray (12); he will contemplate the great mysteries; above all, he has faith in their humble estate:

> . . . we'll wear out,
> In a wall'd prison, packs and sects of great ones
> That ebb and flow by th' moon. (17–19)

The humble know their limits and get hold of the lasting reality. And here we come to another of the paradoxes by which the play is penetrated: the blind see, the unprotected survive, those who resemble the milder animals and those who are treated like animals learn to endure. And in earning his humanity, man gives up his pride—and thus gains sight of final truths.

In a just cause the weak vanquishes the strong.

> Sophocles, *Oedipus at Colonus*

*   *   *

Now also when I am old and greyheaded, O God, forsake me not. . . .

> Psalm 71

CHAPTER VI

IF YOU DO LOVE OLD MEN

THE AGE AND JUSTICE THEMES

B Y W A Y of recapitulation: the preceding two chapters
have been an examination of those passages in the play
which, taken as a group, constitute an inquiry into the nature
of man and of the framework of reality within which he acts.
In terms of animal imagery and of the language of sex the
play makes constant reassertions of the human potentiality
for evil; both in the enthronement of impulse and in conscious, planned action man exhibits bestiality. He is not
exclusively bestial, but he is never safely out of the shadow
of bestiality. This shadow is a double one, for man may act
the animal or by the agency of others be reduced to animal
status. Perhaps in this aspect the play may be read as a statement of man's liability to damnation. Yet damnation implies salvation; and an Inferno, a Paradiso; and *King Lear*,
if it has little of the light of beatific vision, does not become
cynical, does not regard evil as the inevitable end of human
experience; it speculates always in terms of a *nature* of
which evil is a violation, and which will ultimately bring
about a restoration of order in the human world.

The way in which man answers these questions, the point
of view from which he tries to grasp reality, his mode of

understanding—this is the ultimate issue of the play, and all the structural conditions which we are now investigating lead us to that core of the drama. But before we come to the organizing center which establishes the relevance of the language patterns with which we are now familiar, we need still to follow out several other themes that can be discerned in the dramatic and verbal symbols of the play. All of these in some sense are attached to, or are extensions of, the nature theme whose ramifications we have just been tracing.

The problem of the natural, we have seen, is elaborated in part by means of the imagery of injury and disease. A comparable symbol of the vulnerability of human nature is age, and of age there is significant awareness throughout the play. Further, the constant thinking in terms of what is natural and of the violation of the natural would suggest, we might expect, the subject of justice; and, as a matter of fact, the subject is a recurrent one in *King Lear*. Finally,—to anticipate Chapter VII—in a world in which standards of justice differ and in which we must find methods of discrimination, it is but a step to the problem of values. Through the problem of values we shall approach what we have already said is the basic theme of the play—the problem of understanding.

AGE

In the age pattern, as in other patterns, we find the large dramatic fact conjoined with verbal recurrency. The fact is the great age of Lear, and the age of Gloucester. That Lear and Gloucester are old might simply be a part of the dramatist's inherited material; it was not obligatory upon him to make something of it. The fact of age could be quickly conveyed and then ignored. Such a line as the Servant's with reference to Gloucester—"Let's follow the old earl" (III. vii, 103)—would say everything needful. But age is a pressingly recurrent subject, the insistence of which, we must assume, comes from some element in the dramatist's consciousness. Perhaps that element cannot be more than guessed at or crudely restated, but we do need to attempt to see in what way it complicates the problems which in their astonishing complexity have been compacted into *King Lear*. But if the addition of another problem complicates the dramatic whole, the new problem, it is also true, may be dealt with in a way that will sharpen our sense of the general structure. The age theme does just that: it deepens the structural outlines of the play because Shakespeare makes the same kind of use of it that he makes of the nature theme to which it is related. He presents it dualistically: age is not a mere physical fact to be prosaically defined and conventionally treated: rather it is a means of evoking two kinds of responses from those who must deal with age: and these responses help characterize the men and women in whom they occur and help elaborate the systems of value which compete in the play.

In *King Lear* we find, then, a twofold view of age. On the one hand age is allied with Nature: it has a certain position to which a certain response is obligatory. If man adheres to the order of the whole, he cannot withhold from age what is its due from an ordered humanity—respect and loving-kindness. On the other hand, age becomes an isolated fact whose significance lies only in its relevance to the situations of those who must deal with it, and they are under no obligation to apply to it any other standard than that of interest. Their view is pragmatic; the pragmatists are Goneril, Regan, and Edmund. Nearly all the other characters in the play regard age as having established rights within the realm of humanity. These characters are those who understand Nature as *nomos*, and in whom, as we shall see, there is a strong religious sense.

Age is first of all a subject of which Lear himself is very conscious, and by means of which we can trace certain changes in his consciousness. At the start, age is to him simply a time of rest:

> To shake all cares and business from our age,
> Conferring them on younger strengths, while we
> Unburthen'd crawl toward death. (I.i, 40–42)

Then there is the first trace of youth-age counterpoint.[1] Lear speaks of Cordelia's "young love" (I.i, 85), and in the statement of his subsequent disappointment in her there is a carry-over, with a pun, of the same idea: "So young, and so untender?" (I.i, 108) What he says of Cordelia is inevitably called up by a part of his curse on Goneril: may she have a "child of spleen" that will "stamp wrinkles in her brow of youth" (I.iv, 304–306). Lear's inquiry about the disguised Kent's age, and Kent's answer (I.iv, 39–42) continue the theme. What now begins to come over Lear, as understanding of Goneril and Regan is forced upon him, is the realization that the position of age is not exactly the small assured portion of human privilege that he once thought, and here he finds what is an extra twist of the horrifying violation of nature. He says he is "a poor old man,/As full of grief as age" (II.iv, 275–76), a "despis'd old man" (III.ii, 20), "So old and white as this"[2] (III.ii, 24), and "Your old kind father" (III.iv, 20). At one level this repetition of *old* is an index of self-pity, as various critics have seen;

in either sentimentality or violence, Lear can fall very short
of dignity and manliness. He is never whitewashed. Yet at
the same time the recurrence of *old* has another effect, one
produced by poetic suggestion: it is a way of expressing incredulity that such experiences could happen to an *old* man.
That is, to age the "offices of nature" (II.iv, 181) are more
than ever due; age has certain prerogatives in the order of
things; viciousness to age is therefore a rupture in nature.
Since this is Lear's unexpressed assumption, it is no wonder
that in the quieter mood which precedes the final scene, Lear
is inclined to accept age as almost the equivalent of folly.
"I am a very foolish, fond old man" he says (IV.vii, 60),
and "I am old and foolish" [3] (IV.vii, 84).

Now, Lear's conviction that age strengthens "nature," so
to speak—that is, especially obligates others in the perform-
ance of duty—is shared by many of the other characters.
They regard age as of itself exacting compassion. Kent calls
Lear "the old kind King" (III.i, 28); Albany calls him "a
gracious aged man" (IV.ii, 41) and says he will assign his
power to "this old majesty" (V.iii, 299). Cordelia says
French arms are incited by love "and our ag'd father's
right" [4] (IV.iv, 28). When he is about to be tortured by
Regan and Cornwall, Gloucester can speak of Lear's "poor
old eyes" (III.vii, 57) and "poor old heart" (62). Gloucester has already seen Edgar's imagined injury to him in
terms of his age: he has told Regan that his "old heart is
crack'd, it's crack'd!" (II.i, 92) Now, when Cornwall
moves toward him, this awareness of age bursts forth into
Gloucester's climactic cry of anguish: "He that will think to
live till he be old,/Give me some help" [5] (III.vii, 69–70).
His prayer exactly parallels an earlier one of Lear's:

O heavens,
If you do love old men, if your sweet sway
Allow obedience, if yourselves are old,
Make it your cause! Send down, and take my part!
(II.iv, 192–95)

When Kent, deprecating the stocks, says to Cornwall, "I am too old to learn" (II.ii, 134), he speaks for Lear as well as himself. All the old men do learn, of course; what Kent really does is to make a choral commentary on the destructive difficulty of the learning process. The educating experiences through which Lear and Gloucester have gone are "out of nature." So, while at one level we have the irony of old age's receiving treatment the opposite of what it might expect, at another we have an enrichment of the nature pattern: the stress upon age, and upon its due, is a way of reinforcing our sense of a Nature of things to which violence has been done. Yet through some instrument or other Nature continues to function: it is very effective, after all the stress on injured age, to have Gloucester, after his blinding, led by an Old Man who has been his and his father's tenant "these fourscore years" (IV.i, 14). In the Old Man's service we have a symbol of order at the cosmic level, and, at the same time, of the continued sustaining power of the old order which seems to be going to pieces. This is one of the hints of a clash between orders, a historical crisis, of which we shall see more.

AGE: THE PRAGMATISTS

When Edgar says to Gloucester, "Away, old man" (V.ii, 5), we have already seen enough of Edgar's devotion to know that the tone is kindly. But we also come upon an entirely different order of response to age. When Oswald calls Gloucester "Thou old unhappy traitor" (IV.vi, 232), and Regan says she cannot accommodate "the old man and's people" (II.iv, 291), and Cornwall that Gloucester "Follow'd the old man forth" (II.iv, 298), we have either contempt or an indifference close to it; likewise with Oswald's reference to Kent's "gray beard" (II.ii, 68) and Cornwall's addressing him as "old fellow" (II.ii, 91). The single small word always helps delineate the speaker; and these speakers are looking out for themselves. To them there is no obligation to be undertaken; no Nature, no moral reality, is involved.

Of Goneril, Regan, and Edmund we learn a great deal through their attitudes to age, since, aside from the overt actions of theirs that help determine the main lines of dramatic development they say enough about age to constitute almost a systematic discussion. When Lear has barely finished the division of his kingdom, Goneril and Regan engage in an analysis of him so detached that it borders on the "scientific." Goneril begins it: "You see how full of changes his age is; . . ." (I.i, 291). Regan adds " 'Tis the infirmity of his age; . . ." (296). Yes, continues Goneril in effect, he has always been rash, and age will make it worse; further, we must expect "the unruly waywardness that infirm and choleric years bring with them" (302–303)—a characteristic piece of rationalization, that is, a statement of recognizable fact but yet a statement of fact of which the cold objectivity itself becomes an advance defense of whatever steps their plans may compel them to take. They view age entirely in terms of its effect—its effect upon them. "Idle old man," Goneril calls Lear to Oswald (I.iii, 16), and then she generalizes again:

> Old fools are babes again, and must be us'd
> With checks as flatteries, when they are seen abus'd (19–20) ;

that is, she becomes the practical psychologist. So we are not surprised by the kind of logic with which she approaches Lear directly: "As you are old and reverend, you should be wise" (I.iv, 261). His followers should be "such men as may besort your age" (I.iv, 272). His curse on her she explains to Albany, "But let his disposition have that scope/ That dotage gives it" (I.iv, 314–15), and she justifies her opposition to the hundred men on the ground that on every whim "He may enguard his dotage with their pow'rs/And hold our lives in mercy" (I.iv, 349–50). That her pragmatic test is actually rationalization is pointed by Albany's brief rejoinder, "Well, you may fear too far" (351).

In the next act Regan takes up the debate with Lear and uses the same terms:

> Oh, sir, you are old!
> Nature in you stands on the very verge
> Of her confine. You should be rul'd and led
> By some discretion that discerns your state
> Better than you yourself. (II.iv, 148–52)

She adds "I pray you, father, being weak, seem so" (II.iv, 204)—that is, agree with us. And further,

> For those that mingle reason with your passion
> Must be content to think you old, and so—
> But she knows what she does. (II.iv, 237–39)

Age is to her a fact which means, simply, an instrument to use toward her own ends. When Lear expresses his disillusionment by saying, "I gave you all," Regan actually interrupts, "And in good time you gave it" (II.iv, 253)—leaping in with an implied self-exculpation. After Lear and his followers rush out into the gathering storm, she makes her final rationalization, "This house is little; the old man and's people/Cannot be well bestow'd" (291–92). In the meantime Goneril has got in one more blow. Goneril has joined Regan and Lear at Gloucester's castle, and Regan has welcomed her. When Lear expresses shock at Regan's taking her hand—an instance of his sensitiveness to the symbolic which suggests how powerful a shock the loss of his retainers must be—Goneril coolly asks "Why not?" and justifies herself: "All's not offence that indiscretion finds/And dotage terms so" (II.iv, 198–200). *Dotage* is Goneril's favorite word for age: it is her way of denying that age has dignity or deserts, and that it has a place in Nature; she conceives of it only as a state which compels submission to her and her sister's desires.

Edmund, too, sees in nature no intensified claim of Nature but only an aspect of the physical world to be properly estimated and used. In a manner identical with Regan's when she tells Oswald that Gloucester's blindness has aroused popular feeling (IV.v, 9 ff.), Edmund sees only a practical danger in "the old and miserable King,"

> Whose age has charms in it, whose title more,
> To pluck the common bosom on his side. (V.iii, 46–49)

This is the same cool calculation that he showed earlier when he decided to betray his father to Cornwall:

This seems a fair deserving, and must draw me
That which my father loses—no less than all.
The younger rises when the old doth fall. (III.iii, 24–26)

The rationalism of Goneril, Regan, and Edmund, which
we shall investigate further in Chapter IX, is tellingly reduced to its essence by Lear when Regan suggests to him
that he apologize to Goneril. He ironically rehearses the
prayer that he might make:

Dear daughter, I confess that I am old.
Age is unnecessary. On my knees I beg
That you'll vouchsafe me raiment, bed, and food.
(II.iv, 156–58)

This is much more than the "unsightly trick" that Regan
calls it; it is a brilliant speech, brilliant in its own cutting
to the heart of the matter and in its imaginative links with
other elements in the play. If Lear actually kneels, as Regan's phrase "unsightly trick" suggests, his physical action
combines with his words to initiate very effectively a series
of prayer scenes: here he is the ironic critic of a violation of
Nature which is symbolized by the father's being a suppliant
to his child; in the storm he says that he will pray and then
makes his "Poor naked wretches" speech (III.iv, 27 ff.)—
evidence that the very convulsion of Nature is a means of
bringing him to new insights; and near the end he tells Cordelia that he will "kneel down/And ask of thee forgiveness"
and that both of them will "pray" (V.iii, 10–12). His mockery is gone; he has a new humility; and his second kneeling
to a daughter is so different from the first that, as a symbol
of the moral world, it has a reassuring rather than a horrifying quality. Again: in Lear's speech to Regan the words
"Age is unnecessary" stand out, and they anticipate Lear's

passionate speech to Regan which begins, "Reason not the need." Throughout the scene the sisters apply to him a rational standard of necessity which fails to take account of other values which are equally real; their hard, shallow calculation is constantly brought home to us.

But most important of all, Lear's ironic prayer is a ruthlessly logical display of the doctrine of the survival of the fittest. Lear "confesses" that he is old: age is a crime in a world where the chief value is physical force. The sisters really accept a Darwinian universe—and thus they fall in exactly with the doctrines set forth or implied in Edmund's prayer to his goddess Nature. In fact, the age pattern is almost an exact logical extension of the nature pattern; the two views of age virtually coincide with the two interpretations of Nature. One Nature is an ordered, meaningful world, which implies set relationships, duties, obligations, and sanctions; the other is the Nature of individual will and force, where the strength of desire and the duration of rude power are the measures of conduct. The former can accommodate age; the latter outlaws it.

AGE: CHORUS

Edgar, who has many of the "sentences" of the play, several times talks chorally about age. When he sees the recently blinded Gloucester being led on the heath by the Old Man, he exclaims:

> World, world, O world!
> But that thy strange mutations make us hate thee,
> Life would not yield to age. (IV.i, 10–12)

Men do not like to grow old, but they become resigned to age because the ups and downs of fortune make them hate the world. Life punishes; suffering is aging. Yet Edgar does not become cynical; he fights against his father's despair; and he understands that his father's final suffering—being blinded—is morally meaningful. Then there are Edgar's concluding lines, which we have already noticed in their contribution to the sight pattern:

> The oldest hath borne most. We that are young
> Shall never see so much, nor live so long. (V.iii, 325–26)

Here again is a suggestion, significantly at the very end, of the system of paradoxes in the play. The oldest have borne most—but at the same time learned most, acquired greatest spiritual stature. Those who should be brushed aside by the survival of the fittest have survived in a very fundamental way; weakness has shown its own sort of strength. In the long run, fitness consists not in power and in calculation, but in capacity for illumination.

Why will the young never see so much? Not, surely, because the world will offer less of redemptive suffering. Is it, perhaps, that the world itself has undergone some change, that an age is passing? Gloucester says earlier, "We have seen the best of our time" (I.ii, 121–122). These are only slight suggestions of a historical crisis, but we shall come back to the subject later for further investigation.

JUSTICE

Lear, as we have said, regards his daughters' ingratitude, which he mentions several times, and their lack of compassion for age as a violation of the essential order of things. His awareness of this "breach in nature" should lead him, we would suspect, to the subject of justice: as a king he is almost bound to think in terms of that category. As a matter of fact, this is just what he does. Indeed, not only Lear, but other characters, think repeatedly of justice; [6] some ignore the subject entirely, but those who are conscious of it never lose faith that justice is being done or will at some time be done. Yet justice is treated complexly; human beings are not just at all times; and injustice is a fact, a fact which Shakespeare obviously treats with great fullness. Indeed, the patent injustice of some of the characters in the play leads Shakespeare again to the reliance upon paradox which is characteristic of this play: the justice which is meted out in the mad trial scene (III.vi) is in some ways better conceived than the justice which is done under circumstances which are apparently far more propitious. Thus the mad trial scene affords one of the early suggestions of the reason in madness which is one of the main structural elements in the play.

Even when his mind goes to pieces, Lear does not lose the sense of himself as the official dispenser of justice: in his most important mad scene, he says, "When I do stare, see how the subject quakes" (IV.vi, 110). But if it is a long time since Lear has really made anybody quake, the subject of justice has never been wholly out of his mind. We may conjecture that the problem first presents itself to him as such when he finds Kent in the stocks, for the fact that another is involved makes the matter legal rather than personal; that is, the appearance of another victim emphasizes better than one's own grievance that a principle is at stake. Lear has to ask about Kent's situation three times—"Who put my man i' th' stocks?" (II.iv, 185); "Who stock'd my servant?" (II.iv, 191); and "How came my man i' th' stocks?" (II.iv, 201)—before he can pry out Cornwall's in-

145

solent answer, "I set him there, sir; but his own disorders/ Deserv'd much less advancement" (II.iv, 202–203). Then there bursts upon Lear the fact that Regan and Goneril are really in league against him. He first promises himself revenge upon both (II.iv, 282) just as he has already prayed for revenge upon Goneril (II.iv, 164 ff.). But in the suffering of the storm the desire for vengeance gives way to a brooding sense of injustice and an agonized crying for justice. He calls upon "the great gods" that govern the storm to find their enemies:

> Tremble, thou wretch,
> That hast within thee undivulged crimes,
> Unwhipp'd of justice (III.ii, 51–53),

and he urges the murderer, the perjurer, the incestuous, and all other criminals to "cry/These dreadful summoners grace" (58–59). He concludes this speech with the familiar assertion, "I am a man/More sinn'd against than sinning" (60), and later he adds, "But I will punish home" (III.iv, 16). He is, paradoxically, both the victim of injustice, and also, as he sees himself at different times, the dispenser of justice. But this irony is complicated by still another element—the co-existence, in Lear's mind, of a feeling of injustice and, on the other hand, a better sense of justice than he has had. This better sense of justice takes two forms. In the first place, he says that he will pray (III.iv, 27)—which is to acknowledge a principle of divine justice that is permanent and unalterable, unaffected by the evil in the immediate world; and then, as though this very resolve had given him new insight, he continues with the famous speech of sympathy that begins "Poor naked wretches" and ends, "That thou mayst shake the superflux to them/And show the heavens more just" (28–36). The pity, and the specific concern with distributive justice, show Lear's deepening sense of right and wrong: justice has become more than the guaranteeing of personal prerogative. Secondly, his better sense of justice shows itself in the fact that, even while expressing the bitterness which he feels toward Goneril and Regan, he can say, "Judicious punishment! 'Twas this flesh begot/ Those pelican daughters" (III.iv, 76–77). Indirectly he acknowledges some complicity in his situation, if only through a reference to the physical fact of paternity; a kind of judgment has come upon him. What is apparent to us is another hint of the moral relationship between Lear and his daughters.

This development of Lear is a necessary part of the preparation for the scene which all these passages anticipate— the farmhouse "trial" of the daughters that begins when, in the presence of Kent, Gloucester, Edgar, and the Fool, Lear says,

> It shall be done; I will arraign them straight.—
> Come, sit thou here, most learned justicer.—
> Thou, sapient sir, sit here.—(III.vi, 22–24)

Then, amidst apparent irrelevanices by Edgar and the Fool, he continues to station the legal officials, and, employing legal terminology, to arraign Goneril and Regan and make charges against them (37–50). But the trial comes to a sudden end when Lear calls, "Corruption in the place!/False justicer, why hast thou let her scape?" (58–59) Ironically, of course, she does not ultimately escape, although all of Lear's experiences up to the present naturally do suggest to him that she has "got away with" her deeds. In this matter, as in others, he later shifts emphasis.

This concrete dramatization of the theme of justice not only shows how Lear's deranged mind is working but serves as another brief commentary upon the present state of affairs in the world which the play depicts. Now this scene certainly gains some of its effectiveness from the fact that it is in part a duplication of the "trial" scene of Act I, in which Lear is also (besides being judge) the prosecuting attorney and his daughters are the principals before the bar, and in which, also, the chief malefactors "escape"; hence, when Lear makes a charge of "false justicer," he is in one sense commenting upon himself. His falseness consisted, of course, in his misreading all the evidence upon those brought before him for judgment. But the mad trial scene receives its finest amplication in the fact that in the next scene, less than one hundred lines further on, another "trial" takes place—this time not in Gloucester's farmhouse but in Gloucester's castle, with Gloucester not as an observer but as the defendant. Gloucester is being tried, ironically, for his newly achieved assistance to Lear, a belated loyalty, and the prosecutors and judges include the daughters whom Lear has just been arraigning. Whereas Lear, as we have seen, gave up revenge as a program, the trial of Gloucester is inaugurated and carried through in the spirit of revenge. "I will have my revenge ere I depart his house," asserts Cornwall (III.v, 1), and he tells Edmund that he ought not to see "the revenges we are bound to take" (III.vii, 7). "Hang him instantly" and "Pluck out his eyes" cry Regan and Goneril (III.vii, 4, 5)

even before Gloucester is brought in: all this prepares for
Cornwall's revealing statement of intention:

> Pinion him like a thief, bring him before us.—
> Though well we may not pass upon his life
> Without the form of justice, yet our power
> Shall do a court'sy to our wrath, which men
> May blame but not control.—Who's there? the traitor?
>   (23–27)

The abusive, vituperative inquisition and torture which follow in the trial conducted by the formalists is of course as
much of a travesty as the trial conducted by the madman; in
fact, a trial that goes on in a madman's mind may embody a
better approximation of justice [7] than an apparently legal
procedure by the constituted authorities—a fact which is at
once further evidence of the complexity of the total statement which is being made by the play, and a powerful symbol of the state of affairs in Lear's kingdom. The two scenes
interanimate each other. Gloucester, the defendant, actually
"arraigns" the daughters in language like that in Lear's
arraignment of them (Lear: ". . . she kicked the poor king
her father"—III.vi, 49–50; Gloucester: "Because I would
not see thy cruel nails/Pluck out his poor old eyes; nor thy
fierce sister/In his anointed flesh stick boarish fangs"—III.
vii, 56–58); both times the justly accused daughters "escape," as they did on the comparable occasion at the beginning of the play; and whereas Lear inquires what "makes
these hard hearts" (III.vi, 81–82), Gloucester experiences
an incredible application of the hardness of heart. Gloucester's trial, too, helps point a later boast of Goneril's to
Albany: ". . . the laws are mine, not thine" (V.iii, 158).
Her lines and those of Cornwall just before Gloucester's trial

149

describe nicely the state of the external political world behind which the characters grope toward a stable and sustaining reality: "the form of justice," "our wrath, which men/
May blame but not control," "the laws are mine." Here we
see not only cynicism but a justification of the individual
will that harmonizes with Edmund's view of Nature; here is
a moral tone wholly different from anything that Lear or
Gloucester ever subscribed to. The speaking of such words
symbolizes the presence of a world wholly different from
that of the *ancien régime*.

It is no wonder that Gloucester's final attack upon the
daughters expresses itself in the hope that he will "see/The
winged vengeance overtake such children (III.vii, 65–
66). Cornwall openly derides this possibility: "If you see
vengeance—" (72). Then Albany says, addressing the absent Gloucester, "I live . . . to revenge thine eyes" (IV.ii,
94–96). Gloucester is sure that the gods will eventually in-
tervene; Albany hopes to requite the "wickedness" (IV.ii,
91). Both, that is, have faith in justice—a faith which remains unquestioned to the end of the play. Upon hearing of
Cornwall's death, Albany has already said,

> This shows you are above,
> You justicers, that these our nether crimes
> So speedily can venge. (IV.ii, 78–80)

The "venging" here is official rather than private; it is jus-
tice. "The gods are just," says Edgar (V.iii, 170), comment-
ing on the fates of Edmund and Gloucester; and the death of
Goneril and Regan leads to another comment from Albany:
"This judgment of the heavens, that makes us tremble,/
Touches us not with pity" (V.iii, 231–32). In the minds of

those who survive to see the dramatic situation resolved, there is no doubt that justice has been done, and that it evidences the working of divine authority [8]—a matter of which more must be said later. Lear himself is too much in the situation to pass upon it; if he is in part aware of his complicity in the lot that has fallen upon him, that lot is so crushing that he is no longer capable of responding to anything but the immediate experience. But earlier, as we have seen, he has made a tacit correction of himself and thus implied a kind of guilt; further, he is reunited with Cordelia and has her love, and speaks happily of going to prison with her; and it appears that he dies in the belief that she is still alive. Even in the midst of torture Gloucester does not question the operation of divine justice, and his "I stumbled when I saw" implies his own guilt. He too is reunited with a loving child, and he dies happily (V.iii, 196 ff.).

Goneril and Regan do not say anything at all about justice. Cornwall regards it as a formality. They participate in injustices—so harsh that in Lear's mad trial scene the carrying out of justice is no more empty than at their court. This is one of the minor paradoxes of the play. But as a whole the evidence of the justice pattern coincides closely with that of the nature pattern: there is, despite all the horrifying chaos of phenomena, a substantial universal order upon which men may rely.

*W*hen once the mind's corrupted it brings forth unnumbered crimes, and ills to ills succeed.

Sophocles, *Philoctetes* (Francklin's translation)

* * *

Reason is the enumeration of quantities already known; imagination is the perception of the value of those quantities. . . . The great instrument of moral good is the imagination. . . .

. . . the vessel of the state is driven between the Scylla and Charybdis of anarchy and despotism. Such are the effects which must ever flow from an unmitigated exercise of the calculating faculty.

Shelley, *A Defence of Poetry*

CHAPTER VII

LARGEST BOUNTY AND TRUE NEED

THE VALUES PATTERN

W H A T W E have seen so far is a Lear who is inclined to accept human behavior at its face value (the sight theme) compelled to distinguish more sharply between appearance and reality and to attempt a sharper evaluation of humanity (the sight theme, the clothes theme), struggling to find expression for incredible human conduct (the animal theme, the sex theme), to place the human being in a comprehensible order of things (the nature theme) while trying to make sense of the apparent loss of certain supports of the order that had seemed unassailable (the age theme, the justice theme). The heavy problem that faced Lear is presented to us, as far as the evidence of language is concerned, in one other set of terms. These terms deal with what may be called, loosely and inconclusively, the problem of values.

The whole play, of course, *acts* values; it is a metaphor for the values of human experience. Besides, each deed is a value judgment, for it shows the kind of choice a character makes. We must never forget either the total statement or the significance of the actions. But nor should we forget the minuter but no less persistent evidence of language. For in

addition to the operations of character there are also certain
verbal approaches to the problem that contribute to the total
statement of the play about values. Different characters make
statements about what is valuable; sometimes they speculate
on the question. We find them using both familiar metaphors
and abstract terms for value, or discussing directly the kind
of possession, tangible or intangible, that is desirable and
useful.[1] When Kent calls the rumored division between
Albany and Cornwall "a dear thing" (III.i, 19), he of course
comments only upon a minute portion of the historical flux.
A more durable object of concern is human relations. Of
his love for Edgar, Gloucester says, "No father his son
dearer" (III.iv, 174), words which become far more than a
conventional statement of parental love when they are picked
up a few lines later in Cornwall's assurance to Edmund:
". . . thou shalt find a dearer father in my love" (III.v,
24–25). Further, we must see as a part of the picture the remark of the jauntier Gloucester at the beginning of the play
that he has, besides Edmund, another son, "some year elder
than this, who yet is no dearer in my account" (I.i, 20).
Combined with the actual working of father love as we see it
in variable practice, the phrases suggest that father love,
conventionally regarded as a stable and clearly defined
entity, is susceptible of sharply differing interpretations.
Edmund forfeits a father's love; his new "father," Cornwall,
soon meets a violent death. Gloucester must learn about the
sons dear to him; his love is returned, finally, better than he
expects.

In another passage an evaluating phrase is picked up more
rapidly. Showing annoyance at not being enthusiastically
met by Albany, Goneril remarks sarcastically, "I have been

worth the whistle," and Albany retorts, "You are not worth the dust which the rude wind/Blows in your face" (IV.ii, 29–31); thus he skillfully extends her own wind metaphor to characterize her. The implications about value are still wider when Lear speaks to himself of having let folly in "And thy dear judgment out" (I.iv, 294): that judgment is precious becomes doubly apparent when it has been so badly used. When Edgar reports that he met his father "with his bleeding rings,/Their precious stones new lost" (V.iii, 189–90), his words not only tell us that sight is precious and remind us of the ironically bad use that Gloucester made of the precious stones; but they also summarize the stress of the whole play upon the moral insight which, like Lear's judgment, has seriously malfunctioned. Another line of Edgar's, that "conceit may rob/The treasury of life" (IV.vi, 42–43), contributes briefly to one of the ironic ideas of the play—that to man, even though he may be a pauper in well-being, life still seems full of riches.[2] When the Gentleman describes Cordelia's sorrow on hearing about the mad Lear's situation, he uses language more complex that that of any of the other passages I have quoted. Her tears, he tells Kent, left her eyes

> As pearls from diamonds dropp'd. In brief,
> Sorrow would be a rarity most belov'd,
> If all could so become it. (IV.iii, 24–26)

This says, of course, that Cordelia is enviably beautiful in sorrow, which, if it would so affect everybody, would paradoxically come to have the value of a rare gem; but it says equally that in this callous world compassion has the value of a precious stone. Tears of compassion are pearls; eyes are diamonds, and, as we have already seen in Edgar's comment on his father, precious stones. Insight is of the highest value.

There is somewhat fuller discussion of riches and poverty, a subject which comes up because of Lear's loss of the perquisites of royalty. When Edgar says that he will

> . . . take the basest and most poorest shape
> That ever penury in contempt of man
> Brought near to beast . . . (II.iii, 7–9),

he implies that poverty can destroy man's essential humanity (the definition of which, as we have seen in the chapters on nature, age, and justice, is one of the major problems of the play). The Fool ironically tells Lear what kind of wealth— "dolours," i. e., dollars—he shall have, despite the poverty which will make unchaste Fortune close the door to him:

> But fathers that bear bags
> Shall see their children kind.
> Fortune, that arrant whore,
> Ne'er turns the key to th' poor.

But, for all this, thou shalt have as many dolours for thy daughters as thou canst tell in a year. (II.iv, 50–55)

Tell belongs to the pun: Lear can "count dollars" or, as he actually does, "recount sorrows." Later the Fool adds,

> That sir which serves and seeks for gain,
> And follows but for form;
> Will pack when it begins to rain,
> And leave thee in the storm. (II.iv, 79–82)

All the talk about riches and poverty, of course, is in part literal, in part a figurative comment on the ways of a materialistic world; but chiefly it is an implied exploration of the whole subject of what actually constitutes riches and poverty, of the kind of circumstances which humanity can find endurable. The experiences of Lear which lead to the Fool's exegesis, after they have been intensified by later events, and the comparable experiences of Gloucester produce in the old men reflections—reflections which are remarkable in their close similarity. In the "pitiless storm" Lear asks how "poor naked wretches"—that is, both pitiable and poverty-stricken—can defend themselves against such seasons. Then he exclaims:

> Oh, I have ta'en
> Too little care of this! Take physic, pomp;
> Expose thyself to feel what wretches feel,
> That thou mayst shake the superflux to them
> And show the heavens more just. (III.iv, 32–36)

A speech of Gloucester's, as Dr. Johnson long ago observed, comes very close to this. Gloucester speaks shortly after he has been blinded:

> Heavens, deal so still!
> Let the superfluous and lust-dieted man,
> That slaves your ordinance, that will not see
> Because he does not feel, feel your pow'r quickly;
> So distribution should undo excess
> And each man have enough. (IV.i, 67–72)

In such speeches is a concern for distributive justice which, as we have already seen, amplifies the justice theme. Yet, in the problem of computing values, these speeches notably do not adopt a purely material standard. They point to inequalities that need rectifying; they do not imply that the rectification will be a panacea for the radical ills of society. They indicate a widening of sympathy, a deeper perception of the values that life must embrace. But this is only one of

the ways in which Lear learns. Looking at his straw and
hovel, he reflects,

> The art of our necessities is strange,
> That can make vile things precious. (III.ii, 70–71)

Many things are becoming precious to Lear that were not
precious: the values pattern here points to the experience of
revaluation which he undergoes between the beginning and
the end of the play. At the start, his concept of the precious
was at fault. We must now attempt to define, as closely as possible, his initial misconception of values.

LEAR AS VALUE MAKER

The value passages already considered indicate the existence throughout the play of an evaluative attitude to life.
Experiences, kinds of possession, qualities, physical properties, and so on, are not merely named, or dealt with pas-
sively as they occur in the plot; but often, by a rather
unobtrusive use of language, their value to man is suggested.
We are reminded, repeatedly, of the preciousness of parental and filial affection, of judgment, of sight and insight, of compassion; of the world's attitude to poverty; of
misfortune as a producer of insight. By these means the play
always maintains our consciousness of its concern with the
problem of values. Yet such passages as we have been re-
viewing are secondary in importance to two closely related
scenes in the first two acts, scenes which deal primarily with
values and which largely determine the subsequent course
of the plot. When, at the beginning of his most powerful
madness scene, Lear says, "No, they cannot touch me for
coining. I am the king himself" (IV.vi, 83–84), he is of

course experiencing the first of a series of hallucinations; but at another level we feel the implication that the King is the source and guarantee of values. Now this is, ironically, just what Lear has not in fact been (just as he has not been dispensing the justice which belongs to the kingship). Or, still more ironically, he has succeeded in bringing into play values which he has repudiated and would now gladly nullify but cannot. For, on the one occasion in the play when he attempts a formal determination of values, he goes conspicuously awry. This is in the first scene of the play (I.i), where Lear's introduction of inapplicable standards sets off a whole train of woes. Now this first scene, in which Lear divides the land, must be taken together with the later one in which Lear is finally deprived of his followers by Goneril and Regan (II.iv), for the scenes are pointedly affiliated: in both we see the dominant figures, in their own interest and in willful disregard of protest, substituting, for the human actuality which must be imaginatively grasped—for, that is, filial love (I.i) and the meaningfulness of Lear's retainers to him (II.iv)— a verbal, quasi-logical equivalent which grossly misstates the realities it purports to represent. Both are haggling scenes: in both, the characters try to measure in material terms what is not materially measurable; thus these characters do injury both to others and themselves; hence the further course of the play. But the linkage of the bargaining scenes also involves ironic reversals: although, in both, Lear is in a state of wild frustation because his sense of values is not accepted by others, in the first he inflicts injury, whereas in the second he is the victim of injury; further, his intemperate application of a wholly irrelevant system of computing values in Act I is what makes possible the recoil of a comparably irrelevant system upon himself in Act II. Indeed, by Act II Lear has undergone a major intellectual clarification. Even in Act I his "O most small fault,/How ugly didst thou in Cordelia show!" (I.iv, 288–89) indicates his awareness that the apparent "size" of Cordelia's error is the product of his own miscalculation, that is, of his introduction of a wholly alien measure. His passion for measurement is now gone, and the restoring of his imagination is under way. He is beginning to see things in perspective; he can make the leap from conduct to its meaning, as he could not before; he is beginning to grasp values. But the calculating tendency in himself has been set free in the world by his putting Goneril and Regan into power.

Act I is full of the problem of values. The play opens with the question of Lear's judgment of the relative merits of Albany and Cornwall: Gloucester says that "in the division of the kingdom, it appears not which of the Dukes he values most" (I.i, 3–5), and the assumption is that any differentiation between them would be—and *could* be—apparent in the division of the land.[3] Now this prepares for the formal division scene in which the matter of daughter love is first introduced. Some commentators assume that Lear does not seriously introduce his demand for avowals of affection but is merely passing the time and is unconsciously motivated by a desire for reassurance that the division scheme is sound. It has also been argued that this demand of Lear's is evidence of madness.[4] However the demand may have come up, the fact is that Lear does act on it seriously, and our business is to see the symbolic significance of his action in the context of the whole play. Lear asks

Which of you shall we say doth love us most?
That we our largest bounty may extend
Where nature doth with merit challenge. (I.i, 52–54)

He assumes, that is, that there are (1) verbal symbols and
(2) property symbols which can denote quantity of love; he
seeks an exchange equivalent for an entity which by its
nature is not marketable. He wants to make a trade where
there can be none; he rationalistically introduces a mensura-
tional standard where there can be none. He forgets that love,
if it is to prove itself, cannot prove itself in a way alien to its
very nature. He treats love as if it were a material quantum
of a certain size and weight; in his intellectual confusion he
forgets that deeds rather than words are the symbols of love.
This confusion may be described quite literally as a failure
of imagination; love must be apprehended by images, and
the images are richly available to him—not in verbal short-
cuts and formulae, but in the lives of daughters whom he has
observed from infancy.[5] Now this kind of evidence, when it
is not abstracted by literary art from the full and resistant
texture of experience, is vast and inchoate and difficult; Lear
shirks a demanding task—the imaginative apprehension of
symbols, we know, is not always easy—and seeks an easy,
rationalistic way out. Lear's failure is exactly duplicated by
Gloucester's a little later when Edmund accuses Edgar:
Gloucester too might have consulted his nonrational, ex-
periential awareness of Edgar's quality, the images of
devotion which he could find in Edgar's life. But the pains-
taking imaginative transcendence of the moment was too
much for him. Finally, we should observe that Lear's failure
of understanding here is analogous to his failure to perceive

161

that a king cannot be a king without a crown and cannot maintain his perquisites by a kind of oral recipe or contract, that is, a purely rationalized formulation of a status which involves responsibilities as well as rights. This first failure, which is presented in part by the clothes pattern, is also one of imagination: Lear fails to grasp important interrelationships which are nowhere logically specified but are implied by the nature of man and society. In his two first errors—giving up the throne and treating love as measurable—he is acting with complete consistency.

That Lear's "largest bounty"—the gift that upsets the moral world—is rooted in a terrible misconception is apparent to Cordelia, who refuses to try to translate the non-marketable into a currency that can buy property, and possibly to the sisters, although they are willing to profit by it. If they do not actually grasp Lear's error at the level of conscious definition, at least they illustrate the falseness of his hypothesis by doing such a bad job of taking verbal measurement of the abstraction love.[6] Goneril's "I love you more than word can wield the matter" (I.i, 56) and "Beyond what can be valued" (58) are ironically useful phrases, for they express, despite the absence of love in her, a truth about love: it cannot be quantified; inevitably, the words which she chooses—abstractions which, as anyone less determined on a logical impossibility than Lear could see (Cordelia and Kent do), neither weigh nor define—exactly fail to "wield the matter." Those of Regan similarly fail, though, with further ironic effect, she talks *about* love in the abstract terminology of value: "I am made of that self metal as my sister,/And prize me at her worth" (71–72)—words which palpably do not prove love but do tell more about Regan than she supposes.

Cordelia comments outright upon Lear's error: " I cannot heave/My heart into my mouth" (93–94). Then comes the climactic irony of the daughters' speechmaking: whereas the sisters have been dressing up their selfish feelings in high-falutin abstractions, Cordelia expresses her real feelings in a most matter-of-fact metaphor from the world of business and law: "I love your Majesty/According to my bond; no more nor less" (94–95), that is, "as I am bound by the terms of a definite filial relationship." It appears safe to assume that she implies, also, "That relationship has been a happy one; therefore you understand how much I mean." Yet, as I have said earlier,[7] Cordelia here practices a withdrawal not unlike her father's in abdicating: she will not play the game his way, and hence the world is turned over to the evil characters. Lear has his mind set on an impossible evaluative scheme: he wants amounts, quantities overtly specified, spacious hyperboles, and he will pay off with his "largest bounty." Cordelia actually feels, the text suggests, that she is in an impossible dilemma; for, although she cannot do what Lear wants, she goes as far as she can: she will not give loose, expansive assurances, but she will go as far as to give him a metaphor—"According to my bond." If he will not read the image offered by her life, she will give him an easier image. But his mind is still set upon calculation, and upon a calculation to which the answer is predetermined; his imagination is blocked—the imagination which is later to function so intensely—and he misses the import of a concrete image which says more than the sisters' facile abstractions.[8] In one sense, then, the scene initiates a lesson in language, a lesson which Lear learns—too late for practical purposes, not too late for salvation. In his expiatory phase we see him, the man who here fails to grasp a possibly saving image, coming to an intense imaginative grasp of experience and using the most powerful imaginative language.

Lear, then, invites tragedy by three errors: he mistakes the nature of kingship; he establishes a wrong method for evaluating love; and he misinterprets the value of certain statements about love. In each case he is calculating an advantage; his imagination is not working. Then: these errors are not the negligible slips of a mere observer who has time to check and prove and correct; they are the terrible mistakes, not of an acquiescent "average" man like Gloucester, but of a man of action, and of a man whose action is a public action. Lear *imposes* his erroneous conclusions about children and court. We now see him carrying through his scheme of calculation, measuring love by words and property.

Lear had expected Cordelia to "draw," by her speech, a kingdom "more opulent" (88) than those already delimited for Goneril and Regan; after her according-to-my-bond speech he fears that she "may mar your fortunes" (97). When she persists in her stand, he exclaims angrily ". . . thy truth then be thy dower" (110), a judgment more fitting than Lear supposes, in that it is only in some such terms as "truth"—her character, her actions—that love can be valued. Yet he feels that in disinheriting her—in depriving her not only of "largest bounty" but of all bounty—he has found the right symbol for some defect in her, a conviction of his which is qualified by the attitudes to it of Burgundy, who, though he hates to be smoked out, is a bargainer like the Lear of this scene; of Kent, who reproves Lear directly; and of France, who by his deed—his choice of Cordelia—shows a different set of values. Much of the rest of the scene can be understood as a series of efforts to improve upon Lear's bungling in the expression of values. When Burgundy is finally driven to admit his stand, Cordelia says, "Since that respects of fortune are his love,/I shall not be his wife" (251–52). "Respects of fortune" deny love: her words are really another commentary on Lear's mistaken system of measurement. This is even more true of France's

> Love's not love
> When it is mingled with regards that stands
> Aloof from th'entire point. (241–43)

Lear's metaphors continue to stress his misconception: "When she was dear to us, we did hold her so;/But now her price is fall'n" (199–200), and "I tell you all her wealth" (211). It is excellent, the way in which the language pattern itself—especially Lear's use of it—keeps harping on his ironic misestimation of her value. It is exactly fitting, too, that Cordelia should speak of the "want of that for which I am richer" (233) and thus by her own paradox point to the intrusion of irrelevant standards: one better have nothing by the wrong measure. Lear tries to mislead France, but France, ironically, evaluates Cordelia better than Lear does: "She is herself a dowry" (244), "Thy dow'rless daughter, . . . /Is queen of us, . . ." (259–60). Twice he too has recourse to paradox: "Fairest Cordelia, that art most rich, being poor" (253), he says, and none, he adds, "Can buy this unpriz'd precious maid of me" (262). The language of Cordelia and

165

France shows imaginations whose alertness is in fine contrast with the inertness of Lear's. And at the same time their paradoxes remind us again of the predominance of paradox in the play: the clear-sighted do not see, and true values are not valued.

The language pattern of the scene is skillfully carried on by Cordelia's vocative in her next-to-last speech to her sisters, "The jewels of our father, . . ." (271), an ironic comment on Lear's mistaken evaluation of them. Regan's immediate taunting of her with her poverty (280–82) on one level symbolizes the kind of understanding of good and evil of which Regan is capable; and, since Regan thus uses exactly the scale of values which Lear has imposed throughout the scene, we see hinted that relationship between daughter and father which must be understood if the structure of the play is to become clear. Lear's calculation is his elder daughters' calculation. On another level, Regan's taunting Cordelia with her poverty establishes the pattern which will be skillfully used later when the Fool derides Lear for having nothing (I.iv, 130 ff.). As always, the Fool's brilliant lines have overtones: besides having nothing because he gave it all to ungrateful daughters, Lear had publicly taunted Cordelia with having nothing and on that ground had tried to discourage her suitors.[9]

Lear's three errors of calculation are the first links in the chain of tragic events. They are failures of the imagination, and they soon come home to him. The retraining of his imagination makes its biggest advance when he must face his daughters' theory of values as it is applied to his retainers. He finds them using virtually his own calculus.

ALL THE KING'S MEN

It is apparent even in Act I that the unimaginative spirit of calculation which Lear has set loose in the world is beginning to show itself in unexpected ways: for Lear hears apparently reasonable complaints made about the hundred followers whom he had specifically reserved for himself, and then finds that Goneril has cut off half of them (I.iv, 220 ff., 316 ff.). But matters do not come to a head until he must face both Goneril and Regan in Act II. Then we see again an effort to measure an abstraction in material terms, with ironic similarities to and divergencies from the earlier bargaining scene: this time Lear's daughters apply his fallacy against him; Lear in each case is made frantic by real or imagined contumacy; yet Goneril and Regan subject him to the same kind of indefensible deprivation to which he has subjected Cordelia. Lear, who wanted to make practical application of values that are not related to practicality, now learns that in some areas the intrusion of practicality may be intolerable. It comes home to him that quantification is irrelevant. For the value of his followers is symbolic, not pragmatic; they denote his status, his position emeritus; symbols cannot be quantified, and his daughters' metrics are perverse. Whatever their motive, their failure of imagination is in effect exactly comparable to his own.

When he protests against the stocking of Kent, Gloucester shows a clear understanding of the symbolism of the retainers: ". . . the king must take it ill," he says, to find that he is "so slightly valued in his messenger" [10] (II.ii, 152–53). Lear's own phrase "to scant my sizes" (II.iv, 178)

shows his sense of the situation; yet even here he is not wholly
free of the heresy of material equivalents. Regan, he thinks,
he can count on. Why? "Thy half o' th' kingdom hast thou
not forgot" (183)—a mode of thought whose fallacy Goneril's conduct should, and Regan's conduct quickly does,
demonstrate. The impact of Regan's treatment of him, which
parallels Goneril's, is indeed enlightening, and Lear shows a
new subtlety of apprehension when he brings France into
his tirade. To return to Goneril, he tells Regan, is impossible, and as a symbol of the impossible he mentions his beg-
ging a "pension" of France, "that dowerless took/Our
youngest born" (II.iv, 215–16). That is, he no longer relies
upon his *quid pro quo* rationalism, but senses that the less
tangible matter of attitude is a determinant of relationships:
he had treated Cordelia and France with contempt, and he is
therefore not in a moral position to ask aid of them.

The daughters, meanwhile, introduce purely practical
arguments with regard to the reduction of his retainers: [11]
there are not accommodations for all of them, and various
sets of followers will come to blows (II.iv, 240–52). Lear, as
I have said, is coming to insight, but he is still muddled: there
is a brilliant touch in his decision, at one point, to go with
Goneril because the fifty retainers she will allow him double
the twenty-five Regan will permit (261–63). This is the same
kind of haggling which he himself had introduced in the
land-distribution scene. But he is finally driven to a sharper
grasp of the values involved when the daughters introduce
the harshly utilitarian argument of *need* (242 ff., 264).
Their position is brought to a logical conclusion in Regan's
"What need one?" (266) Now if need, taken at its narrowest possible meaning, is to be a criterion of human desert

and privilege, human values will come tumbling. The low philosophy of need is met directly by Lear's fine closing speech, a speech which first marks his ability to grow from the defender of his own privilege into a philosophic observer of experience and a student of values:

> Oh, reason not the need; our basest beggars
> Are in the poorest thing superfluous.
> Allow not nature more than nature needs,
> Man's life is cheap as beast's. Thou art a lady;
> If only to go warm were gorgeous,
> Why, nature needs not what thou gorgeous wear'st
> Which scarcely keeps thee warm. But for true need—
>
> (267–73)

His last phrase, "true need," is very important, for it underscores the existence of values entirely different from demonstrable material needs—higher needs (his own need, at the moment, is for symbols of respect and love) which must be imaginatively grasped and cannot be mechanically computed. There is no relationship between largest bounty and true need. Now Lear not only defines the effect upon humanity of the use of mere need as a measuring stick for perquisites, but he shrewdly demonstrates that his daughters do not themselves observe the canon of need; their values are wrong, and they themselves are dishonest in the bargain. Further, the language of his speech is very interesting: *need, cheap, beggars, superfluous* connect his lines with other passages that approach values through economic terms; *nature* and *beast's* introduce the nature and animal themes; *gorgeous* and *wear'st,* the clothes theme. If the well-dressed have values suitable only for the animal kingdom, they will not survive. The characteristic nexus of patterns shows the

169

weaving together of the different themes into a single strand of meaning which finally *is* the play.[12]

Lear's detection of his daughters' inconsistency adds weight to the fact that their real purpose is, by hook or crook, to keep him in his place. They hope to establish a formal justification for themselves by getting Lear to assent to their action as reasonable—reasonable, that is, for him; consistent with his circumstances; to his own advantage. What we have, then, is a most interesting coincidence of the two common meanings of *rationalization*—the traditional meaning of *giving rational form to,* and the latter-day meaning of *self-justification.* Our conclusions follow rationally from the facts, the daughters say; actually, of course, they simply want to keep things under control. This ambivalence helps weight the final meaning of these scenes—that the daughters' evil consists in the application of rationalistic methods where they do not belong. To measure, to quantify, is rationalization. Perhaps we may say that Shakespeare is commenting upon the problem of scientific rationalism—not being "antiscientific," of course, but indicating the nature of the problem. Some entities are subject to the quantitative norm, and some are not; and terrible results may follow from the application of the norm to matters not susceptible of such treatment. Some areas of reality can be represented only by images or symbols and apprehended only by insight—or by what I have called the imagination, the power of grasping symbols and images and of meaningfully combining them. The basic irony of the play is that Lear himself refuses an imaginative act when it is essential and introduces an inapplicable rationalism. Thus Goneril and Regan come to power, and with them comes to power the spirit of calculation. Lear wanted to measure love, which is a state of the soul, in material terms (property); his daughters wish to deal with a symbol (Lear's retainers), which represents a state of the soul, in terms of material need. Instead of relying on imaginative insight, they apply the techniques of the bargainer. There are various ingredients in Lear's tragic flaw, but the most important is his failure to recognize what areas of value are not capable of rational formulation. That error becomes the whole being of Goneril and Regan, who represent, as I have argued, one element in Lear in its full untrammeled effectiveness.[13] It is often said that ingratitude is the theme of the play; and doubtless Goneril and Regan should be called ungrateful. But we ought also to understand precisely what course of action they take in their ingratitude: they seize an occasion which Lear in his error has given them, and then they take the method of evaluating conduct which led him to give them the occasion, and, in applying it against him and whoever seems to stand in the way of their own plans, carry it to a ruthlessly logical extreme. What they use came from him: this is the deepest symbolic meaning of their kinship.

The Lear who introduced rationalistic procedures soon becomes irrational. Yet in his very irrationality he is capable of an insight which he did not have when he was apparently in full command of his faculties. This paradox is the burden of the madness pattern, which is the structural core of the play. To it we now come.

". . . and this is what you call your salvation. Lunacy, just lunacy, that's what it is!"

"Only truth without perception is lunacy, this has to do with the truth of perception . . . in such reality there is no lunacy."

Hermann Broch, *The Death of Virgil*

* * *

. . . but there is also a madness which is the special gift of Heaven, and the source of the chiefest blessings among men.

Plato, *Phaedrus* (Jowett's translation)

CHAPTER VIII

REASON IN MADNESS

THE MADNESS PATTERN

L E A R ' S   M A D N E S S overshadows the play—because it is shocking and terrible, of course, but in a more fundamental manner because it is at the center of the meaning of the play. It is too easy merely to be aware of the pathos of the scenes of madness; and indeed pathos alone, even at such an exalted level, would be incapable of creating the overwhelmingly powerful impression which for centuries has been made by the mad king. Nor could even terrifying madness, and a terrifying storm, of themselves create much of the force of the central scenes of the play. Beneath the superficial aspects of these scenes there must be felt, by even a casual student, a reverberation of underlying meanings which constitute the inner reality of the scenes.

The reader soon becomes aware that the madness functions in more ways than one. In its most palpable aspect it is a psycho-physiological phenomenon, the ultimate collapse of a high-strung but unstable personality brought, by a habitual unrestrained emotional violence, to a pitch of utterly frustrating discords at which it can no longer maintain its identity. But seen from another point of view—which the play presents with equal fullness—madness is an intellectual phenomenon, the expression of a failure of understanding before the extraordinarily complex situation in which the problem of evil is embodied. A good deal of the imagery of the play which we have been examining has been a richly elaborate statement of that complexity of situation. The madness, however, exists not only at the naturalistic level but also at the moral: here it is a part of the vital middle link in the tragic process—the expiatory phase [1] which in *Lear* is of such bitter intensity as to confound sentimental critics. Finally, the madness is also a symbol, a symbol of a disordered and distraught world where expectancies are defeated and norms contemned; it is and it signifies a "breach in nature." Here it collaborates with the storm: these two phenomena so often thought of as existing primarily in relationship to each other are actually most important in their common function as indices of the spiritual state of the world.

To go still further, we find that the madness is not an isolated fact, any more than are the storm, the nakedness of Edgar, and the blindness of Gloucester. Just as the blindness focuses the sight imagery of the play and the nakedness the clothes imagery, so the madness brings together and is to be read along with the assumed madness of Edgar, the folly and wisdom of the Fool, a great many comments on madness and folly throughout the play, and, finally, the powers of reason of those of whose technical sanity there is no doubt— Goneril and Regan, whose rational activity we have already had a glimpse of in Chapter VII, and Edmund. To the other patterns of meaning which we have seen, then, we must add a madness pattern, and we must trace the interrelationships of this pattern and the meaning which they appear to set forth.

What we must come to, it is obvious, is some consideration of the kinds of mental balance, the kinds of human wisdom.

THE OTHER PATTERNS

The configuration of verbal and dramatic elements of which Lear's madness is the center is of course not a solitary system the meaning of which is to be added to the meanings of the other systems within the play to produce, as a sort of sum, the total meaning of the play. The various systems are constantly interrelated, are often scarcely distinguishable parts of a whole, and should not undergo the separation which is one of the dangers of the present schematized discussion. But since the separation is inevitable here, it may be well to review once again the mode of interrelationship and interdependence of the constituent thematic elements. With the exception of the sight symbolism the other image and word patterns which we have examined have, as their general function, the setting forth of the complex universe with which man, as a perceptive and understanding creature, must deal —a universe which includes, in one aspect, humanity, and, in another, the principles, whether natural, moral, or theological, which he invokes in the determination of order; a universe, too, in which, in a variety of phenomenal emergences, the problem of evil is always the ultimate irreconcilable antagonist. The clothes imagery suggests some of the intricacies of the human reality—the disguise and trickery which must be penetrated, the defenses needed for preservation, the nakedness which means not only defenselessness but a kind of loss of the minimal tokens of humanity; so that here we have figured forth, in wonderfully apt concrete

175

form, a paradoxical truth at the center of human conduct, namely, that the necessary protective movement has in it the seeds of, and can with deceptive ease slide over into, the cynical aggrandizement of self. The animal imagery, which is plentiful, is used almost exclusively to emphasize another complication in humanity—its capacity for abjuring its especial characteristics and taking on the rapacity and ruthlessness of the beast; the animality in man receives further expression in the direct and figurative use of sex. The problem of age serves to amplify our picture of a scarcely accountable moral variability in man, in whom this one phase of experience may evoke responses that range from tender compassion to a hard sense of opportunity for profitable manipulation. Such, says the language of the play, are the enigmas of man as a moral agent. On the other hand, viewed with respect to his status in the world, man seems hardly to justify the complacency with which he often regards himself: the animal imagery says repeatedly that his position—the result of his treatment by fellow beings—is like that of animals; and often it seems possible to describe him only in the language of disease, decay, and injury. Does man, then, live in an ordered universe, or is he simply buffeted about in a meaningless chaos? The justice pattern points out not only the miscarriage of principles of justice by deliberation, but the liability to act unjustly even in those who do not intend evil. This is of course not to deny that justice exists or to assert cynically that it is always accidental or too little or too late, but rather to point out that in practice it is far less simple than as an abstract conception. Likewise the value pattern, although incidentally it may assert the preciousness of the compassion and power of seeing which are not the most frequent of human gifts, is largely devoted to showing how "honest confusion" may in its effects coincide rather closely with the most clear-minded intention to govern all considerations of value by the possibilities of immediate profit. The distinction of false and true is not easy, and the discovery of an infallible method of making the distinction is still more difficult. If man is unwilling to deal, or incapable of dealing, with experience imaginatively, and substitutes rationalistic procedures where they cannot be successfully used, he will get into trouble: rational man is in the greatest danger of rationalizing essential values out of existence. Finally there is the nature pattern, which includes on one hand the symbolic storm and on the other, direct, literal philosophic inquiries. What appears to be implied by the nature pattern is that trickery, cruelty, injustice, a value system dominated by the spirit of calculation, though real and ever-present to be reckoned with, are to be regarded as disorder, a violation of the nature of things, ab-normal. "Nature" still *is*, even though obscure and elusive; it is ever the measure of the world of accident.

What we have here is an immensely inclusive anthropology, an effort unequaled in drama to get at the problem of man from every side and in every aspect, to give it the fullest and most variegated possible expression in differentiable and yet collaborating strands of poetic and dramatic structure; so we have an almost overwhelmingly complex accumulation of phenomena and of the metaphysical problems which they introduce. The play does not attempt, at least in prosaic and logical form, final answers to the problems; it is primarily bent upon evoking a sense of their magnitude and of the well-nigh intolerable burden which they place upon the human mind. But if the play, since it is not didactic, does not announce answers, it at least implies answers; and its method of implication is a very elaborate system of contrasts. The materials of practically all the patterns which we have examined are presented dualistically; life resolves itself into alternatives. This is not only to say that we always have options, but it is to say that a man in search of understanding finds alternatives as empirical realities. Nearly every pattern has its dichotomy, and the dichotomies tend to coincide and even coalesce into a general definition of reality. There are two natures—Lear's Nature which is order, and Edmund's which is impulse and will. There are the two views of man—that man may be a human being (by conforming with order) or an animal (falling into Edmund's view of nature). Man may view age as the possessor of certain prerogatives (established in Nature) or as mere obsolescence, to be utilized for the profit of the fittest, the up-to-date (the view consistent with Nature as defined by Edmund). There are the two aspects of the problem of justice —the belief in an eternal, unswerving justice (Nature as order), and the fact of actual injustice (inflicted by man as animal). There are the naked and the overdressed—both of whom represent different contradictions of Nature. What we are always kept aware of is the qualitative distinction between the two opposing possibilities: to be on one side of the fence may mean being terribly beset in an actual world, but what happens in the world is never allowed to obscure our sense of intrinsic absolute value. By such means the play moves toward its final statement. Indeed, we are always reminded of the paradoxes of experience: the naked may survive better than the well-protected, those who become beasts

178

of prey may perish before their victims, age may endure and come to a saving understanding, the hidden justice may upset the insuperable temporary power.

Then there is the paradox of man's grasp of the complex world. Again we have the dualism: there are the clearsighted in the world, and those who are blind. But the blind come to sight, and the clear-sighted do not see far enough. The rational may be too rational. But the imaginative may be reduced to complete incompetence in affairs, even to mental incompetence. What is said about them is the burden of the madness pattern.

THE SIGHT AND MADNESS PATTERNS

The clothes, nature, animal, age, and justice patterns present the complex *world that is to be understood;* the sight and madness patterns (of which the values pattern is an auxiliary) are concerned with the *process and method of understanding* and coming to terms with that complex world. What means does man have to cope with its complexity? The shift is from humanity as object to humanity as subject. In the living drama, of course, the two are one, and the present separation is necessarily artificial; but it should serve to show that the objectively single drama is ambivalent, and that the problem of understanding is brilliantly illuminated from two points of view.

The very extensive imagery of sight that permeates the play keeps our attention focused on the quality, and especially the failure, of man's seeing; thus we are aware of Lear's and Gloucester's blindness to important circumstances, symbolized in Gloucester's subsequent real blindness, and of the scornful eyes and tearful eyes, respectively, of Goneril and Cordelia, which represent the kind of seeing, that is, grasp, of experience of which the individual sisters are capable. Since sight is constantly the symbol of insight and comprehension, it may seem that the sight pattern exhausts the possibilities of comment upon man as an observer and student of man and the world and of the evil in man. It is true, indeed, that the sight pattern and the madness pattern often do coincide functionally, and that the kind of sight man has keeps turning our attention toward the kind of wisdom he has; yet, as a general thing, the sight pattern tends to take man at the level of the *recognition and identification of phenomena,* that of the immediate practical decision. At the start of the play, for instance, Lear and Gloucester both miss the point of what is going on around them; they do not see the events properly, as, in contrast, Kent and Cordelia do (Cordelia at least sees through her sisters). The madness pattern, however, is concerned with the ways in which men *interpret phenomena,* the meanings which they find in experience, the general truths which they consciously formulate or in terms of which they characteristically act, the kind of wisdom, or sophistication, which they achieve. What men see and what men believe, of course, are intimately related; yet it is possible to focus attention on what goes on in the foreground or on what lies behind. The latter is the special area of the madness pattern. Its materials are men's philosophic attitudes to the world of which they are a part, their grasp, more specifically, of the problem of evil. Lear's madness is, in one respect, a result of his inability to bring an obdurate universe under intellectual control: the difficulty is too great, and his mind fails. Gloucester, the typical man of despair, formulates a pessimistic position which makes only suicide meaningful. The implied metaphysics of Lear's elder daughters is, as we shall see, something quite different. Other minds mould the materials of life in still other ways. The play, indeed, puts together an almost schematic pattern of the relationships of minds to experience. In this structure, the madness of Lear is focal; hence the term *madness pattern*.

Of certain fairly obvious structural relationships among Lear's madness, Edgar's assumed madness, and the Fool's ambiguities, much has been said by many commentators. What we may profitably notice here is the patterns of internal structure in the three characters, the varying relationships between the sound and the unsound or quasi-unsound state.[2] Edgar, who gradually becomes a sententious, almost formally philosophical moralist, makes a meaningless hash of his mad speeches (though Shakespeare makes some of Edgar's language support several meaning patterns of the play); his highest integration is at the level of conscious, logical formulations. Lear, who in the normal state is a man of feeling passionately aware of the immediate object but weak on implication and synthesis, shows, amid the irrelevancies of madness, an organizing imagination of considerable power and actually puts together a coherent general view of experience, a symbolic formulation of the problem of evil as set forth in the world of the play; the mental failure caused by the pressure of circumstances is not only a failure but an escape, a means of liberating for full flight an imagination that was hampered before.[3] Edgar's gifts are logical and disappear when he takes to antilogic; Lear's are imaginative and are freed by his departure from the world of normal order and logic. The Fool has the imaginative power which the mad Lear achieves [4]—that is, the ability to read image and symbol, to leap from the concrete manifestation to the meaning, to the values implied; but by definition the Fool is outside the world of normal order and logic, so that his imaginative insight into the meaning of phenomena is always free to find immediate expression. He both forgoes the prerogatives and is free of the responsibilities of the normal everyday world; thus he is known by a term of contempt, lives at the mercy of others, and is hardly taken seriously in the great workaday world of adults; but at the same time no conventions restrain him from putting his grasp of realities into words. In view of the evidence of Lear and the Fool, and of other evidence to be considered later, we might almost treat *King Lear* as a dramatic presentation of the fate of the imaginative grasp of truth in a wholly practical world. Lear's own imagination failed in Act I; the rest of the time his really powerful imagination is contrasted with the rationalistic spirit—for the introduction of which, by his imposition of the love test, he was responsible—of Goneril, Regan, and Edmund. The man of imagination does not have an easy time in the world. But that, as we shall see, is not the only truth that may be told about him—nor the most important truth.

FOOLS AND FOLLY

The play says a good deal about fools and folly, nearly all of it useful in determining the attitude of the play to the problem of man's mode of understanding experience. Once again, in fact, we find the characteristic union of the dramatic fact and the verbal pattern: the dramatic fact is the role of the Fool himself, and the verbal pattern is what the Fool and other characters have to say about fools and folly. The different elements work together closely in contributing to the meaning of the play, so that within the madness pattern we have actually a complete Fool pattern.

There is a decided tension between "folly" as it is exhibited and described by the Fool and as it is understood by various other characters. Kent introduces the folly theme in the first scene, almost as soon as he starts protesting against Lear's disinheriting of Cordelia; his phrase is "When majesty falls to folly" (I.i, 151)—the words *majesty* and *folly* suggesting the counterpoint between King and Fool which is presented directly in Acts I, II, and III. As used by Kent, *folly* is a corrective term spoken by a devoted follower; Kent is privileged by his devotion. The next time such a word is applied to Lear, it is used by Goneril: "Old fools are babes again" (I.iii, 19). It is ironic that Kent and Goneril should hit upon similar words, since the feelings with which they speak are entirely opposed; to Goneril, Lear's folly is not his failure to consult his own best interests, but his running athwart hers. Lear soon understands what Kent meant, as his own words show. After Goneril first complains of the behavior of his men, he cries, presumably striking his head, "Beat at this gate that let thy folly in/And thy dear judgment out" (I.iv, 293–94) ; and just before he runs into the storm he prays to the heavens, "fool me not so much/To bear it tamely" (II.iv, 278–79). That is, do not put me into the position of the Fool, who must endure contempt.[5] Lear might have found some other image to express his fear of falling into an unregal submissiveness, but the very fact that he

183

compares himself with the Fool gives his speech secondary meanings: he has been foolish, and, ironically, it is the Fool who has already been pointing his folly out to him.

Except in Goneril's usage, folly is elementary careless-ness of well-being and honor. Goneril's understanding of the term becomes clearer in the scene in which Albany condemns her actions. With an ironic juxtaposition characteristic of the method of the play, Albany's first outright recognition of the evil in Goneril is accompanied by her violent attack on him—an attack in which she applies to him a remarkable series of terms of contempt. As we have already seen, she accuses him of lack of manhood. Then there is her amazing repetition of the term *fool*. "My fool usurps my body," she says first (IV.ii, 28), perhaps within the hearing of Oswald. Then, after Albany has criticized her, she turns upon him di-rectly: "The text is foolish" (37); "Fools do those villains pity who are punish'd/Ere they have done their mischief" (54–55); ". . . thou, a moral fool" (58); and "O vain fool!" (61) The clatter of *fool* through the passage can hardly be mere chance, and the word actually functions in a double sense. On the one hand, Goneril condemns, on ra-tional grounds, her husband's disapproval of her cold schemes for getting on in the world. Again we see the ration-alistic attitude which the sisters also show with regard to age, justice, and values; the sisters' intellectual pattern is highly consistent. But if we thus see it made unmistakable that to Goneril *folly* is failure to practice a sensible, unsentimental opportunism, we also see that Albany is a fool in another sense: he has been treated as if he were politically inconse-quential, like the Fool, and yet he has come to the insight into affairs which, as we have long seen, is characteristic of the Fool. The man who can say to Goneril, "Wisdom and goodness to the vile seem vile;/Filths savour but themselves" (38–39) is getting beneath the surface of things and reading peoples' symbolic actions in terms of the moral quality from which the actions emerge. Goneril's mistake is not to realize how terribly dangerous to her it is that Albany, whose position makes him capable of political action, takes the view of her that he does. It is her folly to consider him a mere fool.

Edmund contributes to the folly pattern by his sneer at his "noble" and unsuspecting brother, "on whose foolish honesty/My practices ride easy!" (I.ii, 195–98) That is, not to be alert to worldly machinations is folly. Edmund is, as often, intellectually correct (Edgar has to make up for his being fooled by an especially intensive alertness later), but his correctness is of short range; the limits of his vision become evident in his implicit extension of his sure recognition of folly into a justification of the worldly machinations which foolish honesty does not detect. This is Edmund's mental habit: to see a truth, and then to interpret it in a programmatic way that is a distortion of the observed truth.

We have, then, two implied definitions of folly. As the word is used by Kent, it implies that the wise man will protect himself at least negatively, so to speak, by the mere avoidance of such needless actions as putting one's enemies into power. As Goneril applies the word *folly* to Albany's arguments, she implies that the wise man's duty to himself is taking affirmative, self-aggrandizing action, regardless of who gets hurt in the process. Yet these definitions have one sense in common: folly is not looking out for oneself in the world. Looking out for oneself in a worldly sense is at best a slippery business, in which one may slide almost imperceptibly from thoughtless mistakes to an overlooking of injury to others. Thus in his folly, as in his introduction of a wrong scheme of values, we see the relationship between Lear and his daughters. At the same time we are fully aware of the ultimate moral distance between them. For the time being, however, we ought to be quite conscious of both the resemblances and the differences in the conceptions of folly which we have so far seen, because this awareness is essential if we are to grasp all the echoes and emanations of the inner drama on folly that is an important part of the whole *King Lear*. For the Fool's main business is to hit off the folly of others who are supposedly competent in a world of action from which he, by definition, is excluded.

In the scenes with Lear, the Fool functions in a number of ways.[6] At one level he may be understood as the conscience of Lear, the inner voice—externalized, as Empson says—which will not cease in its condemnation of error. At another level he is a tutor, the intellectual master of the world who lessons Lear in the way of the world. In this role he accents the irony hinted in Kent's earlier phrase, "when majesty falls to folly." Lear falls to folly; the fool rises to wisdom. He becomes king in the sense that he sees things in the perspective which ideally should always belong to royalty—a counterpoint which is always emphatically present in the scenes between the two. But there is still something more in the Fool: it is his love for Lear and his devotion to Lear when there was every "practical" *reason* for his getting aboard the political band wagon ("Take the fool with thee," he calls to Lear—I.iv, 339—when he knows very well how badly things are going). Here the Fool is the man of imagination who by imagination grasps a value that cannot be demon-

strated rationally and whose deed is the dramatic opposite
of the conduct of the rationalists in the play. His speech is
consistently the imaginative speech of poetry: he is always
ironic, he depends on symbols (the coxcomb, the crowns of
the egg, "the hedge-sparrow fed the cuckoo so long"), on
riddles and analogies, on similes ("like the breath of an un-
fee'd lawyer"), metaphors ("truth's a dog"), and paradoxes
("thou mad'st thy daughter thy mother"). The Fool's education of Lear is in part a re-education of his imagination, an
implied attack upon the calculating rationalism by which
Lear had inaugurated all his troubles. Lear's imagination
is recovering: he understands the Fool's poetry, he is learning rapidly to grasp the symbolic meaning of action (as he
could not at the beginning), and he is moving toward the
imaginative syntheses which he will make in his madness.
The closer Lear moves to madness, the more he comes to
exercise the gifts of the Fool.

The most inclusive paradox, then, is that the despised
Fool—he is always subject to the whip (I.iv, 124 ff.)—
exposes the folly of the supposedly wise master of men, the
King. Now, within the confines of the Fool pattern, we find a
great many remarks about folly made by the Fool himself,
and we need to examine them briefly to see how they comment upon the concepts of folly held by Kent, Lear, and
Lear's daughters. The Fool first offers his coxcomb to Kent
for "taking one's part that's out of favour" (I.iv, 111), and
he adds, "If thou follow him, thou must needs wear my coxcomb" (115–16). In this passage he is reasoning exactly as
Goneril and Regan might: folly is not looking out for oneself
in terms of immediate, material opportunities. Later the
Fool returns to this theme—when he and Lear have found

Kent in the stocks before Gloucester's castle. The Fool lectures Kent:

> Let go thy hold when a great wheel runs down a hill, lest it break thy neck with following it; but the great one that goes upward, let him draw thee after. When a wise man gives thee better counsel, give me mine again. I would have none but knaves follow it, since a fool gives it.
>
> > That sir which serves and seeks for gain,
> > And follows but for form,
> > Will pack when it begins to rain
> > And leave thee in the storm.
> > But I will tarry; the fool will stay,
> > And let the wise man fly.
> > The knave turns fool that runs away;
> > The fool no knave, perdy. (II.iv, 72–86)

At the end of this passage [7] the Fool becomes explicit: though knavish, it is wise to run away from one's loyalty to a lost cause, and foolish to adhere to it. But the Fool and Kent, whom we admire, do adhere: and folly thus becomes admirable, and the wisdom of the world itself folly ("the knave turns fool"). The Fool's jingle imperceptibly slides into the complexity of poetry, and it imposes upon us the task of the reader of poetry: the Fool uses *fool* ambiguously, and his communication is complete when we have disentangled and distinguished his two senses.

The Fool is parodying the rationalistic wisdom of Goneril, Regan, and Edmund. Wisdom ultimately lies in loyalties, or in adherence to tradition. At the same time, however, there is an actual world in which one lives, and in it one may conduct oneself in such a way as to be very foolish about one's own interests. The Fool chooses, as his wisdom, the folly of staying with a King who has fallen from power; but he berates the King for the folly of his falling from power. *Folly*, as it is used to describe the King's conduct, implies as its opposite a good sense in the world which nevertheless the Fool himself eschews and which he stigmatizes as knavish folly. Nearly all of his lines on fools and folly, and there are many of them, are a chastisement of Lear for his bad management in the world. After the Fool sings a lyric about Lear's folly in giving away his land, Lear asks, "Dost thou call me fool, boy?" and he is answered, "All thy other titles thou hast given away; that thou wast born with" (I.iv, 162–64). Throughout the scene the Fool continues to call Lear a fool in a variety of ways (172–206). In the next scene he says, by means of a joke, that Lear has no brains at all (I.v, 8 ff.), praises him as a "good fool" (41), and summarizes, "Thou shouldst not have been old till thou hadst been wise" (47–48). Twice in the storm [8] he refers to Lear and himself as "a wise man and a fool" (III.ii, 12–13, 40–41)—leaving the matter of identity indeterminate; and he speaks another epigram, "He that has a house to put's head in has a good headpiece" (25–26).

The Fool pattern constantly poses questions: what is folly? who is fooling whom? And precisely as in the areas of meaning developed by the other patterns, Shakespeare presents the relevant material in all its complexities,[9] with all the ironic contradictions that may easily lead us to conclude that he is resting in a detached presentation of the ambiguities of experience. But eventually he resolves—or at least suggests a resolution of—the equivocal. Folly is, as we have seen, the ignoring of worldly interests; but inattention to the world may take quite different forms. The Fool parodies the cynical *un*foolishness of Goneril and Regan; but he also ridicules Lear's folly. In following Lear, he himself is not doing well in the world; but he attacks Lear for foolishly not doing well in the world. But in one lyric he concludes that worldly wisdom, being knavish, is folly. Thus worldliness is folly, and unworldliness is folly.

But we are not caught in an insoluble dilemma. Actually, the words and deeds of the Fool develop further the meaning of the values pattern: the real problem is not at all one of worldly success, which is secondary, but of the values in accordance with which one acts. This is where one is basically wise or foolish. Goneril's and Regan's worldly wisdom is folly because their values are wrong; Lear's failure in the world is also folly, not because it is failure, but because it is the result of wrong values. He has unnecessarily introduced a calculating spirit which incidentally has ruined his worldly position; but what is worse is that he has thus given full scope to the ability of his daughters to profit by acting in terms of this spirit. He has made a qualitatively inferior choice. As we have seen, he failed imaginatively, failed to understand Cordelia in terms of the action symbols of her love—the reason why he had come to love her most; in another sense he failed in his imaginative awareness of loyalties—to both his office and Cordelia—precisely as Kent and the Fool retain their imaginative grip upon their loyalty to the King. They unquestioningly accept it, in the only possible way, as an absolute and undemonstrable value. Lear, in his folly, lost sight of essentials, and thus turned the world upside down; the state of affairs is symbolized in the Fool's prediction that Lear's daughters "will make an obedient father" (I.iv, 256).

Folly is to mistake the short-range for the long-distance—

the error of Lear and the three evil characters. The Fool, as
I have said, starts Lear off on the imaginative restoration by
which he will grasp again permanent values. First he must
be humble and see what he has done, and to this painful recognition, the preliminary to salvation, the Fool brings him
by a use of figurative language which stimulates him to a
revaluation of what has happened. First the Fool makes the
heel-and-shoe joke of which the import is that Lear has no
brains; then he prophesies, "Shalt see thy other daughter
wilt use thee kindly"; then, to contrast the other daughter
with Goneril, he uses the simile, ". . . she's as like this as
a crab's like an apple" (I.v, 11–15). The Fool, of course,
is talking about Regan and ironically prophesying that she
will treat Lear as Goneril has treated him. But the mention
of "other daughter" and the introduction of a comparison of
daughters are sparks which ignite Lear's imagination: he
thinks about Cordelia. He hardly listens to the next two
speeches of the Fool, who jokes about the position of eyes
and nose; after the second speech, Lear comes out with words
that have no relation to what the Fool has just said but do
express thoughts that come from the Fool's earlier stimulus
—"I did her wrong" (25). He is not yet finished calculating
his rights, as we know; but his imagination is beginning to
work. We recall Gloucester's flash of illumination after he is
blinded: "O my follies! Then Edgar was abus'd" (III.vii,
91). Gloucester's folly was also to choose the short-range
values which appear to promise much in the world.

The Fool, who by his own methods directs us to a definition of folly which the play as a whole dramatizes, stays in
the play only to the point at which the results of Lear's folly
drive him to madness. Amidst the pseudo-mad lines of

Edgar and the increasingly irrational remarks of Lear, the Fool says, "This cold night will turn us all to fools and madmen" (III.iv, 79). The association of cold and madness is heightened by Edgar's recurrent "Tom's acold" (56, 85, 152, 178). Lear is sinking into insanity—a means of relief from the intolerable burden of an enigmatic world. Although he is in constant dread of losing his mind, insanity is paradoxically an escape. Thus there is an ironic parallel between Lear and Edgar, who affects incoherence as a badge of innocuousness in the face of danger, and the Fool, who if he feels at any time that he has gone too far in telling the truth, retreats into nonsense or apparent nonsense. In the world of calculation, of rationalistic measurement, aberration, real or assumed, must be the refuge for men of insight—of those who actually have and use it, and of those like Lear, whose gift it is though they have failed in the use of it.

WRONG IMAGINATIONS: LEAR

The Fool is the center of the folly pattern, and what he says takes us close to the heart of the play. But the heart of the play must appear finally in the Lear plot. Now Lear is dealt with both by the folly pattern and by the larger madness pattern of which the treatment of fools and folly is really a subdivision; and there is some difference between Lear as fool and Lear as madman. His whole career, of course, is of a piece; it is the record of a mistake and the consequences of that mistake, and we need not attempt too-finicky distinctions between what is foolish and what is mad. But it is safe to say that Lear's folly is his mistake, and his madness is the consequence—and at the same time, paradoxically, the rectification—of that mistake. As fool, Lear loses his imaginative

192

grasp of truth, and tries to express truth in the wrong way; he fails to discriminate between the kinds of truth and the ways in which they may be apprehended. The horror of the world that his folly creates, the senselessness and meaninglessness of it, drives him to madness; yet in that very madness there is a powerful lucidity, a tremendous exercizing of the imagination that failed him before. Even before the madness comes on we are made to see it as a potentiality; in fact there is throughout the play a special awareness of mental states —brought about not only by Fool-ishness and madness as dramatic facts but by the large amount of talk about folly and madmen—which is itself a symbolic way of stressing the problem of understanding which is structurally the center of the play. When Kent says, early in the play, that "Lear is mad" (I.i, 148), he is of course speaking figuratively; yet the metaphor begot by Kent's incredulity takes on the ominousness of a word to which later events ironically give a literal truth. What is more significant, however, is Lear's own growing awareness of the psychological dangers by which he is beset, and upon which he makes a continual commentary.[10] At first he also speaks figuratively; Goneril's initial indications of attitude to him lead him to remark of himself, "Either his notion weakens, his discernings/Are lethargied" (I.iv, 248–49). But when the situation becomes clearer, and the Fool has turned his bitter magnifying glass upon it, Lear turns from incredulity to prayer, to prayer in which his agony is expressed by the repetition so often used in the play:

> O, let me not be mad, not mad, sweet heaven!
> Keep me in temper; I would not be mad! (I.v, 49–50)

Next time his prayer is addressed to Goneril: "I prithee, daughter, do not make me mad" (II.iv, 221). The alteration in Lear's state is marked by the fact that he prays no more: he now gives up trying, as it were, to avert insanity; from now on, his statements are all declarative. "O fool, I shall go mad!" he says (II.iv, 289), the juxtaposition of *fool* and *mad* reminding us of the counterpoint between the Fool who intellectually is master of the situation and the King who has lost his grip on things. In the storm he comments, "My wits begin to turn" (III.ii, 67); his awareness of the storm is dulled by "the tempest in my mind" (III.iv, 12); and with terror he turns from brooding on his daughters' ingratitude: "O, that way madness lies; let me shun that!/No more of that!" (III.iv, 21–22). A minute later Edgar appears to the others for the first time, and his quasi-madness holds the stage and powerfully affects Lear, who in a series of lines expresses great interest in "this philosopher" (159, 162, 177, 181, 185). As Lear begins to escape, there is, besides his own words and actions, a trail of guideposts to his loss of mental balance, as if Shakespeare were taking especial care to keep the situation and its implications unmistakable. Kent speaks of Lear's "bemadding sorrow" (III.i, 38); to Gloucester he says, "His wits begin t' unsettle" (III.iv, 167), and Gloucester replies "Thou say'st the King grows mad" (170). Kent follows up the case: "All the power of his wits have given way to his impatience" (III.vi, 5–6) and "his wits are gone" (93). Albany accuses Goneril and Regan of having "madded" Lear (IV.ii, 43). Several times later Lear refers to his own mental state. After his central climactic mad scene he exclaims, "Let me have surgeons;/I am cut to th' brains" (IV.vi, 196–97); and after he has partially recovered he says, "I am . . . very foolish" (IV. vii, 60), "I fear I am not in my perfect mind" (IV.vii, 63), and "I am old and foolish" (84).

I have already noted, in the first section of the present chapter, the various levels of meaning in Lear's madness. In this rich complex of meanings there is still one other possibility: considered as a product, the madness is expression of a certain conflict within Lear. Throughout Acts I and II Lear still tries to act in terms of his original rationalistic disposition of the territory; he still tries to sustain what I have called his heresy of material equivalents. That is, he still believes that the larger share of property which he gave to Goneril and Regan ought to guarantee him his stipulated privileges, and this belief determines all his major actions in Acts I and II. Even after he is out in the storm he cannot wholly get rid of this logic; that actual fact is at variance with logic preys upon his mind. Were he able to renounce his untenable expectations, to recognize that the treatment of him is a logical consequence of his treatment of Cordelia, and to meet this terrible disappointment with resignation, his purgatory would be of a different sort. It is of course not his nature to act in such a way. He still holds, dimly but tenaciously, to his original calculation. Yet at the same time he undergoes a great deal of enlightenment before he goes mad; the Fool, as we have seen, stirs him to a better perception of truth: and two sets of values conflict in him. He is told that he is a fool, yet he still hopes his folly will pay off. He begins to read his daughters in terms of their actions rather than their words, but still hopes for actions that will conform to their original words of assurance. He calls on Nature for punishment of his daughters, but still tries to argue with them. Even in Act I he is beginning to understand Cordelia (I.iv, 288–89; I.v, 25). By the end of Act II, as we have seen, his reason-not-the-need speech (iv, 267) in effect repudiates his philosophy of calculation. His imaginative apprehension of truth is constantly becoming better. In the storm (III.ii and iv) he becomes more and more both the philosophic observer and the sympathetic human being; in the farmhouse near Gloucester's castle (III.vi) he conducts the trial which manifests an insight into the world far superior to that which he had at the beginning of the play. His conflict is being resolved in madness: the closer he comes to it, the further he is from his original fallacy: in his madness he exhibits an acute vision; and after his madness he has forgot about Goneril and Regan and thinks only of his relationship with Cordelia and of the truths which they may perceive together.[11]

All the comments on madness, by both Lear and the others, have technical utility—as realistic details, as guides to psychological states, as tonal elements. But in Lear's own comments on his mental state there is a special significance: they show that he knows what is happening to him. Not only does he know what is happening; he also knows, at least in part, why it is happening. That Lear has this knowledge is important for the interpretation of the drama, because in the possession of the knowledge Lear is in contrast with his daughters, who *never know what is happening to them*. For all of his early violence and injustice, Lear has a sensitive awareness that extends to his own mental states and his complicity in the terrible situation in which he is struggling; he has recovered, or perhaps brought to life for the first time, the imaginative insight by which, in the final mad scene in

IV.vi, he will paint a figurative picture of the world and endow it with frightening brilliance. His self-awareness is one of the dramatic indications that he is a tragic character. The daughters' callousness, on the other hand, prevents their seeing themselves objectively, their having any intimation of what is happening to them morally; they have no saving iota of self-consciousness. Lear's possession of such an awareness is of course an element in his suffering, but at the same time it is potential redemption, a way to moral wholeness. Some introspection is necessary to humanity, to the human as distinguished from the animal. In virtue of it Lear is able also to comprehend Regan and Goneril in a way in which they can never comprehend Cordelia or him. If he cannot manage or bear up under his knowledge, he is at least better off than those who do not know that there is a problem of knowledge. To suffer under the weight of recognized evil is qualitatively better than not to recognize evil.

WRONG IMAGINATIONS: THE SYNTHESIS SCENE

The lines about madness that I have so far quoted are only the fringe of the pattern: the center of the pattern is the powerful culmination of Lear's madness in IV.vi, in which Lear appears for the first time since he conducted the imaginary trial in a farmhouse in III.vi. In the interim Gloucester has been tried, blinded, reunited with Edgar, who is still Poor Tom; Albany and Goneril have quarreled; the French forces are ready for battle; Cordelia is searching for Lear near Dover. In IV.vi we have the climax of the Gloucester plot and the climax of the Lear plot; Gloucester, won from despair by Edgar, reaches his philosophic heights, and

Lear comes to his most penetrating vision. Not only are their experiences parallel, but the men are then brought together physically—a dramatic indication of the unifying function of the scene. It is just after Gloucester has promised Edgar to "bear/Affliction till it do cry out itself" that Lear enters, crowned with weeds, and, with Gloucester and Edgar as audience, speaks about one hundred lines—his most important in the play.

In these lines there are few irrelevancies; almost every phrase of Lear's relates in some significant fashion to the experiences which he has had. What we become aware of first is the irony of his demonstrating a kind of "understanding" of the very world which had been too much for him when he was in possession of his mind; before, he could but exclaim in anguish, now he incisively goes to the heart of the Goneril-Regan world, of all human evil as it is incarnate in them, and even apparent in himself. Outside the limits of everyday rationality he displays immense imaginative resources and finds exact forms for his devastating insight into the moral reality of the world, and, by implication, into himself and the situation of mankind generally. The language of his disillusionment, and of his compassion, makes one of the most powerful scenes in the play. At the most obvious level this is true because his image and symbol are neither conventional nor timid, because they are exactly adapted to the effects, and because the different kinds of image and symbol, instead of being isolated media of expression, collaborate among themselves in the production of those effects. But there is a still greater source of strength in these speeches by Lear, and that is the fact that they are *a nexus of all the main lines of development in the play;* all the patterns of image and symbol are focused here; the result is a compelling synthesis of all the individual systems of meaning whose ramifications we have been tracing. Almost every line of Lear's, instead of having, by the relations within itself and with the rest of the passage, to create its own poetic momentum, has a very strong initial impulse; this impulse is the prepared meaning and suggestion that can come only from the author's utilization of language patterns already developed and therefore eliciting a special kind of imaginative co-operation from the reader. For Lear expresses himself almost entirely by drawing upon patterns which, at this late time in the play—the next-to-last scene of Act IV—have been well established. Here we find, united in a single impact, the sight, smell, clothes, sex, animal, and justice themes that move throughout the play. And they are organized by means of the madness theme; through them the mad Lear, in what is virtually a soliloquy, gives verbal form to his bitter comprehension of an ugly and deceptive world and of the human capacity for evil that has made it so and to his pity for the sufferers in the world. In his madness there is unity.

Gloucester, relatively passive and unimaginative, is in IV.vi a foil for Lear—the role which in one way or another is his throughout the play. When he first sought Lear out in the nocturnal storm, Gloucester said to Kent:

> Thou say'st the King grows mad: I'll tell thee, friend,
> I am almost mad myself. I had a son,
> Now outlaw'd from my blood. He sought my life
>
> .   .   .   .
> The grief hath craz'd my wits. (III.iv, 170–75)

But going mad is precisely what Gloucester is incapable of. When Gloucester next mentions madness, he is blinded and is about to be led by Edgar; he says, " 'Tis the time's plague when madmen lead the blind" (IV.i, 46). Gloucester speaks pungently and truthfully, but again he makes a statement in which the reader finds a secondary meaning: the situation of the times may not be desperate when the madmen who lead are the brilliant madmen of *King Lear*. But the brilliance of Lear is lost upon Gloucester—as it is not lost upon Edgar; and after listening to all Lear's great lines in IV.vi, Gloucester only comments:

> The King is mad. How stiff is my vile sense,
> That I stand up, and have ingenious feeling
> Of my huge sorrows! Better I were distract.
> So should my thoughts be sever'd from my griefs,
> And woes by wrong imaginations lose
> The knowledge of themselves. (IV.vi, 286–91)

As a statement of bare fact, what Gloucester says is unimpeachable: Lear is mad, and his "wrong imaginations" may be said to blot out his woes. But the wrong imaginations are not mere nonsense; they embody a kind of very real knowledge in Lear's mind, and so they have an authentic rightness. For the reader they pull together the whole play, as the happy babbling of a well-adjusted lunatic could never do; Lear's escape is only partial; if his everyday consciousness of reality is obscured, he still experiences a painfully thorough recognition of essential truth.[12]

After a few lines of incoherent images,[13] Lear moves into the fierce climax of his madness, in which hardly a word is irrelevant. He sees Gloucester and exclaims, "Ha! Goneril with a white beard?" (97)—a line in which we see Lear's possible recollection of the fact that Gloucester had at first tried to preserve peace between him and the new regime, and which is an ironic reminder of Regan's plucking that beard and sneering at Gloucester, "So white and such a traitor!" (III.vii, 37). Lear unmistakably comments on his own experience with his next statement, "They flatter'd me like a dog, and told me I had white hairs in my beard ere the black ones were there" (97–99)—words which bring more than one aspect of the play into focus. Most important, perhaps, is Lear's self-understanding—his understanding that he had been a willing victim of flattery, willing to believe that he possessed wisdom from youth. We recall the Fool's "Thou shouldst not have been old till thou hadst been wise" (I.v, 47–48). It is only now that he is coming to wisdom—a wisdom which the rest of the scene makes evident. Further, Lear's sentence on flattery picks up the animal imagery of the play and thus reminds us of the whole problem of the nature of man. ". . . like a dog" has a very interesting ambiguity. It may mean, "They fawned on me as a dog fawns on its master"; in that sense the phrase continues the body of imagery which defines the daughters as animals— willing to flatter for what they could get. Again, the sentence may mean, "They petted me as if I were a dog," suggesting, ironically, that they possessed a kindly consideration for creature life. But a still more effective irony enters in the association of this image and Lear's dog imagery a few lines later, ". . . a dog's obeyed in office" (162–63). Lear is thinking of tyranny in general, and specifically of his daughters' tyranny, but: he too has been a dog in office—as an object of flattery and as a passionate and selfish exercizer of official authority. So by his use of an old image pattern

201

he moves further into a confessional, into self-understanding.

Lear continues, "When the rain came to wet me once, and
the wind to make me chatter; when the thunder would not
peace at my bidding; there I found 'em, there I smelt 'em
out. . . . They told me I was everything. 'Tis a lie—I am
not ague-proof" (101–107). Here he introduces the storm
—the nature pattern—and in so doing describes precisely
what happened: only when he was finally driven out into the
storm did he understand how he had been mistaken in his
daughters. His *ague-proof* picks up the disease pattern: the
ague is probably a literal fact, but at the same time it is a
symbol of his vulnerability in the face of the onslaughts of
life. The final pattern which is used in this complex sentence
is the smell pattern—which, like the sight pattern, is concerned with the problem of perception, but which also implies the evil smell of that which is to be perceived. Lear is
beginning to detect what is unsavory. Just at this moment
(108) the blind Gloucester breaks in, a fact which, as we
have already seen, shows how much is to be compacted into
the scene. For Gloucester is Lear's only interlocutor in the
main body of the scene: thus are brought together climac-
tically the two main tragic characters, the central figures, respectively, in the sight and madness themes, whose blindness
and madness are symbols of the initial failures from which
the tragic action has sprung. By restricting the dialogue to
Gloucester and Lear, Shakespeare keeps our attention on
their analogous tragic flaws, yet at the same time lets us see,
through Lear's mania, the whole moral world which is the
context of, and which becomes an inevitable element in,
their private suffering.

Gloucester's phrase "the king" leads to Lear's "every inch a king" (109), which, like various other lines we have seen, is paradoxically both true and untrue. Lear is not actually exercising the functions of royalty; yet he is a completely dominant figure who makes all other personalities look small and who attracts the loyalty of all those who are capable of loyalty. Lear then goes into an intensified denunciation of the daughters—and really of the human category to which they belong—by a complex interweaving of three familiar patterns (111–34). As a king he conceives of himself as dispensing justice: "I pardon that man's life" (111), "Thou shalt not die. Die for adultery? No" (113). His role as judge brings into perspective the distribution scene of Act I, the arraignment of his daughters by the mad Lear in Act III, and the "trial" of Gloucester in Act III, that is, all the events of the justice pattern. Here Lear is the bitter ironist, talking in quasi-judicial fashion of adultery and copulation ("Let copulation thrive"—116), which for the moment he affects to praise. The total effect of bitterness is heightened by Lear's justification of adultery:

> . . . for Gloucester's bastard son
> Was kinder to his father than my daughters
> Got 'tween lawful sheets (116–18);

for these words are heard by Gloucester, who knows how far they are from the truth. Lear's real subject, of course, is human evil, of which his awareness has become acute, and which he presents through two familiar means, the sex symbolism and the animal imagery. His figurative setting forth of the bestiality in man gains weight from the whole dramatic context—the adultery of Gloucester, the viciousness of the bastard Edmund, the uncontrolled passion of both Regan and Goneril for Edmund—which is introduced by the sex references. Likewise Lear's defense of sexuality on the ground that it is characteristic of animals (the wren and fly, 114; the fitchew and the horse, 124) calls up all the fluent metaphors which the play regularly uses to suggest that as moral agent man is often an animal. These lines pack together, into one dense speech, all the suggestions of the play that man can lose his essential humanity, can break with the Nature which is universal order, and identify himself with animal nature. The passage on sexuality and animality is fittingly climaxed, as we saw some time ago, by the Centaur image (126–29) which so vividly depicts the horror of the subservience of the godlike in man to the animal. Lear ends this speech by the reintroduction and elaborate use of olfactory imagery (the *fourth* pattern in this unbroken twenty-four-line passage). He describes his daughters "Down from the waist": "There's hell, there's darkness, there's the sulphurous pit; burning, scalding, stench, consumption. Fie, fie, fie! pah, pah! Give me an ounce of civet, good apothecary, to sweeten my imagination" (130–34). In his next speech Lear says that his own hand "smells of mortality" (136)—a further indication that he is somehow involved in the evil that flesh is heir to, evil that can be symbolized by a stench.

Two other aspects of this first part of the scene deserve a word. After Lear says that his hand smells of mortality, Gloucester ejaculates, "O ruin'd piece of nature! This great world/Shall so wear out to naught" (137–38), and thus reinforces what the whole passage has been implying—that there is a Nature, an order, from which Lear, and with him his society, has fallen away. This is the burden of the nature pattern in the play: that experience must be judged in the light of a norm and that the consequences of a violation of norm must be taken into account. Equally important, because it also has a summarizing value, is Lear's request for "an ounce of civet" and his evocative statement of the use to which the civet shall be put—"to sweeten my imagination." The simplest meaning, of course, is that he wants incense or perfume to take away an evil smell; but more than this lies beneath the semantic surface. Once Lear had too sweet an imagination; he had a spiritual sweet tooth, and expected life to be heavily sugar-coated; hence he was a victim of his daughters' flattery. Now he has discovered unsweetness and stench: he is coming much closer to the truths of human experience. He can cry, very understandably, for relief: yet he goes right ahead and unhesitatingly continues to recount the evil realities of which he was once insufficiently aware.

Gloucester's "Dost thou know me?" (138) leads to an ironic reply by Lear. Of all the ways in which he might remember Gloucester, the one he picks is his eyes: "I remember thine eyes well enough" (139). We enter with an ironic shock upon a new movement in which the sight pattern is dominant. The pattern has already been active in the mere fact of Gloucester's presence, so that structurally what we have here is less a break than a re-emphasis, a direct calling upon resources already felt as available. Lear's harshness continues as he moves into the orbit of the sight symbolism. On the surface his remarks on Gloucester's blindness appear brutally inconsiderate; yet it is plain that what actuates his mental processes is his groping for the meanings that Gloucester's eyeless face suggests. And we should recall, too, that in various parts of the play Lear himself is treated as blind and that we must therefore see him a sharer of Glouces-ter's specific fate. That is, what he says about Gloucester is, like other lines of his elsewhere, also applicable to him-self. All their talk about eyes brings in the problem dealt with by the sight pattern—the problem of what and how well man sees. Now at last Gloucester and Lear are both seeing very well. Lear in his sensitiveness reads a meaning even into the expressionless eye pits of Gloucester. *Squiny* may mean *squint,* which would suggest a careful scrutiny; but it may also mean "look scornfully"; [14] both meanings are in ironic contradiction with the fact, for Gloucester is staring vacantly rather than scrutinizing, and pitying rather than scorning. But the second meaning comports very satisfactorily with the rest of the passage. For one thing, it shows Lear, ever on guard now, transferring Goneril's "scornful eyes" even to his friends. If that reading is sound, the reference to "blind Cupid," which is natural enough, is more than casual: for it is a recollection of Goneril that would make Lear especially averse to love. Only a scornful Cupid could have made him blind to Cordelia's love, and willing to accept the merely verbal love of Goneril and Regan. Hence he will protect him-self now, that is, he will "not love"—a denial which symbol-izes his cut-off state: when he is restored, he will again find love, the love of Cordelia; and his love for her, and reunion with her, will symbolize both his psychological and his spirit-ual recovery. Then when Lear, who has subconsciously recog-nized Gloucester's blindness, is finally brought, by Glouces-ter's pathetic insistence (143, 147) to a conscious aware-ness that Gloucester cannot see, he exclaims, "No eyes in

your head, nor no money in your purse? Your eyes are in a
heavy case, your purse in a light. Yet you see how this world
goes" (148–51). Two aspects of this speech seize our attention. Here is an outright statement of the ironic fact which we
noted earlier; the paradox that the blind man sees how the
world goes reflects the literal fact that for Gloucester blindness coincided with insight. He and Lear both saw too late,
and now in their respective blindnesses—of eyes and of mind
—they see almost more than they can bear. Further, the reference to the purse is much more than an irrelevant intrusion or an occasion for a pun, for it introduces the problem
of distributive justice which keeps coming up in the play; in
fact, it belongs to the general values pattern, especially as a
reminder of the material values that dominate the everyday
world. Lear's comment on Gloucester's purse resembles the
Fool's earlier comments on Lear's own penniless depend-
ency, and they recall Mad Tom, who was a beggar. Yet to
be poor in the world is not to be ignorant of it.

These sardonic remarks of Lear to Gloucester anticipate
the next lines of both men, lines in which the whole problem
of seeing, of perception, of understanding, is brought out
sharply. Gloucester replies, "I see it feelingly" (152). He
is saying, of course, that now he must see, that is, perceive,
by other senses than that of sight; but at the same time his
words convey the fact that he now "feels," that is, has a
sensitiveness to values, which he did not have before, and
hence a better insight into the world. For his words here pick
up an earlier speech of his which also belongs to the sight
pattern: it was just after being blinded that he called for
justice upon "the superfluous and lust-dieted man" who "will

not see/Because he does not feel" (IV.i, 68–70). He was concerned for, he "felt for," humanity; and in that sense he saw and sees. "What, art mad?" (153) Lear flashes back, thus by word mentioning, as if it were a detached entity, the very state which he also presents in his deed: in thus presenting madness at two levels, Shakespeare does the very thing sometimes regarded as experimental in modern fiction. As Lear and Gloucester are thus virtually identified, madness becomes the direct subject of the madness pattern. Lear's remark is ambiguous; but he implies, I take it, that to understand—"to see feelingly"—makes a man mad, a bitter observation which ironically reverses the dramatic fact that to be mad is to understand. Lear has caught, incidentally, the figurative "see feelingly," and he caps the phrase with his own variant of synaesthesia, "Look with thine ears" (154). The copiousness of the terms of perception—"A man may see how the world goes with no eyes. . . . Hark in thine ear" (153, 156)—brings to a head the problem of perception with which the whole play deals. Gloucester and Lear both now perceive well enough, and Lear continues to demonstrate the quality of his own seeing and understanding. He launches off into a dramatic word picture of the world; this climax of the scene, instead of being a rant, is related to the play structurally by being held within the sight pattern. The sight pattern and the madness pattern coincide: Lear tells what one must see and understand in order to get on in the actual world. But the organization is made still more tight by the internal relationships of the speech, for all the facts of the seen world are recorded, as before, in terms of existent patterns—justice, animals, sex, clothes, values. Here the patterns are all brought together in a remarkably controlled synthesis, in a central definition into which flow all the meanings of the carefully channeled streams of symbol and image which we have seen moving in all parts of the play.

"Look with thine ears; see how yond justice rails upon yond simple thief. Hark, in thine ear. Change places and, handy-dandy, which is the justice, which is the thief?" (154–59) Here the justice theme is used again for a comment upon the perversions that justice undergoes in practice; but it is used for more than that: Lear grows from the castigator of the evils of "great place" into a contemplator of tragic life — of the liability to evil in all. Thus the deepening of Lear's understanding gradually becomes apparent. That deepening is also indicated in a slight way, I believe, even when Lear returns to the animal pattern and uses it as his next means of crying injustice. "Thou hast seen a farmer's dog bark at a beggar? . . . And the creature run from the cur? There thou mightst behold the great image of authority: a dog's obeyed in office" (159–63). These words do more than cynically mock at injustice: they suggest the excessive reverence for office which helps account for injustice; and at the same time, since Lear himself has already been identified with the dog in office ("They flatter'd me like a dog"—97–98), they imply a self-criticism. Lear continues to develop the justice theme that came up early in the passage when he was ironically praising adultery (we now have the sex theme serving the justice theme, and the justice theme in turn serving the sight theme):

Thou rascal beadle, hold thy bloody hand!
Why dost thou lash that whore? Strip thine own back.

Thou hotly lusts to use her in that kind
For which thou whip'st her. The usurer hangs the cozener.
(164–67)

At first glance we note Shakespeare's grasp of psychological complexity—of the relationship between sexuality and flagellation and of the desire of human beings to whip in others the vices which they themselves possess. But more important is that Lear is again transcending the melodrama of injustice and rising to a consideration of the tragedy of life; his theme is, "Let him who is without blemish cast the first stone"; and the poignancy of it is that, as an officer of justice, Lear had been no more immune to imperfection than others such as the imaginary beadle whom he here addresses. He had, for instance, accused Cordelia of a pride which was conspicuous in his own conduct. Then, shifting to the clothes theme to continue with his indictment against the world, he once again, also, reminds us of a failure of his own:

Through tatter'd clothes great vices do appear;
Robes and furr'd gowns hide all. Plate sin with gold,
And the strong lance of justice hurtless breaks;
Arm it in rags, a pigmy's straw does pierce it. (168–71)

Here is the whole clothes pattern in little: clothes are either a defense or a disguise: in one sense necessary to life, in another the means for hypocrisy and deceit.[15] Lear, along with the Fool and Edgar, has been in rags, either literally or figuratively, and has especially felt the injustice which man visits on man and which has constantly been a cutting edge to him; but likewise he has failed to see through the "Robes and furr'd gowns," the "plighted cunning" and the "gorgeous" dress, of Goneril and Regan. His failure is also given expression by the tag end of the values pattern which crops up here: "Plate sin with gold"; gold-plated words had been his undoing, and "plainness" he had spurned. Some such awareness of failure must explain the universal pardon which he announces in his next line: "None does offend, none, I say, none; I'll able 'em (172)—almost his last words as a justice. Lear speaks not only as the scourge of injustice but also as the practicing humanitarian: he shows the sympathy with humankind that he exhibited earlier in the storm: in fact, the earlier episode and this are bound together by the clothes pattern, for then he had pitied "Poor naked wretches" just as now he pities those in "tatter'd clothes" and in "rags." In less than a hundred passionate lines Lear has given us an excoriating picture of the world that has been laid open to his sight and to his imagination; yet at the same time, as some of his figures have clearly implied, Lear has participated in the guilt which he sees in others and which hence becomes a general human possession; thus he has given a summary expression of the complex world which the clothes, animal, age, sex, and justice patterns have set forth. An awareness of man's perceptual difficulties lies behind his final sardonic cry to Gloucester:

> Get thee glass eyes,
> And, like a scurvy politician, seem
> To see the things thou dost not. (174–76)

These words are addressed to the same Gloucester who said, long before, ". . . if it be nothing, I shall not need spectacles" (I.ii, 35–36). But it turned out to be so much more than nothing that spectacles could not have been much help. Lear, of course, is not taunting Gloucester; rather, the false

semblance of sight which is the meaning of "glass eyes" belongs to a world at large; and Lear himself had "seemed to
see" things that he did not. Growing milder, Lear shifts to another kind of "seeing" of which the play also makes considerable use: "If thou wilt weep my fortunes, take my eyes"
(180): weeping shows compassion, the weeping eye sees into
the truth of things. The eyes which he will now give away to
weep are the ones he once threatened to pluck out if they
wept. "Thou must be patient," Lear tells Gloucester (182)—
an ironic echo of Edgar's own advice to Gloucester.[16] Then
Lear summarizes, his earlier savageness reduced almost to a
quiet reflectiveness:

> We came crying hither.
> Thou know'st, the first time that we smell the air,
> We wawl and cry. I will preach to thee, mark.
>
> . . . .
>
> When we are born, we cry that we are come
> To this great stage of fools. (182–87)

"Smell the air" must, in the context of the play, suggest an
evil air. At the same time crying is a necessary sign of life:
to be alive itself is to have to face grief and evil. It is
the human condition; hence Gloucester must be patient.
". . . this great stage of fools" takes us back again to the
Fool and to the implied but never formulated relationship
between him and the rest of foolish mankind who regard him
at best as but a plaything. Folly has been thoroughly defined
as the misjudgment of values, the giving up of everything but
the immediate, tangible profit: the stage of fools is the world
of fumbling humanity. But fumbling humanity deserves
pity; and, further, among the fools is the Fool, the man of in-

sight whose very presence makes the stage hold something more than a cruel farce. Hence one may call for patience.

Thus the madness pattern, in its climactic scene, concludes by means of the fool pattern; it has now bound all the other patterns together. The synthesis takes place for the reader; but it is also an imaginative process that goes on within Lear. He has put together again the world that has fallen apart; when he awakens after a curative sleep, he is at peace. Achieving unity involves purgation: as he has gone through his own purgatory, Lear has literally purged his mind of the images of Goneril and Regan—or at least so reduced them that they are now in proper perspective. When he awakes, the agony caused by thoughts of them is gone (just as, after being blinded, Gloucester never again thinks of Edmund) : he mentions them only once more, and then almost casually (IV.vii, 73–74). Then, when Cordelia asks "Shall we not see these daughters and these sisters?" (V.iii, 7) Lear replies quickly, "No, no, no, no! Come let's away to prison" (8). To forget them is one of the things he has learned. To the full meaning of his madness, however, we shall return after several other relevant matters have been brought into view.

Like Gloucester's blindness, Lear's madness evokes different responses from those who observe it. Cordelia's references to it are fraught with love and concern (e.g., IV.iv, 2 ff.; IV.vii, 14 ff.), whereas to Regan he is simply "the lunatic King" (III.vii, 46), just as to Goneril he was simply in his "dotage" (I.iv, 315, 349). The latter daughters are coolly correct, or at least fairly close to correctness. This is a fact of importance in the unfolding of the madness pattern, for, when dialectics give way to the full exchange of human living, correctness is not enough.

THE UNDERSTANDING OF CORDELIA
AND KENT

What we have seen Shakespeare doing, thus far, is exhibiting the efforts of a sensitive but, in its haste and passion and initial inflexibility, not very well-equipped, mind to come to terms with, to master, a cosmos whose complexity and recalcitrancy we have always tangible and solidly visible before us. The cosmic resistance to intellectual conquest is vividly figured in the symbolic system of the play: the symbols are not fixed equivalents of concepts but rather suggest a highly fluid and elusive reality never wholly susceptible of prosaic formulations such as are attempted in the present analysis; they demand, as does the world which they shadow forth, an unflagging imagination such as that of the Fool and of the later Lear. As the multivalued clothes pattern suggests, behind the phenomenal action surface of the play are vast bodies of meaning tapped in different places and at different times by symbolic outlets of different capacities. As Lear is compelled to see into the ever-retreating depths coming into view beyond the one-dimensional reality that he is prepared to deal with and that his old order has narrowed into, the new perspective is too much, the novelty of vision is overwhelming, and he goes under. The easiest conclusion to draw is that life is intolerable at a rational level, that it is irrational, and that madness is the proper symbol for it. To draw such a conclusion, however, would be greatly to oversimplify the dramatic evidence: there are important elements in the structure of the meaning that we have not yet examined. Even in the parts we have already examined there is evidence that life, although it may make crushing demands of him, does not habitually treat man with a monstrous, meaningless treachery before which his mind must give way. Lear, as we have seen, overcomes even while being overcome. Gloucester's experiences are meaningful to him; and if the weight of retribution drives him to despair, even his despair is successfully countered by Edgar's expert and ingenious tenderness. Gloucester's suffering, which he does understand, has its origin in an initial failure of understanding, a loss of integrity of point of view, a slipping away from his own co-ordinates. For the early Gloucester is a trimmer: not a matriculated opportunist, but a man who tries to operate with two methods of understanding at once. There are the imperatives of status and tradition, to which he decides at last to adhere; but with these he tries at first to equate the claims of the new, flimsy, rationalistic order. He gets the *de facto* and the *de jure* confused; his is the rationalism of appeasement. Yet ultimately, after paying, like Faustus, a great price for it, he reaches clarity of understanding.

Now in the total structure of the play it is very important that Cordelia and Kent do have this clarity of understanding, this imaginative vitality, at the outset and never lose it: their position is medial with reference to those who do not understand clearly enough and those who, as we shall see, may be said to understand too well (and who see too well and are dressed too well). Cordelia and Kent reason, so to speak, with their blood; that is, they have an immediate understanding, as sure as if it were instinctive, of the situation which Lear has precipitated; they are clear not only intellectually but morally, so that to each—without the conscious mapping of itinerary that is necessary for Gloucester—his road is unmistakable, and each never swerves from it. Cordelia acts as daughter, as a member of organic family; Kent as vassal, as a member of organic society; both are "in" the "nature," the rupture of which is a leading motif of the play. One does not say of them "Theirs not to reason why," for that would be to sentimentalize them, to make them primitive child types, whereas their adherence to status and tradition, that is, to "bond" as Cordelia puts it, is a valid way of thinking about experience. They are adults. Neither is blind or stupid or naïve; neither is fooled by Goneril and Regan as Lear is, and as Gloucester is by Edmund; and neither is entirely without "practical" intelligence in a world which calls for exceptional portions of it. Their understanding is their mode of action toward Lear, and thus they are wholly integrated; if finally they do not have worldly "success," their failure must be understood as extrinsic to their character. The point is that their understanding is sound, and by sound understanding they save their honor.[17]

To say this of Cordelia and Kent is not to idealize them— or to sentimentalize them in the manner of an occasional critic who thus deprives the play of some of its depth. Kent is a human being who does not manage well in his efforts to secure admirable objectives: his direct rebuke of Lear for his division of the territory—perhaps Kent, like Cordelia, has no other way—infuriates Lear and in no way helps the situation; nor does he render much aid to Lear's cause by his brawling in front of Gloucester's castle.[18] He is no improbable Grandison; but he is absolutely faithful to his bond. Cordelia, by her nonparticipation in Lear's trial of his daughters, is partly responsible for everything that happens later. She is a creature of this world: she is caught in a dilemma which compels her to make a choice, a choice which must be imperfect. This is what happens to men: but it does not happen to all men to receive injury, to understand that it comes from error, and still to love him who commits the injury. There are two ways in which to oversimplify Cordelia: to forget her complicity in the situation, and to forget the clear-sightedness with which she views her father even after he has treated her in a way that might easily make her blind with resentment. Just before she leaves with France, she says to her sisters, "Use well our father" (I.i, 274). She cannot expect that they will do so, yet she cannot refrain from hoping. She has every reason to regard Lear as a vindictive old scoundrel. But her imagination is better than his: with it she sees behind the present and sees him more truly than he has seen her; and with her imagination she perceives the value of the "bond."

The Fool has the same kind of comprehension that Kent and Cordelia have; he too knows what kind of devotion is required of the man who would realize his humanity. By voluntarily responding to this demand, even from his own special world, he emphasizes the enveloping claims of the "bond" to which, in the adult world of full participation, Cordelia and Kent have already shown their allegiance. The imperatives are the same; in accepting the imperatives they show their philosophic code; and though they lose all in the world, they save everything essential.

REASON IN MADNESS

Now that we have seen the schematic place of Cordelia and Kent, and the Fool, we can return for a further consideration of Lear and other components of the dramatic structure which gives form to the meaning. Lear's original failure, we have seen, has an intellectual form: he endeavors to introduce quantitative norms where the questions are entirely qualitative. This mistake may be rephrased: Lear himself paves the way for the breakup of the organic order, represented in comparatively unadulterated form by Cordelia and Kent, by making contractual relationships basic. In his *quid-pro-quo* rationalism, however, he fails to provide substitutes for the old sanctions; thus his new system allows infinitely greater scope to latent human evil. Lear thinks badly, unimaginatively. Were he not content to pause at the appearance of things, he would understand that it is impossible to be king-in-name without being king-in-fact (not that this error justifies those who take advantage of the king-in-name-only); he attempts an abstract, theoretic separation characteristic of his early rationalistic temper, and for stability counts upon a contract which cannot be enforced. As he *divests* himself of the symbols of royalty, he forgets that there are no naked kings; he neglects both himself and his society. It is ironic that Lear—and Gloucester too, for that matter—is terribly put upon just at the moment when he feels he is being very clever. Like Faustus, he proposes to beat the game in which the nature of man is his opponent. Thus he evinces his pride. It is not the conscious pride in reason of, say, Oedipus or Faustus; but it is implied by his arbitrary imposition of his scheme of values and relations. He takes on too much. Precisely by being too clever he evades his adult responsibility, which should be intensified in one of position and authority, not to be gulled by every Mr. Plausible bent on profit, and not to give the Mr. Plausibles political power.

But having taken the world apart, Lear very soon has a terrifying vision of what he has done; and he tries, intellectually and morally, to put it together again. He calls upon the certainties of the old organic world (from which Kent and Cordelia derive their impulses), but he has invalidated the old imperatives, and disintegration has gone so far that nothing happens in accordance with his expectations. That this is the form of his problem appears in one passage that stands out among the many that embody his incomprehension and incredulity: ". . . by the marks of sovereignty, knowledge, and reason, I should be false persuaded I had daughters" (I.iv, 252–55). Sovereignty, knowledge, reason, and filial relationships all connote an absolute order. But that such an order is gone, at least as far as Lear is concerned, is pointed by the Fool's immediate witticism: "Which they will make an obedient father" (I.iv, 256). The irrevocable passage of things is underscored by the pathetic irony of Lear's subsequent lines:

> Thou shalt find
> That I'll resume the shape which thou dost think
> I have cast off forever; thou shalt, I warrant thee.
> (I.iv, 330–32)

But a historical turnover has taken place; Lear does not, and cannot, resume his old shape. Hence on, his kingliness will show itself only in his moral force among his followers. The old order is gone, and under the shock of its loss, Lear loses the powers of reason which he has not used well.

But Lear's un-reason accommodates a kind of reasoning; we see, in place of his earlier calculative spirit, a restored imagination which, even though at his death he is still battling fundamental enigmas, is capable of effecting austere syntheses out of the materials of the new disorderly world.

In place of his old myopia there is a new uncompromisingness of insight. In the experiences before his madness, in the
storm scenes during which he goes mad, but most of all in the
synthesis scene which we have analyzed at length, Lear has
developed an imaginative awareness of evil which he did not
have when he was making the trial of his daughters; he has
come to a compassion for humanity—a compassion which,
as Cordelia's tears indicate symbolically, is a kind of insight;
and, as both his direct statements and his figures show, he
has come to some knowledge of himself and his liability to
error.[19] He is a very different man from the Lear of Act I;
and it is safe to say that if the Lear of Act I had had the kinds
of awareness to which he has now come, he would not have
acted as he did. At the start, he had no insight into, nor did
he question, himself; if he had the power of compassion, he
did not show it; and he was so confused that he had no real
sense of evil. He was the man of calculation instead of the
man of imagination.

But his imagination is restored. If such a process were not
going on, the madness scenes would have been merely pathetic or grotesque or sardonic. Yet they are no such thing.
Not that the madness is not real; but it is ambivalent, and the
meaningfulness is as authentic as the clinical detail. Shakespeare takes pains to point out literally that Lear is as much
a man of understanding as he is a raving lunatic, or rather
that lunacy of demeanor can co-exist with a most penetrating
insight. The key speech is significantly given to Edgar, who,
after his pretended madness, has already begun to exhibit
the force and clarity of mind which are his to the end of the
play. His words are: "O, matter and impertinency mix'd!/

Reason in madness!" (IV.vi, 178–79) *Reason in madness:*
no single line has a more important bearing on the structure
of the whole play.

Shakespeare so qualifies and amplifies *reason in madness*
that he avoids having, at one polar extreme, a mere surreal-
istic laudation of lunacy. Along with Lear's burning knowledge we must take the insight of the Fool and Edgar, which
is an essential part of the madness pattern. Madness becomes, then, not merely clinical insanity but the whole realm
of what is, from the conventional point of view, mental and
worldly incompetence. Shakespeare takes three very "unlikely specimens," [20] as the world might view them—a crazy
old man long told that he is in his dotage, a Fool who may be
clever but is probably unbalanced and is certainly a no-
account, a naïve young man who manages so ill that he can
save himself only by becoming an outcast bedlam—and
makes them, as far as the reflective and imaginative world
is concerned,[21] his three wise men. Lear's interpretative
union of symbolic patterns, the Fool's keen perceptions of
fact and imaginative inferences from fact, and Edgar's
gnomic observations constitute, certainly not a formal philosophic commentary on experience, but a very solid aggrega-
tion of wisdom about it. That it should come from the humble, the scorned, and the exiled produces almost a Christian
transvaluation of the values of Lear's pagan world. This
is Shakespeare's central paradox, by which he unites the
other paradoxes into an inclusive paradox: the blind see, the
naked survive, and wisdom belongs to the mad. By these
paradoxes he presents the dilemma of the World: humanity
must live in it, and wishes to do well in it, yet the better man

does in it, the more likely he seems to come to ultimate grief. To have little and to be outside the sphere of the great seem the surest way to salvation.

What of the other side? Shakespeare presents madness not merely as psychologically "realistic"; he goes far beyond this and presents madness, which in one sense is a negation of all values, as itself containing value. But since we are quite evidently not to be told that this value is absolute, we look immediately for the contrapuntal statement; since Shakespeare is a master of the world of polarities, we automatically seek the alternative necessary to the tension of the play. At one pole, we find *reason in madness;* at the other, indeed, is *madness in reason.* Here we come to a balancing set of paradoxes. We have already seen the ironic contrast between the blind who come to insight, and the sharp-seeing who see so complacently well that more escapes their eyes than they know. We have seen, too, the paradox of the wild animals who are destroyed, and of those in proud array who have neither warmth nor protection. They are the wise in the world, and they have their own kind of madness.

. . . superficial perception may be increasing, while the kernel of perception may be shrinking. . . .

Hermann Broch, *The Death of Virgil*

* * *

But the thing which in eminent instances signalizes so exceptional a nature is this: though the man's even temper and discreet bearing would seem to intimate a mind peculiarly subject to the law of reason, not the less in his soul's recesses he would seem to riot in complete exemption from that law, having apparently little to do with reason further than to employ it as an ambidexter implement for effecting the irrational. That is to say: towards the accomplishment of an aim which in wantonness of malignity would seem to partake of the insane, he will direct a cool judgment sagacious and sound.

These men are true madmen, and of the most dangerous sort, for their lunacy is not continuous, but occasional; evoked by some special object; it is secretive and self-contained: so that when most active it is, to the average mind, not distinguished from sanity; and for the reason above suggested, that whatever its aims may be (and the aim is never disclosed) the method and the outward proceeding is always perfectly rational.

Herman Melville, *Billy Budd, Foretopman*

CHAPTER IX

MADNESS IN REASON

GONERIL, REGAN, AND EDMUND

A T T H E other pole from the outcasts who have understanding or come to it, we have three rationalists, shrewd citizens of the world—Goneril, Regan, and Edmund (in between, we should recall, are Kent and Cordelia, whose thought is act, and in whom we rarely see, as we do constantly in both of the structurally opposed trios, the thinking process as such),[1] and we need now to see how these three are presented with reference to the problem of understanding. We need hardly labor the fact that they are "evil"; probably no other characters in all literature, although Edmund has his admirers, have called forth such complete vocabularies of denunciation from the critics. But our business is to try to define the evil, or at least to find the dramatic terms in which it is presented. Since *King Lear* is concerned with the problem of understanding, we may expect that it will give a rather thorough interpretation of the minds of Goneril, Regan, and Edmund. What is their method of thought? By way of preliminary we may consider what use they make of such words as *reason* and *wisdom,* which come to their mouths more than once. Goneril, we remember, applied the term *fool* to Albany a number of times, and by it she meant one who permits the inhibitions of conscience to interfere with an apparently profitable course in the world.

When Edgar speaks of "reason in madness" and when France says in an elaborate theological metaphor that to believe great evil of Cordelia "Must be a faith that reason, without miracle,/Should never plant in me" (I.i, 225–26), they provide a contrasting background for the use of reason by others. When Goneril sends Oswald to Regan to explain her "fear" of the "harms" Lear and his men may do, she orders Oswald, "And thereto add such reasons of your own/ As may compact it more" (I.iv, 361–62). Reasons are *ad hoc* arguments, justifications for desire; or, as with Edmund, for the thing done: after Edmund has plotted the death of Lear and Cordelia, he says he has locked Lear up lest the old king arouse the public against them, and he adds, "With him I sent the queen./My reason all the same . . ." (V.iii, 51–52). Likewise Regan, arguing with Lear: "For those that mingle reason with your passion/Must be content to think you old . . ." (II.iv, 237–38). Reason is *our* view of *your* situation; it is the quasi-logical form in which one dresses up one's plots and passions. Thus the elder daughters make what are, at the literal level, at the level of everyday logic, almost unanswerable cases for their intention to deprive Lear of his followers. But after listening to their insistent rationalizing, which will ultimately help drive him mad, Lear cries angrily, "Oh, reason not the need; . . ." (II.iv, 267). Their reasoning is beside the point, and he calls for extrarational categories of understanding as a means of grasping the human truth involved. The daughters who make reason their partner and instrument also claim wisdom for their own. By way of contrast: Cordelia speaks of "man's

wisdom/In the restoring his bereaved sense" (IV.iv, 8–9);
Kent professes "to converse with him that is wise" (I.iv, 15–
16); and the Fool tells Lear, "Thou shouldst not have been
old till thou hadst been wise" (I.v, 47–48). To them, wisdom may be professional skill or personal insight. Against
these illuminating uses of *wise* and *wisdom* we find Goneril
telling her father, "I would you would make use of that good
wisdom/Whereof I know you are fraught . . ." (I.iv, 240–
41); that is, wisdom is falling in with the plans of someone
else who has authority, and who brazenly uses *wisdom* to
mean acquiescence in her own profit. Goneril likes the word;
again she tells Lear, ". . . you should be wise" (I.iv, 261)
—by giving up these disorderly and unnecessary followers.
His "wisdom" is the rationalization of her own advantage.
She censures Albany—

> You are much more at task for want of wisdom
> Than prais'd for harmful mildness (I.iv, 366–67),

using an inappropriate Machiavellianism in defining, as
"want of wisdom," his very mild questioning of her arbitrary treatment of Lear. Shakespeare's final stroke in charac-
terizing the evil sisters by their vocabulary is to have one of
them turn their favorite word against the other: thus the
inevitable break between the opportunistic allies is marked
by the language of reason as well as by the sight pattern and
the animal pattern.[2] Regan explains to Oswald that Edmund
is really destined for her and indicates her expectation that
Oswald will report as much to Goneril. She adds:

> And when your mistress hears thus much from you,
> I pray desire her call her wisdom to her. (IV.v, 34–35)

It is a neat ironic twist that Goneril is now to be "wise," just as she herself demanded that Lear be "wise." Regan's speech contributes usefully to the exposé of the sisters' reason-wisdom credo.

The preceding examples of the language used by Goneril and Regan are fairly good preliminary evidence of their essential quality: they are rationalists whose considerable shrewdness is used entirely for the gratification of their desires.[3] In one aspect they represent Edmund's view of Nature: that is, the uninhibited individual will—the dominance of which, in them, is apparent in all their major actions in the play. Their relationship to this Nature is almost continuously emphasized by the animal imagery used to describe them (Chapters IV and V). They are subject to none of the discipline which is important in establishing the quality of Cordelia and Kent (Chapter VIII). At the same time they have keen and ruthless minds; they see with wonderful clarity how, in Lear's phrase, "the world goes." The animal and the practical intelligence are joined in a calculating mechanism which, within certain limits, is terrifyingly efficacious. Now, by way of keeping in mind the total structure of the drama, we may recall that the spirit of calculation was first set free, so to speak, by Lear, and that the kinship between him and his daughters symbolizes his responsibility for them, and his momentary, but inaugural, participation in the fallacious method of judging values (Chapter VII). If they are considered as a kind of extrusion from him, a developing into life-size of a part of his personality, freed from the counterbalance of the rest of the personality,[4] we can see how tight the unity of the play is. Lear, by expiatory suffering, undergoes a spiritual recovery, an imaginative wakening; Shakespeare pictures him as coming again to an apprehension of values of which he had lost sight (Chapter VIII). What remains to be seen, then, is how Shakespeare dramatically indicates the limits of the Goneril-Regan-Edmund way of life, how he suggests the missing element in them, what it is that he makes catch up with them. How far will their sharp reason, their unshrinking minds, go? [5]

THE MINDS OF GONERIL AND REGAN

The rationalism of Goneril and Regan first appears in full action when they discuss their father's division of the property (I.i, 287 ff.). It is significant that instead of bursting into warm enthusiasm over the windfall, as well they might and as one might in a way sympathize with them for doing, they view the situation with cold understanding and calculation—a mood which is, after all, consistent with that in which they had served up the warmed-over protestations that had won the legacy. It is still more significant that they speak in prose, for the prose is symbolic: it is the language of analysis rather than imagination. Goneril and Regan record facts, and they see in them only the most immediate significations. Their prose here at the end of I.i is exactly comparable with their language in expressing their love to Lear: in those speeches, it is true, they speak in iambic pentameter, but what they speak is inflated prose. It is in pointed contrast with Cordelia's metaphor, "According to my bond." From the start Goneril and Regan are shown to lack the imaginative capacity which might save them.

They speak truths, as far as their perception of truth goes. Regan tells Cordelia, "You have obedience scanted" (I.i, 281), which is in one sense perfectly correct. Goneril and

Regan estimate their father as calmly as a board of inquiry. ". . . how full of changes his age is; . . . he always lov'd our sister most; . . ." (291–94). They can even censure him, making especial reference to his powers of reason: ". . . with what poor judgment he hath now cast her off appears too grossly" (294–95). It is cuttingly ironic that their calm assessment of the situation resembles a sympathizing with Cordelia. Everything they say about him is correct: " 'Tis the infirmity of his age; yet he hath ever but slenderly known himself" (296–97). Their absence of enthusiasm predicts their cool evaluation of prospects: it continues from the calm opportunism with which they had accepted Lear's imposition of a literal quantitative standard in the measurement of love. Their minds are so incisive that it is they who give expression to Lear's tragic flaw, or at least to one possible formulation of it. Goneril says, "The best and soundest of his time hath been but rash; . . ." (I.i, 298–99), and Regan later echoes the word *rash* [6] (II.iv, 172). What gives substance and form to the play is the intelligence of Goneril and Regan; were they simply stupid monsters, the essential polarity would be lost; Shakespeare has liberally endowed them with a certain kind of virtue which in a different context might be highly prized; then he sets about the complex task of exploring the deficiencies of that very virtue. The sisters rarely make errors about matters of fact, and they even have a certain predictive skill. But their sanity is turned all upon immediate business. From that point of view their plans follow perfectly logically from the evidence that they see. They expect "unconstant starts" (I.i, 304) from Lear and decide to take action against "the unruly waywardness that infirm and choleric years bring with them" (302–303).

Yet even in this close observation of the frailties of age, the insufficiency of their instrumentalism begins to appear, for important aspects of human life are not apparent to them. How much they do not understand becomes clear when they utilize his age (his weakness, his dotage, etc.) as a logical justification of their depriving him of the symbols of status (II.iv, 148 ff.). For what gradually becomes evident is that age cannot be accommodated by a strictly rational order. Lear puts it with fierce compactness: "Age is unnecessary" (II.iv, 157). Yet in dramatic terms we see age, with its expectations and prerogatives, as an empirical fact that cannot be ignored, and that receives a justifying homage from Kent, Cordelia, Edgar, and even Albany, who has to resolve a conflict of loyalties. The sisters argue only from "need"; other values they do not admit. Thus their clear-headedness is not enough; it simply does not enable them to gather in all the essentials of experience. Their reliance upon clear vision muddles them. They are correct but incomplete, and their incompleteness is morally fatal.

Goneril shrewdly plots to bring about the complete powerlessness of Lear which she desires. She tells Oswald that he and his fellows may adopt a "weary negligence" in attending Lear because she "would breed . . . occasions" (I.iii, 12, 24). To Lear she makes an apparently reasonable complaint about the behavior of his men (I.iv, 220 ff.). Her objections to the Fool are bred of an understanding of him which appears overtly when she calls him "more knave than fool" (I.iv, 337). Regan nicely exhibits the strategy of finding "reasons" when Gloucester sorrowfully recounts Edgar's supposed villainy; she asks a leading question, "Was he not companion with the riotous knights/That tend upon my father?" (II.i, 96–97) But the direction which sharpness of mind, rational skill, takes when it owes no allegiance beyond the moment and beyond the scheme on foot is brilliantly illustrated by the reasoning with which the sisters make their father's going out into the stormy night appear inevitable. Goneril says, " 'Tis his own blame; hath put himself from rest/And must needs taste his folly" (II.iv, 293–94), and Regan elaborates:

> O, sir, to wilful men
> The injuries that they themselves procure
> Must be their schoolmasters. Shut up your doors.
> He is attended with a desperate train;
> And what they may incense him to, being apt
> To have his ear abus'd, wisdom bids fear. (II.iv, 305–10)

This speech is quite magnificent in its own way: it characterizes a woman who sees so far and yet misses so much. As we have already seen, Regan, without any moral sensitivity to tragic quality, has actually succeeded, in her sentence about willful men, in making one possible statement of the tragic process. In fact, what she says about her father roughly parallels what Edgar later says about his father:

> The gods are just, and of our pleasant vices
> Make instruments to plague us. (V.iii, 170–71)

Yet there is an obvious ironic distance between the two passages. Edgar speaks as a philosophic observer; Regan makes a sanctimonious self-defense. That she is rationalizing is somewhere in the borderland between what she grasps and what she does not; she has not the moral perspicacity to recognize the spiritual defect of her convenient statement, but in her cynical sharpness she may well relish the fitting solemnity of what she knows is a "sentiment" rather than a conviction. Finally, of course, behind the sentiment there is another ironically unperceived substance, an unsuspected fitting solemnity—the applicability of the words to the sisters themselves: they too are willful, and, although unable to learn, must be schooled. The "desperate train" is a more obvious part of Regan's rationalizing game; but again one must toy with the possibility of her sardonically grasping the double entendre of "being apt/To have his ear abus'd." They who first abused his ear achieved, by doing so, a position where they can urge the folly of his ear as a justification for taking defense measures against him. Her final words are "wisdom bids fear"; *wisdom,* that is, is looking out for oneself—a meaning wholly in harmony with all we have seen of the sisters who keep their minds strictly on business. Here a veritable exaggeration of cool sanity is transmuted into moral madness.

The ultimate irony proceeding from the sisters' rationalism is not so much its moral fatuity, which has the immediacy and inescapability of the axiomatic, but its insufficiency precisely where, in the eyes of the world, the best case might be made for it—in the management of the practitioner's "interests." The practical is the ultimate test for the pragmatists. Goneril's and Regan's interests, though their dominant form is political, are inextricably identified with their passion for Edmund, a passion which can be neither controlled nor manipulated in a satisfactory way. Here we have the most clear-cut illustration that in the sisters, mind is combined with "nature." Even before the seductive Edmund comes in to tangle their schemes, it is apparent that their clarity of mind has its limitations in the practical world and may be interfered with by unexamined, nonrational motives. Goneril and Regan have hewn firmly to a cool control of the situation and of themselves throughout their dealing with the frantic Lear: but the very next time we see them—in the scene with the "traitor" Gloucester—they are beginning to lose their grip. They are furious at Gloucester, whom they treat savagely; Regan's words fall little short of a wild rant. If they felt convinced they had a case against Gloucester, they might dispose of him quietly and with the appearance of order; in fact, every rational consideration would demand their refraining from the vengeful abuse which they might expect to have serious political repercussions. But they are weak in the imaginative anticipation of mankind's moral responses. "Nature" takes over; the hot, unplanned, unregulated response will leap out. So the whole scene may be read as a symbol of the crack-up of the schemers. When, then, Goneril and Regan face the problem of dealing with a passion far more powerful than that evoked by Gloucester's aid to Lear—their lust for Edmund—we are prepared for their failure to master it. Ideally, their calculating minds should be able to reject this passion for Edmund as inconsistent with their "interests." Their difficulty is that they are without the only kind of values—moral or religious—by means of which the passion could be disciplined. Their minds know no such imperative. They are what we now call rootless. But the paradox is that these free minds, unburdened by any conventional or traditional allegiances, become slaves to the uncontrolled animal desire, mechanisms for the attainment of irrational objectives. Now this has been true of Goneril and Regan from the start—this union of reason and uncontrolled impulse—but the truth is given the most ex-

234

plicit dramatic form in the love triangle. Neither Goneril nor Regan endeavors to reject Edmund; both, on the contrary, regard him, like sovereignty in the kingdom, as a desideratum toward which the mind must work. Their decisions are appetitive (whereas Kent's and Cordelia's are instinctive-traditional); their minds are merely instrumental. Hence the portrayal of the sisters in the triangular passion is a dramatic elaboration of Lear's metaphor for them—*Centaurs:* we see rational mind unmistakably in conjunction with, and what is more, in the service of, animal body. Such an outcome was inevitable.

The devotedness of Cordelia and Kent sets off not only, at the obvious level, the central conduct of the unfilial trio, but also, more subtly, the failure of devotion between Goneril and Regan. The latter are not joined by a common cause which transcends the individual but are allied by reasoned considerations of advantage; but the reasoners are not immune to the nonrational, and, since their nonrational impulses find no discipline in a nonrational loyalty such as that which binds Kent to Lear, the partnership disintegrates. Each goes her own rational way, driven by her own impulse and scheming against the other precisely as both schemed against Cordelia and Lear. Goneril and Albany are informed jointly that Gloucester has been blinded and Cornwall killed. While her husband is expressing outraged incredulity at the blinding of Gloucester, Goneril responds to the news only by falling immediately into close calculation of how Cornwall's death affects her chances with Edmund (IV.ii, 83 ff.). The very next thing we see of either sister is Regan's effort to intercept Goneril's letter to Edmund, to persuade the messenger not to complete his journey, to win his support for her own suit (IV.v). Soon after, we see her again, questioning Edmund bluntly, and quite indifferent to her self-exposure (V.i, 1–17). A moment later Goneril gives us a clue to the breakdown of the Goneril-Regan order of things when she says, aside, "I had rather lose the battle than that sister/ Should loosen him and me" (V.i, 18–19); the breakdown actually comes about when Regan and Goneril quarrel openly over Edmund (V.iii, 62 ff.). Meanwhile the cold scheming has gone on, and Regan's illness turns out to have been caused by Goneril's poison. They are defeated by their "nature" despite their sharp minds, for their Nature is "red in tooth and claw," and in its service their minds must become purely destructive. This is the outcome of their calculation of profits. They have lacked the power of imagination by which they might get hold of disciplinary, saving values. That they are morally lost was clear from the start; the final little joke upon them is that they are also practically lost. In their reason is a double madness.

THE MIND OF EDMUND

In the madness-in-reason pattern Edmund is of course a main strand. In our very first view of him we see Edmund as a reasoner, the possessor of a detached mind; the essence of his first twenty-one lines is a rational attack upon the traditional modes which Lear represents and in terms of which Kent and, later, Gloucester act. In his libertine view, the accepted order of things is merely "the plague of custom" (I.ii, 3). We must, Edmund implies, see things as they are (that is, that a bastard may be the physical and spiritual equal of a legitimate child), and think inductively from the evidence of the facts. But even at this stage Edmund is presented ironically, for his inductivism is only partial; actually, he repudiates one deductive procedure (the argument from the superiority of legitimacy) and adopts another (the argument from the superiority of illegitimacy) (I.ii, 11 ff.). What we now see, indeed, is a phenomenon that, as we have already noted, occurs also in the mental processes of Goneril and Regan: the coalescence of the two meanings of *rationalize*.[7] For, whereas Edmunds appears, on the one hand, to be disinterestedly seeking a *ratio*, an intellectually tenable position, with regard to certain facts of experience, it is clear that what he is actually doing, on the other hand, is seeking justification for an emotionally determined course of action: he has already decided to "top th' legitimate" (21), and he is seeking a quasi-logical formulation of an emotive commitment. As with the sisters, his mind is reduced to instrument; this rationalist is a man who lives by his wits. As he says, he will "have lands by wit" (199). That what his mind is the instrument of is "Nature" is of course made explicit: his opening analysis of conventions is addressed to Nature, and, as we have seen,[8] Nature is what he is and what he serves.

A little later Edmund is again conspicuously the reasoner, boldly puncturing, as before, a belief which probably had considerable currency. The occasion is Gloucester's attributing the evil he sees in the world to the influence of the stars; Edmund contemptuously dismisses the theory (I.ii, 128 ff.), and, with a fine incisiveness that is in ironic contrast with the mental fuzziness which he can display with regard to the workings of his own mind, even puts his finger on the "rationalizing" instinct of the believers in influence: ". . . as if we were . . . fools by heavenly compulsion, . . . An admirable evasion of whoremaster man, to lay his goatish disposition to the charge of a star!" (I.ii, 133–40). Edmund is brilliant here; in this speech he shows Goneril's and Regan's gift of acute scientific observation unimpeded by emotional bias; like them, it is worth noting, he points with cold wisdom to a father's folly (the scene provides another of the numerous structural parallels in the play, for it balances the scene in which the sisters comment on Lear's disinheriting of Cordelia—I.i, 287 ff.). He is technically all right; like the sisters, he does not make errors about immediate fact. It is a part of Shakespeare's skill to endow the three liberally with intelligence; to make them stupid brutes would severely limit the meaning of the play. That they reason, to a point, so lucidly, is the clue to Shakespeare's attitude to the phases of human experience which constitute the materials of the play. He gives the three definitely a kind of virtue, a skill which is potentially valuable in humanity's dealing with the universe; the detached mind is an admirable instrument of observation and analysis. But Shakespeare then goes ahead to indicate, in dramatic form, the shortcomings of the analytical mind—its insufficiency as a driving force; its failure to view itself with detachment; its destruction of sanctions which it regards as hollow only to fall prey to the passions which it was the function of the sanctions to inhibit; its weakness in making the imaginative jump from the observed fact to the total significance, in making, that is, the moral inferences to which the bare facts are only prolegomena. It is good to expose Gloucester's faulty morality, but not to conclude, as a consequence, that one is free to impose one's own passions upon society.[9] It is good to detect the *non sequitur*'s of astrology; but not to regard the detection as providing an ample spiritual code for the whole man. As Lear's early lack of it shows, clarity of vision is a necessity; but it is not a good when it is turned only upon the obstacles to one's own progress toward cherished goals. The vision which comes too late, and then only in the synthesis of madness, may be qualitatively superior to the early bright hard seeing, the very concentration of worldly sanity.

Edmund's opening scene has several excellent ironies of vocabulary. Gloucester, the victim of Edmund's cunning, says to him, ". . . frame the business after your own wisdom" (106). Before Edgar's entry Edmund says his cue is to sigh "like Tom o' Bedlam" (147)—the character which, as a result of his scheming, Edgar will have to assume. Edgar finds him apparently in a "serious contemplation" (150–51)—a term which describes Edgar's abilities more accurately then Edmund's. Edmund evidently knows his Edgar and opportunistically adopts the right pose, just as, in talking to Edgar of eclipses, he quickly picks up a cue from his own soliloquy on astrology (I.ii, 148 ff.)—any cue will do —and has the fun of parodying Gloucester while beguiling Edgar.

In Edmund the observer of human folly there is a certain saving directness which naturally cannot appear in Edmund the deceiver. Except for the rigor of calculation which excludes every iota of moral concern (in contrast with Gloucester's strong, although unripened, sense of moral disorder), Edmund's deceptive process is not intrinsically brilliant, depending chiefly upon a sure knowledge of the relatively unperceptive individual to be seduced, and in that respect resembling—in another of the systematic parallels —Goneril's and Regan's method of tricking Lear in the first

239

scene of the play. Edmund does approach genius at one point, that at which, in order to keep him manageable, he must give the overstimulated Gloucester a daring admonition—daring in that it incorporates so accurate a description of Gloucester's conduct that it might well awake him to his folly throughout the scene: "If it shall please you to suspend your indignation against my brother till you can derive from him better testimony of his intent . . . if you violently proceed against him, mistaking his purpose, it would make a great gap in your own honour and shake in pieces the heart of his obedience" (I.ii, 85–92). Thus it falls to Edmund—as to Goneril and Regan—to make a succinct statement of the parental flaw that is to have tragic consequences. After so mastering the situation that he can fling his father's error into his teeth without discovery, Edmund can easily carry the cool headwork over into hoodwinking the less experienced Edgar and so cultivating the split between father and son that his plot successfully culminates in the voluntary exile of Edgar (II.i). The finesse which Edmund exhibits in these dealings is that of what we have come to know as the propagandist—the agent who uses his mind as machinery but is indifferent to the moral quality of his end, who gains technical understanding of how men's nervous systems function and without scruple manipulates them for pleasure or profit. The technician as practical psychologist must have sharp wits; but the irony of his sharp wits is that, though they may enable him to see immediate life approximately straight, they in no way guarantee his seeing it whole. Even lesser wits may achieve a better perspective; the rational trio come to be understood better than they ever understand.

With such materials as the evil of "influencing people" it

would have been easy for Shakespeare to lapse into the homily of oversimplified contrast. But Shakespeare goes far beyond the most obvious possibilities: another of the evidences of his skill is his exactly balancing the scenes in which Edmund "works on" Gloucester by those in which Edgar "works on" Gloucester (IV.i, vi). Edgar appears to fall in with Gloucester's desire to commit suicide, by skillful manipulation makes Gloucester think he has been miraculously saved, and thus rescues him from despair. The point is: Edgar is a practical psychologist too; he subverts the will of Gloucester; but his act is charity. (Comparably, the elder sisters' driving Lear insane is complemented by Cordelia's helping to restore him to sanity.) The simplest dramatic opposition would have been that between the managed will and a fine, exuberant freedom of will, between the exercise of influence and the absence of influence; but that opposition might well have fallen into the callow and the melodramatic. The play holds to a view that is firmly realistic and tragic: Man's weakness puts him often in need of persuasion, and that man is subject to influence is an empirical fact. The question is then of the motive, the sanction, the imperative. If life is simply an open moral field for sharp wits, the profit motive will debase the world. If practical psychology comes at last to be identified with the evil manipulation of humanity for profit, human relations will have finally escaped from the curbs upon the self seeking its most immediate and tangible profit.

The rationalist-plotter appears again in Edmund's decision to betray to Cornwall Gloucester's communication with Lear (III.iii, 22–26) and his arranging for the assassination of Lear and Cordelia (V.iii, 26 ff.). In the latter activity Edmund not only sets forth a characteristic position: "To be tender-minded/Does not become a sword" (31–32); but also calculates the means by which he may evade responsibility for the murder: he will utilize his victim's psychological state. He thought, he says later (V.iii, 254–55), "To lay the blame upon her own despair,/That she forbid herself." Edmund's dispassionate capitalizing upon a state in which there is the deepest pathos is another excellent device for displaying his mind; and Shakespeare ensures the effectiveness of the device by another contrast between Edmund and Edgar. In fact, Edmund's confession of his intended use of Cordelia's "despair" occurs only a short time after Edgar has told how he helped the blind Gloucester, "became his guide,/Led him, begg'd for him, sav'd him from despair" (V.iii, 190–91). Thus there is a structural tension between profiting from despair and combating despair.

With Edmund as with the sisters, the rational prosecution of advantage ironically falls down when the complexity of experience becomes too much for it. As a moral code it is madness; it not only wantonly injures others but ruins the basis of human order; it destroys the soul of its practitioner; yet, at this incredible cost, it cannot even bring consistent profit in the practical world. It is mad, that is to say, even at the lowest possible level of computation. Except for his step against Lear and Cordelia, Edmund the hard schemer has become very ineffectual by Act V: in the vital situation in which he has become ensnared, there are too many movements and countermovements for him to manage. The equipment with which he faces life is too simple to enable him to meet all the complexities of life. Whereas until now he has foreseen or even brought about action, he is now suddenly overwhelmed by actions uncontrolled and even unanticipated —Albany's enmity and strong assertion of leadership, the fierce attack of the unknown challenger who turns out to be Edgar. This collapse of his aggressive mastery of men and strategy—it is notable that the restoration of moral balance begins when the emergence of systemic weakness coincides with resourceful and determined countermeasures by the morally sound—finds its occasion in his involvement with the sisters, just as their own destruction grew out of their passion for him. In Edmund, of course, we do not see "Nature" in a violent unresisted upsurge turning his rational powers into an instrument of destruction; Edmund seems to reciprocate none of the passion which the sisters feel for him; so that the collaboration of his mind and his appetite for position and power has so far been rather "successful." If his chief aim is still land and position, positive action with respect to the embarrassing triangle is called for. Since he cannot indefinitely be the pretended lover of both sisters, what is demanded of him is a realistic assessment of the advantages to be gained by professing love for Goneril or for Regan or for neither, a mapping out of a line of conduct in accord with his decision, and a consistent hewing to that line. But he temporizes and evidently hopes to extemporize as successfully as he did when the situation was, as he should realize, much simpler. The first time after his betrayal of Gloucester to Cornwall (III.v) that we see him for more than a line or two is in V.i, where he has a fifteen-line soliloquy. Here he explicitly considers the problems that face him, and, although he says, with admirable clarity, that his

"state/Stands on me to defend, not to debate" (V.i, 68–69),
he has no definite plans at all except to do away with Lear
and Cordelia (65 ff.). Actually, he does little more than debate; as far as the sisters are concerned, he looks ahead only
to the extent of assuming that Goneril will do away with the
obstructing Albany (V.i, 64–65). He is plainly letting the
initiative pass to others and thus losing his grip upon the situation. What is actually happening is that inroads are being
made upon Edmund's life of reason, if not by love, by other
emotions. There are two forces that may be supposed to be
influencing Edmund and causing him to lose his original aggressive firmness, and each of them, I think, is partially responsible for what happens. One of these forces is a kind of
sentimental vanity or egoism; the other is some latent capacity to respond to traditional appeals—to what Edmund himself calls "the plague of custom." Perhaps the latter has also
a sentimenal cast with him, and what we see in all his final
actions is merely the kind of softness that the hard rationalist
frequently falls into—and that is quite likely to be mistaken
for moral quality. Edmund's sentimental vanity is suggested
by his inability to do anything decisive about the triangle:
he cannot give up the role of heartbreaker, one very flatter-
ing to an ego which has suffered as much damage as Edmund's. When the sisters quarrel over him publicly for
twenty lines (V.iii, 61–81), the confident wit and schemer
says nothing at all. When, some time later, their dead bodies
are brought in, he says not one word about them; his sole
thought is of *himself:*

> Yet Edmund was belov'd.
> The one the other poisoned for my sake,
> And after slew herself. (V.iii, 239–41)

The affair thus ends in his self-congratulation—yet, iron-ically, self-congratulation for being the recipient of an emo-tion which he seems never to have sought or, more important, felt. Perhaps we should take him at the psychological level and say that his whole trouble is that he has never received love. Under any circumstance, however, we see Edmund overtaken by a force which his view of life could hardly accommodate. One can imagine what the contemptuous iconoclast, who wanted land and power, ought to be saying about the value of the passion of two dead women.

The sentimental side of Edmund appears also in another way—in his acceptance of Edgar's challenge. In mere con-sistency Edmund should seek a legal or legalistic escape from an encounter which by his standards can only be ro-mantic tomfoolery; the code of honor must seem to him as flimsy as astrology. "In wisdom I should ask thy name," he does say (V.iii, 141); and, if only to "spurn" it, he does think of the delay which he might have "By rule of knight-hood" (145). There is the shrewd man of action, with his *rule* and his *wisdom* used precisely as they might be by Goneril and Regan. These are the words by which he ought to reject the "plague of custom," and indeed the early Ed-mund is now exactly represented by Goneril, who, when Edmund is wounded, cries with a mixture of frustration, dis-gust, and even desire to console:

> This is mere practice, Gloucester.
> By th' law of arms thou wast not bound to answer
> An unknown opposite. Thou art not vanquish'd,
> But cozen'd and beguil'd. (V.iii, 151–54)

Her words are exactly in character. But Edmund has re-soundingly proclaimed that he who "names me traitor, villain-like he lies" (98), insisted upon his "truth and honour" (101), and retorted to the disguised Edgar, "Back do I toss those treasons to thy head" (146)—terms which belong not to a rebel against but to a faithful observer of the "plague of custom." Edmund, we may assume, expects to win his fight; but hope of victory does not require these verbal decorations from an old code of personal honor. In Edmund there is some residuum of traditional responsiveness, never quite conquered by his rationalism, and yet in its emergence vitiated by its lateness, by the publicness which permits Edmund a histrionic gratification, by the official disgrace (Albany's attack) which compels some bold move to recoup his status, and by the possibility that the words themselves, though manifestly untrue, have been chosen to win him some regard from inimical forces now apparently much stronger than they once seemed. The unreconstructed remnant of the old order in Edmund comes closest to authentic expression, to winning a pure assent from him, in his agreement with Edgar's moralizing comment on Gloucester's adultery (170–73) and his further reply, "Th' hast spoken right; 'tis true./ The wheel is come full circle; . . ." (173–74), which, I have suggested earlier, is virtually a recantation of his nature credo. His words are plain and unspectacular; they come when his being seriously wounded is likely to lead to at least a partial reconsideration of his values. But the sentimental element in Edmund's bowing the knee to the moral tradition is clear, I think, in the few lines which remain to him—those on the sisters' love, which we have observed, and these: "This speech of yours hath mov'd me/And shall perchance do good" (199–200) and "Some good I mean to do,/ Despite of mine own nature" (243–44). Edmund makes an effort to halt the assassination, it is true, when he might sardonically relish the thought of the others' pain on discovering the death of Lear and Cordelia; but he is very slow in his effort—that is, he talks about "good" instead of promptly and directly doing it. He is savoring a feeling, perhaps also enjoying his own death scene.[10]

The thematic significance of the careers of Edmund, Goneril, and Regan is that the practical, expedient, programmatic reason is insufficient, that man cannot sustain himself by it, and that, whatever his moral stature, he will inevitably seek fulfillment by other means. In the latter part of the play we see dramatized, beside the growth of understanding within the madness group, the breakdown of their antagonists' rationalism. In Goneril and Regan the collaboration of reason and appetite breaks down when individual, antagonistic passions, unchecked by any rational or suprarational control, turn the reason into an implement of destruction. In Edmund the realization of "Natural" rights by reason fails when the world becomes too complex to manage by so simplified a program, and Edmund himself comes to act on other motivations that are largely sentimental but have in them some trace of the traditional. The codes of these three are morally insane; and they have no soundness even at the pragmatic level for which they were especially meant. The three show no more fitness to survive than those whom they planned to survive.

It is more than interesting that the madness-in-reason theme should be brought to a climax in the triangular passion which envelops the sisters and Edmund, for the passion is multivalued dramatically. At the plot level it wrecks the political aspirations which are apparently at the threshold of final success; at the psychological and symbolic level it represents an effort of a distorted nature to assume just proportions. Yet itself it becomes a distortion of the central human experience of love: perverse passion in beings who have perverted their humanity, who, with cool minds that are remarkably accurate in detecting the folly of others, have yet fixed on courses that cut off too much of their essential humanity. But the clear-eyed perception of folly does not establish sanity (as we have already seen intimated by the sight theme). In their madness the three have tried to do without love, and love reasserts itself: it cannot be controlled or rationalized, and it is fatal. "To both these sisters have I sworn my love," says Edmund (V.i, 55), and Goneril promises Edmund "a mistress's command" (IV.ii, 21). But like that of the souls in Purgatory, it is a misdirected love—lust or sentimental self-soothing—in contrast with the right love of Cordelia and Edgar and Kent. But here we have no Purgatory, for in these damned souls—whose kinship is to those in the last circle of the Inferno—the misdirected love is a very metaphor of the radical disorder against which it futilely rebels.

OSWALD AND CORNWALL

In Act I, we have seen, Kent shows a clear insight which is not unlike that of Goneril, Regan, and Edmund. "Answer my life my judgment," he says to Lear (I.i, 153–54), "Thy youngest daughter does not love thee least." His insight is combined with no profit motive; yet there is the peculiar irony of his failing just where the evil characters succeed—in exerting influence upon the immediate action. He is not a

practical psychologist; his candor to Lear in I.i is in contrast
with Edmund's deviousness toward Gloucester; his trust to
the logic of truth in contrast with Edmund's use of untruth.
We see Kent similarly unsuccessful after his attack on Oswald in front of Gloucester's castle. During his defense he
has the bitter experience of seeing Oswald look the confident
insider, and he exclaims,

> Smile you my speeches, as I were a fool?
> Goose, an I had you upon Sarum Plain
> I'ld drive ye cackling home to Camelot. (II.ii, 88–90)

Kent, who was ironically called a fool by the Fool, is now
asked by Cornwall, ". . . art thou mad . . .?" (II.ii,
91)—madness being, as it is to Goneril and Regan, opposition to the controlling will.

The initial failures of the understanding Kent help underline the madness paradox: in the world, real insight is apparently doomed to ill success. Early in the play also, Kent's
experiences have an immediate dramatic utility in that he
comes into conflict with both Oswald and Cornwall, who are
on the side which is apparently winning. Kent shows up Oswald as not the brightest of faithful camp followers; Oswald
gets his principles of rational worldliness at second hand,
and he attempts to move in company which is too fast for
him. When Albany calls Oswald "sot" after Oswald has re-
ported to him "Gloucester's treachery" and Edmund's "loyal
service" (IV.ii, 6–8), Albany's word nicely exhibits the
moral and intellectual obtuseness of Oswald. On the one
occasion when his wits impel him to take the initiative to
advance his fortune (by killing Gloucester), he is quickly
killed (IV.vi, 230 ff.). His moral madness is penetrated by

an ironic ray of selflessness as he is dying: he wants Goneril's note taken on to Edmund (254–55).

In Cornwall we find another variation: the man of reason whose emotions are fatally close to the surface. Spurned emotions ultimately betray all the plotters; but Cornwall has so little control that in a scheming world his survival value is small. Compared with Oswald, of course, he is a man of intellectual stature. In analyzing the type to which he thinks Kent belongs, he shows the same kind of brilliance that characterizes Edmund's debunking of astrology:

> This is some fellow,
> Who, having been prais'd for bluntness, doth affect
> A saucy roughness, and constrains the garb
> Quite from his nature. He cannot flatter, he,—
> An honest mind and plain,—he must speak truth!
> An they will take it, so; if not, he's plain.
> These kind of knaves I know, which in this plainness
> Harbour more craft and more corrupter ends
> Than twenty silly-ducking observants
> That stretch their duties nicely. (II.ii, 101–10)

That Shakespeare gave to characters such as Cornwall speeches which are keenly penetrating rather than shocking or absurd has been noted by various critics. But, as this essay has repeatedly said, such sharp, independent minds, although they are often masterly in the analysis of a situation or of the minds of others or of human types, are incapable of transcending this partial profundity to arrive at an understanding of themselves or at tenable standards of conduct. In the passage quoted, of course, Cornwall's skill is in delineating what we might call the pseudo-plain type. He does a brief "character." His fallibility appears in the fact that

Kent does not actually belong to the pseudo-plain type. That Cornwall's analysis is not applicable to its immediate subject is suggested by a startling verbal echo of an earlier half-truth by Lear. Lear said of Cordelia, "Let pride, which she calls plainness, marry her" (I.i, 131); Cornwall's comparable words are of the "knaves . . . which in this plainness/Harbour more craft, etc." In believing that they see through plainness, both men are being too clever. At another time Cornwall reads too much into a character: "Cunning," he sneers (III.vii, 49) at Gloucester's patently candid replies to his inquisitors. Yet his own tendency is to fall in with the casuistry of the usurping sisters; on Regan's obvious rationalization of letting Lear go out into the stormy night and of barring the castle against him, Cornwall comments, "My Regan counsels well" (II.iv, 312).

But if Goneril, Regan, and Edmund are ultimately betrayed by lapses from rationalistic standards, they are, compared with Cornwall, models of self-discipline. When any kind of pressure is applied, Cornwall becomes wholly a creature of emotion: Kent's treatment of Oswald puts Cornwall into a fury (II.ii, 52 ff.); there is evidence that he has quarreled with Albany (II.i, 2–12; III.i, 19–25; III.iii, 8–9); and the news of Gloucester's visiting Lear brings on a frenzy of vengefulness (III.v). When strategic considerations would, for a schemer of better rational control, demand merely the elimination of Gloucester with due orderliness, Cornwall announces that his wrath shall prevail and that the hearing shall have only "the form of justice" (III.vii, 25), insanely abuses Gloucester, finally reaches a hyperbole of violence that excites a servant to attack him, and thus brings about his own death. Here is a man of sharp mind apparently coming into control of a kingdom: but his own kind of madness betrays him. If Cornwall's evil is to be defined, like that of Goneril and Regan, as a combination of reason and nature, perhaps we may say that his nature, his impulse, is definable by the modern term *sadism*. He has a passion for the infliction of physical suffering: thus he symbolizes the appetite for evil generally. In fact, in terms of the play, appetite—man-as-nature, man-as-animal—is appetite for evil; man achieves human goodness when the self is mastered by loyalties and by transcendent insights.

The extended analyses of individuals in Chapters VIII and IX are only incidentally character sketches: their primary function is to trace, by the persons' deeds, and especially their words, those paradoxes of human nature and experience which are the chief structural elements of the drama. *King Lear* dramatizes fundamentally the paradox that wisdom and insight may be found in the outcast and the deranged, and that the powerful and brilliant may be, by both moral and pragmatic standards, insane; it amplifies this dramatic theme by the contributory paradoxes that those best equipped with eyesight in the world may be blind to spiritual truths, that those who in strength and ruthlessness are like animals may have destroying weaknesses, and that the gorgeously arrayed may lose the most important of all defenses. By these very complex techniques Shakespeare sets forth what I have called the problem of The World. The great in the world seem to use their greatness badly or to achieve it at the cost of all spiritual values; these values are preserved best by those whom the world rejects. But if they are the victims of the world, what is their security? Is it merely a romantic retreat into a private reality? Or is there a greater reality that transcends the truth of the world? Such questions, like all the others, are never answered directly, but answers are implied in the recurrent references to the deities. We come finally, then, to an examination of what the characters in *King Lear* say about the gods.

Yea, for the gods lift thee now, but before they were working thy ruin.

Sophocles, *Oedipus at Colonus*

*   *   *

But in truth the gods do exist, and they do care for human beings, and they have put all the means in man's power to enable him not to fall into real evils.

Marcus Aurelius, *Meditations*

*   *   *

They are incredible, these positivists, with their insulated, lucid brains and their blind hearts.

Eliseo Vivas, in *The Western Review*

CHAPTER X

THE GODS ARE JUST

MAN AND THE GODS

T H E   R E L I G I O U S attitudes of the characters are logically the final subject in this essay, for what the play says or
implies about religion ties together the other observations
upon man and gets hold of the nature of man in the most
inclusive terms. Not that the play is an untapped mine of
systematic theology. It is not. But there are many references
to the gods; [1] and in its presentation of man's relationship to
the gods the play carries further and indeed corroborates
what it says by means of the other patterns. In the face of injustice man may believe in justice because the eternal gods
will execute it. Man may speak in terms of a Nature which is
Law because it is ordained by gods whom he can invoke. The
blind man sees because he can have insight into the divine
reality. The sanity of the mad is that they can understand
eternal truth.

Man as a religious creature we hardly see directly, that is,
as an immediate object of full dramatic analysis. At first
glance, indeed, *religious* may seem rather too weighty a term
to denote the phase of personality which comes forward in
curses, prayers to, and observations on the ways of, supernatural powers, especially when the invocations and com-

2 5 5

ments are brief and casual rather than extensive and formally developed. But the fact is that apparently chance
words are a trustworthy index to the soul, and that certain
exclamations easily skipped over and generalizations by the
way are managed so consistently that they constitute a pattern of their own, one whose function is stressed by its integration with other meaning patterns. That the characters are
conscious of deity is likely to elude our attention because
of the absence of formal ritual and observance and of the
familiar Christian nomenclature; and the appellatives used
instead of say *Christ* or *Jesus* or *Holy Spirit* may seem so
general as to be neutral, as insignificant as the mild habitual
oath which comes indifferently out of careless conversation.
But addresses or references to God do not have, in *King
Lear,* the kind of casualness which means that they could be
transposed from the lines of one character to those of another, or systematically replaced, without loss, by expletives
or interjections of different meaning. They are consistent
with other elements in the characterization, and they help
define the point of view which governs characterization.
When France, commenting on his love for Cordelia and his
astonishment at Lear's treatment of her, exclaims, "Gods,
gods! 'tis strange that from their cold'st neglect/My love
should kindle to inflam'd respect" (I.i, 257–58), we see
the pious man's honest shock that in an ordered universe
Lear and Burgundy could so miss Cordelia's value and thus
willingly hand her over to someone else; perhaps he is even
a trifle surprised that it should be granted to him to have the
insight which they lack. When Cordelia prays,

> O you kind gods,
> Cure this great breach in his abused nature!

Th' untun'd and jarring senses, O, wind up
Of this child-changed father! (IV.vii, 14–17),

her prayer expresses not only her anguish but also a reliance
upon divinity that is analogous to her filial devotion; and
further there is the sense of god as the source of the ultimate
order which is always implied by the nature pattern. In the
vigorously self-reliant Kent we see no wavering of faith in
the gods as supporters of the moral order. When Kent, in his
opposition to Lear's disinheriting of Cordelia, first tries des-
perately to gain a hearing from the king, he addresses Lear
as King, father, master, and "As my great patron thought on
in my prayers" (I.i, 144). When Lear in anger swears by
Apollo, god of light, Kent vehemently insists that such an
oath in such a cause—that is, the blind carrying out of an
evil deed—will not work:

Now, by Apollo, king,
Thou swear'st thy gods in vain. (I.i, 162–63)

On the other hand his farewell wish to Cordelia is "The gods
to their dear shelter take thee, maid" (I.ii, 185). In his
soliloquy after he has been stocked on Cornwall's order,
Kent applies an old proverb to the king: "Thou out of heav-
en's benediction com'st/To the warm sun" (II.ii, 168–69);
he does not question, as in their common adversity he might,
the existence of a benediction from heaven. Then we find him
in another clash with Lear, this time amiable: Lear swears by
Jupiter that his son and daughter could not have set Kent in
the stocks: Kent replies in the echoic fashion which he occasionally uses, "By Juno,[2] I swear, ay!" (II.iv, 22) And
after Gloucester has provided shelter for Lear, Kent says
"The gods reward your kindness" (III.vi, 6). In insisting

on a fact or reflecting upon life, in opposing injustice or asking protection for its victim, in avowing loyalty or praising
a good deed, Kent always falls back upon, or implies, his
belief in the gods.[3]

In one of his first lines Albany addresses the gods. He has
heard Lear raging after his first clash with Goneril, and he
exclaims, "Now, gods that we adore, whereof comes this?"
(I.iv, 312) That the words are not casual is shown by the
earnestness of Albany later when he speaks of the gods or
invokes their aid. The very next time we see him, he has come
to understand Goneril, and his second speech to her contains
these words:

> If that the heavens do not their visible spirits
> Send quickly down to tame these vile offences,
> It will come
> Humanity must perforce prey on itself
> Like monsters of the deep. (IV.ii, 46–50)

He finds, indeed, that he can define Goneril only by identifying her with the principle of evil, the opposite of deity. His
next speech is:

> See thyself, devil!
> Proper deformity seems not in the fiend
> So horrid as in woman (IV.ii, 59–61),

and he adds, ". . . thou art a fiend" (66)—words which
gain something from the visions of fiends which Edgar has
been describing in earlier scenes. Then Albany learns of
Cornwall's death and comments,

> This shows you are above,
> You justicers, that these our nether crimes
> So speedily can venge (IV.ii, 78–80) ;

258

and later he says of Goneril and Regan,[4]

> This judgment of the heavens, that makes us tremble,
> Touches us not with pity. (V.iii, 231–32)

"The gods defend her," he prays (V.iii, 256), when Edmund discloses his plot against Cordelia's life. What is conspicuous in his lines is the unshaken faith in the just workings of divine order; here the religion pattern coincides in effect with the justice pattern. Whatever the deviations of empirical justice, whatever the alternatives from which one must in fact choose, Albany's lines imply a metaphysical justice upon which man must finally rely.

Significantly, Edgar's pretended madness takes, in large part, the form of religious mania. When he announces his plan to disguise himself, he remarks that Bedlam beggars "Enforce their charity" in different ways, "sometime with prayers" (II.iii, 19–20). "Away! the foul fiend follows me!" is his opening line (III.iv, 46) when he first appears disguised, and it is repeated and amplified throughout this and subsequent scenes (III.iv, 51 ff., 120 ff., 164; III.vi, 18, 25, 31). At one time he bursts forth with an abridgment of the decalogue (III.iv, 80 ff.), listing at least two commandments which have especial reference to the contents of the play: ". . . obey thy parents; . . . commit not with man's sworn spouse; . . . " His catalogue of vice includes ". . . swore as many oaths as I spake words and broke them in the sweet face of heaven" (III.iv, 90–92); he gives his own version of the Seven Deadly Sins (III.iv, 89 ff.); he identifies and describes different fiends (III.iv, 120 ff., 146, 148–49; III.vi, 7 ff., 33–34; IV.i, 56 ff.). Edgar's use of this kind of madness—for the images of which his creator leans so heavily upon Christianity—is evidence of the religious force at work in the society which the play represents; but, besides this symbolic value, the assumed mania adds another dramatic irony: it is not Edgar at all who is being pursued by the foul fiend but others, the ones who seem least aware of his existence.

As a straightforward observer of the history of the times, Edgar exhibits the same sober devoutness [5] that appears in Kent and Albany. When he sees his blinded father, he says, "O gods! Who is't can say 'I am at the worst'?" (IV.i, 25) He assures Gloucester, who has not been killed by his supposed leap from the cliff, "Thy life's a miracle" (IV.vi, 55), and he describes to Gloucester the diabolical "thing" (a creature with horns, a thousand noses, and eyes like full moons) who, Edgar says, was with him at the top of the cliff (IV.vi, 67–71). Edgar concludes, "It was some fiend" (72) —that is, an infernal tempter to suicide. The episode is very strongly reminiscent of the temptation of Christ (just as Lear, who enters ten lines later with his crown of nettles and weeds, is reminiscent of Christ in another way). Hence there is especial solemnity in the advice which Edgar gives Gloucester:

> Therefore, thou happy father,
> Think that the clearest gods, who make them honours
> Of men's impossibilities, have preserv'd thee (IV.vi, 72–74),

and in his subsequent commendation: "Well pray you, father" (IV.vi, 223). Before the battle he urges Gloucester, "Pray that the right may thrive" (V.ii, 2). But he does not presumptuously expect divinity to be a magical servant, nor does he despair when the battle is lost: it is after the defeat that he says, "Ripeness is all" (V.ii, 11). An important part of his charge against Edmund—it is his first specification—is "False to thy gods" (V.iii, 134), and after the victory, as if Shakespeare were continuing the Christian tone of the speeches of Edgar when he was Poor Tom, Edgar says to Edmund, "Let's exchange charity" (166). This charity, by showing his absolute convictions, mitigates the didactic flavor of the summary of their family history to which he comes immediately:

> The gods are just, and of our pleasant vices
> Make instruments to plague us. (V.iii, 170–71)

Edmund agrees. Of the ineluctability of justice we are again reminded.

GLOUCESTER'S FAITH

When we turn from Kent, Albany, and Edgar, whose religious feeling manifests itself especially in reiteration of the faith in a divinely administered just order, to Gloucester, who calls upon the gods more frequently than any of these, we deal with a man who—as victim of treachery, hatred, and physical torture and as bearer of an uneasy conscience—has suffered more profoundly than any of them, and in whose history there are special complications. It takes all of Gloucester's suffering to awaken his sense of deity. Early in the play, when he has seen the disinheriting of Cordelia and Edgar's apparent treachery, his only approach to the supernatural is his fuddled theorizing to the effect that "These late eclipses in the sun and moon portend no good to us" (I. ii, 112 ff.). Edmund skillfully uses this side of Gloucester by describing Edgar to him as "Mumbling of wicked charms, conjuring the moon/To stand's auspicious mistress" (II.i, 41–42)—a picture ironically at variance with what we have now seen to be Edgar's concept of the supernatural. Gloucester's astrologizing is exactly appropriate to the relative superficiality of his early views of things, and it is therefore a suitable foil for the deepening that occurs in him later. It is a familiar fact that he is the only superstitious character in the play; we should also observe, however, the relationship between his superstitiousness and his religiousness: [6] unlike Edmund, he at least is capable of supernaturalistic thought. When the brutality of the world comes to him, he forgets about astrology.

> By the kind gods, 'tis most ignobly done
> To pluck me by the beard,

he exclaims to Regan (III.vii, 35–36). He thinks of Lear as suffering in "hell-black night" (60) and he prophesies divine justice for Goneril and Regan: "But I shall see/The winged vengeance overtake such children" (65–66). He soon moves from oath and prophecy to prayers: when his first eye is put out, his only cry is "Give me some help!—O cruel! O you gods!" (III.vii, 70) The climactic suffering is mental: he is told that Edmund has betrayed him. He says,

> Then Edgar was abus'd.
> Kind gods, forgive me that, and prosper him! (III.vii, 91–92)

Like Lear, Gloucester reaches a turning point when he feels the need to pray for forgiveness for himself.

The blinding scene (III.vii) is brought to an end by an extremely interesting set of speeches by two servants. They express the hope, and belief, that Regan and Cornwall will come to justice; and the servants are justified by the outcome.

Then the final speech concerns Gloucester: the Third Servant
utters what amounts to a prayer, "Now heaven help him!"
(107) It is sometimes argued that in *King Lear* prayers are
not answered; but here is a good example of a prayer which
is answered. For Gloucester receives a twofold help: he is
reunited with Edgar, and he is saved by Edgar from despair.
His despair, as we have seen earlier (Chapter II), is consistent with his character as a whole. When we consider Gloucester's faith, we see his earlier tendency to think of moral
phenomena as the product of nonmoral causation (eclipses)
translating itself into theistic terms: man is the victim, not
of eclipses, but of the gods:

> As flies to wanton boys, are we to th' gods;
> They kill us for their sport. (IV.i, 36–37)

This point of view he appears to carry further when he says
to Edgar:

> Here, take this purse, thou whom the heavens' plagues
> Have humbled to all strokes; that I am wretched
> Makes thee the happier. (IV.i, 65–67)

Such lines are the expression of a mood—a mood which
leads Gloucester even to attempt suicide but which the play
as a whole does not admit as a valid expression of man's
condition.[7] Even in the depths Gloucester shows that he has
insight by which he can be saved. Immediately after his sardonic remark that his misery makes his guide happier, he
continues with the prayer which so much resembles that of
Lear in the storm:

> Heavens, deal so still!
> Let the superfluous and lust-dieted man,
> That slaves your ordinance, that will not see

Because he does not feel, feel your pow'r quickly:
So distribution should undo excess. . . . (IV.i, 67–71)

Again the religion pattern and the justice pattern coincide
in effect. When, finally, he attempts suicide, Gloucester's
speeches are pervaded by religious feeling. "Fairies and
gods/Prosper it with thee!" (IV.vi, 29–30) is his farewell
speech to Edgar. Then, before leaping, he kneels and makes
a formal prayer:

> O you mighty gods!
> This world I do renounce, and in your sights
> Shake patiently my great affliction off;
> If I could bear it longer and not fall
> To quarrel with your great opposeless wills,
> My snuff and loathed part of nature should
> Burn itself out. If Edgar live, O bless him.
> (IV.vi, 34–40)

Gloucester's motive, that is, is a fear that he may rebel
against divine will; his last thought is concerned with his
relationship to the deity. And he prays for the son whom he
had mistreated. In this context there is a profound meaningfulness in Edgar's statements "thy life's a miracle" (IV.vi,
55) and the gift of "the clearest gods" (IV.vi, 73) and in
Gloucester's becoming convinced that he has been tempted
by "some fiend" (72, 79): what might elsewhere be old,
reliable metaphors for the apparently marvelous are now
reflections of Gloucester's religious convictions. When he
resolves, then, to "bear/Affliction till it do cry out itself/
'Enough, enough,' and die" (75–77), we know that his resolution is grounded in belief. But things are not made easy
for Gloucester. In his self-distrust, he must pray again for
help:

You ever-gentle gods, take my breath from me;
Let not my worser spirit tempt me again
To die before you please! (IV.vi, 221–23)

Edgar's following words, "Well pray you" (223), are to be taken, then, not as conversational filler, but as an expression of his belief and of his profound satisfaction that Gloucester does pray. Edgar promises to find him a place of shelter from the battle, and Gloucester calls a blessing upon him:

Hearty thanks;
The bounty and the benison of heaven
To boot, and boot. (IV.vi, 228–30)

In Gloucester, then, we have seen a gradual transformation from the man in whom a jaunty worldliness is dominant to the man who finds it essential to be in harmony with the will of the gods; and, as we would expect of a character in whom such opposites come into play, there is, even after the transition, a discernible wavering. It is his old dubiety and skepticism, the reactivation of his old susceptibility to despair, once in a secular, now in a religious, context. Between the early and the late Gloucester we can see also an intermediate position which logically bridges the extremes: as the old courtier begins to realize that he and the court are in a serious situation, his first effort to come to grips with it is, in terms of understanding, his eclipse theory, and, in terms of action, the tendency to ride along with the dominant forces as an unpleasant necessity. He is a what-will-be-will-be, spirit-of-the-times man—until he is shaken and forced into the deeper channels of understanding of which he is capable. For the will of history he substitutes the will of god; his sense of authority moves from a temporal orientation to an eternal, from a naturalistic to a divine.

LEAR'S RELIGION

From the start Lear is constantly aware of the gods; in oaths and curses he tempestuously calls upon them as if they were spirits doing his bidding, so that his religious feeling serves, actually, as a perverse expression of the pride which is an ingredient in his tragic flaw. On the other hand, he is bound neither to the world nor to his own reason; to him the supernatural is a reality of every moment. He disinherits Cordelia

> . . . by the sacred radiance of the sun,
> The mysteries of Hecate, and the night;
> By all the operation of the orbs. . . . (I.i, 111–13)

Even in the midst of this tumultuous injustice Lear calls on the "orbs"—the ordered universe, the Nature to which later he will appeal directly. Lear is acting willfully, of course; but not consciously so; he feels in harmony with universal law. Later he repeats his oath in slightly different terms: [8] ". . . by the pow'r that made me,/I tell you all her wealth" (210–11). He banishes Kent "By Jupiter" (I.i, 181). Earlier he has begun an oath, "By Apollo" (I.i, 162) and been interrupted by Kent, "Thou swear'st thy gods in vain" (163); this leads to his calling Kent both "miscreant" (163) and "recreant" (169), terms which, though they may have simply the meaning of "scoundrel," suggest, by the original meanings of "unbeliever" and "apostate," which are difficult to ignore in the theological context, that Lear may be trying, perhaps more than subconsciously, to gain the advantage of being defender of the faith. And in one sense that is just his role in the play, though here he abuses the prerogatives of the defender.

These early speeches belong to Lear's quarrel with his real friends; from now on it is his supposed friends that drive him to call on the gods. When Goneril urges him to be "wise" and to "disquantity" his train, "Darkness and devils!" he exclaims (I.iv, 273) and prepares to visit and ask support of Regan. But before he goes, he calls upon "Nature . . . dear goddess" to bring a terrible curse on Goneril:

> Into her womb convey sterility.
>   . . . If she must teem,
> Create her child of spleen, that it may live
> And be a thwart disnatur'd torment to her.
> Let it stamp wrinkles in her brow of youth;
> With cadent tears fret channels in her cheeks;
> Turn all her mother's pains and benefits
> To laughter and contempt; that she may feel
> How sharper than a serpent's tooth it is
> To have a thankless child! (I.iv, 300 ff.)

It is interesting that Albany's words which immediately follow are also a prayer: "Now, gods that we adore, whereof comes this?" (312) Lear's prayer is a curse; in the early part of the play, as many critics have pointed out, he is full of the spirit of vengeance. It is important, however, to observe that in his spirit of vengeance he still calls upon gods: he is not the secular, self-complete avenger that Edmund is for a time, and Cornwall and Regan always are. Shakespeare has treated Lear's religiousness very complexly, but he leaves us in no doubt that it is a religious spirit. Human beings do pray for revenge. Yet the man who can pray for vengeance instead of summarily executing it can also pray in other ways. Lear's first shift in tone comes at the end of Act I:

Oh, let me not be mad, not mad, sweet heaven!
Keep me in temper; I would not be mad! (I.v, 49–50)

For the first time he humbly asks aid. But Lear is not yet
wholly transformed into the mild suppliant. When he finds
Kent in the stocks, he swears in incredulity: "By Jupiter, I
swear, no!" (II.iv, 21) When he talks to Regan, whose alliance with Goneril is not yet clear to him, he once again
curses Goneril: "All the stor'd vengeances of heaven fall/On
her ingrateful top" (II.iv, 164–65); and he really continues
his original invocation of Nature with prayers to "taking
airs," "nimble lightnings," and "fen-suck'd fogs" to blast
her (165–70). It is the last of his curses. When Regan admits
Goneril, Lear receives another sharp disillusionment, and
again feels the need of support:

O heavens,
If you do love old men, if your sweet sway
Allow obedience, if yourselves are old,
Make it your cause; send down, and take my part!
(II.iv, 192–95)

It is the last of these prayers that is ultimately answered. Perhaps the point made by Lear's prayers is that prayers are
not always answered exactly as or when the suppliant wishes;
he can expect justice, but he cannot dictate terms. Indeed,
what is suggested is that Lear's requests, insofar as they are
demands for a specific kind of revenge, recoil upon himself:
he is the victim of the "nimble lightnings," and his own "ingrateful top" receives the "stor'd vengeances." They are part
of his purgatory.

Lear is still capable of great violence, but in the gods pattern we find signs of his eventual moderation. He seems to
become reconciled to Goneril's treatment of him:

> I do not bid the Thunder-bearer shoot
> Nor tell tales of thee to high-judging Jove.
> Mend when thou canst. . . . (II.iv, 230–32)

But when he finds both sisters allied in obduracy, he bursts forth into his final speech before the storm—a speech that contains a prayer, half for aid in enduring, half for power to avenge:

> You heavens, give me that patience, patience I need!
> You see me here, you gods, a poor old man,
> As full of grief as age; wretched in both.
> If it be you that stirs these daughters' hearts
> Against their father, fool me not so much
> To bear it tamely; touch me with noble anger,
> And let not women's weapons, water-drops,
> Stain my man's cheeks! (II.iv, 274–81)

Always there is the awareness—it surpasses that of any other character—of superhuman beings upon whom man may call. The very storm suggests to him that the gods will bring justice upon the evil, however well the evil deeds have been concealed:

> Let the great gods,
> That keep this dreadful pudder o'er our heads,
> Find out their enemies now. Tremble, thou wretch . . .
> . . . and cry
> These dreadful summoners grace. (III.ii, 49–59)

From now on, however, the modification of Lear's tone is marked. He shows sympathy for the Fool in the storm (III. ii, 71–73), urges Kent and the Fool to enter a protecting hovel first (III.iv, 23–26), and then speaks the line which Granville-Barker calls "the crowning touch of all": [9] "I'll pray, and then I'll sleep" (27). He has achieved a new humility. His prayer is the great nine-line speech which we have already quoted; it begins, "Poor naked wretches," and it ends:

> Take physic, pomp;
> Expose thyself to feel what wretches feel,
> That thou mayst shake the superflux to them
> And show the heavens more just. (33–36)

Lear feels compassion, acknowledges his own failures, and lessons himself in terms of divine justice; like Gloucester, he has come to a new insight.

Even in Lear's madness some of his phrases indicate how thoroughly he is penetrated by religious experience. His daughter's insincere *ay*'s and *no*'s, by which they always agreed with him, were, he says "no good divinity" [10] (IV.vi, 100)—an error which he detected "when the thunder would not peace at my bidding" (103), the thunder, that is, which symbolized to him the working of the "great gods." He defines, in his Centaur-daughters, the "women all above": "to the girdle [they] do the gods inherit" (126–28), and he adds, "Beneath is all the fiend's./There's hell, there's darkness, there's the sulphurous pit; . . . " (129–30). After this application of Christian dualism it is altogether right for Lear to say to Cordelia, as he awakes from his restorative sleep, "Thou art a soul in bliss; but I am bound/Upon a wheel of fire . . . " (IV.vii, 46–47). His final two speeches to her before Edmund sends them off to what he intends as their death are full of religious feeling:

> When thou dost ask me blessing, I'll kneel down
> And ask of thee forgiveness. So we'll live,
> And pray, and sing, and tell old tales, and laugh

At gilded butterflies, and hear poor rogues

. . . .

And take upon's the mystery of things,
As if we were God's spies; and we'll wear out,
In a wall'd prison, packs and sects of great ones
That ebb and flow by th' moon. (V.iii, 10–19)

After Edmund's "Take them away," Lear continues:

Upon such sacrifices, my Cordelia,
The gods themselves throw incense. Have I caught thee?
He that parts us shall bring a brand from heaven
And fire us hence like foxes. (20–23)

Lear is contrite; they will humbly pray; they will think of
eternal things, of truths beyond the reach of the transitory
world; the gods approve of this sacrifice, this yielding of
things of the world—this renunciation which has come so
hard for Lear; Lear and Cordelia are thus united in the name
of heaven and can be separated only by heaven. The passage is permeated by Christian feeling.

As we have said, none of the passages which indicate
religious attitudes is very long, nor does any of them formally develop a theological position. But the passages are
sufficiently numerous to evidence a pervading consciousness
of deity, not a self-conscious adoption of suitable modes of
religious expression, but a largely unconscious, habitual
reliance upon divine forces whose primacy is unquestioned;
the passages occur most frequently in the lines of the chief
tragic characters, who must be chiefly concerned with the
fundamentals of human experience; and enough of them are
spoken by other characters (Kent, Albany, Edgar) to make
clear the religious climate of the action. Now we need to see
the function of that climate in the complete play. In determin-

ing what it is, we must examine the speeches of the remaining characters. Finally we shall see the relationship of the religion pattern to the synthesis of patterns which is the play.

But before we leave Lear and Gloucester we need to return briefly to one phenomenon in their spiritual history: both of them repent. They not only call upon the gods and pray; they also experience the self-abasement that governs the reordering of personality. They are contrite—as the characters to whom we now turn never are.

THE MEN OF THE WORLD

In Oswald there is no slight sign of religious awareness: the time of his death brings forth no prayer or compunction. Likewise with the "fiery" duke: although Cornwall shares Lear's propensity to violence and abusiveness, he does not have Lear's habit of calling upon the gods: at no time does he mention them or show any awareness of them. There is a startling similarity in the ways in which the men-of-the-world Oswald and Cornwall meet death: death is inopportune. Everyman's book of reckoning is all unready. "Untimely comes this hurt," complains Cornwall (III.vii, 99); "O, untimely death! Death!" laments Oswald (IV.vi, 256). Perhaps it is not going too far to suggest that their very use of *untimely* symbolizes the limitation of their interest to matters within time.

In Goneril there is never a trace of oath or prayer or other reference to the gods. To the end she is faithful to this world and her logical view of it: her last words are a defense of her *legal* untouchability. "Who can arraign me for't?" she asks (V.iii, 159). That Lear has already "arraigned" her—it is his word—she cannot know; that a higher power might arraign her never enters her mind.

In only one line does Regan exhibit what might be called religious consciousness. When Lear has come to her in a fury with Goneril and has called down furious curses upon Goneril, Regan exclaims: "O the blest gods! so will you wish on me,/When the rash mood is on" (II.iv, 171–72). But this is hardly a case of a threatened mortal's falling back on higher powers for support, for Regan is obviously in command of the whole situation in which she speaks thus; her words actually become, then, a piece of simulated piety which is consistent with her general strategy of trying to put Lear in the wrong. For a final confirmation of her nontheistic view of life we need only to compare her view of the tragic flaw with Edgar's. "The gods are just," says he, "and of our pleasant vices/Make instruments to plague us" (V.iii, 170–71). Regan's comparable lines are, ". . . to wilful men/The injuries that they themselves procure/Must be their schoolmasters" (II.iv, 305–307). She reduces the concept of divine nemesis to naturalistic terms: the burnt child will dread the fire. As in other ways, Regan is modern.

As in other phases of the dramatic material, Edmund is the most complex of the evil characters. With a piece of Regan-like hypocrisy he can assure Gloucester, concerning Edgar, ". . . I told him the revenging gods/'Gainst parricides did all their thunders bend" [11] (II.i, 47–48), and can say to Cornwall, while betraying his father Gloucester, "O heavens! that this treason were not, or not I the detector" [12] (III.v, 13–14). When he concludes his opening speech by praying, "Now, gods, stand up for bastards" (I.ii, 22), he

has no audience: he is, with his phallic pun, privately enjoying a parody of a conventional invocation. There is less
lightheartedness in the apostrophe with which he begins this
speech: "Thou, Nature, art my goddess; to thy law/My
services are bound" (I.ii, 1–2); but his subsequent lines
indicate that here he hardly goes beyond self-worship—the
essence of his character which brings forth Edgar's accusation, "False to thy gods" (V.iii, 134). Yet Edmund's critique
of Gloucester's astrologizing is not antisupernatural. When
he sneers, ". . . as if we were . . . fools by heavenly compulsion; . . . and all that we are evil in, by a divine thrust-
ing on" (I.ii, 133–37), he might be construed as defending
the gods against moral burdens which irresponsible human
beings want to pass on to them. He demands moral responsibility—at that point giving voice to a Christian concept such
as those we sometimes find in Lear and Gloucester. There is
a familiar echo of Christian terms in his reply to Edgar's
challenge: "With the hell-hated lie o'erwhelm thy heart"
(V.iii, 147), but, as we saw in Chapter IX, all these last
speeches of his, made in public and under pressure, are suspect. The one which seems to me most nearly to escape from
the burden of hypocrisy is his assent to Edgar's "the gods
are just" and his own estimate of his life—"the wheel is
come full circle" (174), which, I have already suggested,
recants his nature worship and implies a submission to universal law.

There are two main interpretations of Edmund: one is
that he is a wholly evil person who can adopt an expedient
hypocrisy, and the other—held by Knight—is that at the end
he acknowledges his error and becomes a proper tragic
character. Both these views, I believe, do not give due weight

to the ambiguity which makes Edmund more elusive than either view implies. Both have some rightness. Edmund is evil and hypocritical. On the other hand, as we saw in Chapter IX, there is a soft spot in his rationalism, one which manifests itself largely in sentimentality. Yet, in one form or another, he does show much more awareness of the idea of divinity than any other evil character. He hardly becomes religious—or a tragic figure. But in him there is some residuum of a mythic habit of mind which is one of the marks of the old regime against which the revolution, though the revolutionaries attend only to immediate and "practical" objectives, is actually being made. He can for a moment before death feel that the gods do rule. That is all. But such a residuum we do not find in Oswald, Cornwall, Goneril, and Regan, even though the insufficiency of Goneril's and Regan's rationalism is dramatically demonstrated by their falling, without, of course, an intentional change of direction, into irrational modes of conduct. Thus they "weaken"; but they do not weaken to the extent of calling upon the gods. Unlike Gloucester, in whom adversity awakens a dormant religious sense, the sisters in their downfall still rely stubbornly upon themselves. There is no diminution of their pride, as there is in that of Gloucester and Lear. Suffering transforms Lear from an angry king, vehemently demanding divine support, into a suppliant. Cordelia, Kent, Albany, and Edgar pray.

Remember that the best and greatest among mankind are those who do themselves no worldly good. Every successful man is more or less a selfish man. The devoted fail.

Thomas Hardy, *Jude the Obscure*

*   *   *

Nay, since he hath found a blessed end, my children, cease from this lament; no mortal is hard for evil fortune to capture.

Sophocles, *Oedipus at Colonus*

*   *   *

But death certainly, and life, honor and dishonor, pain and pleasure, all these things equally happen to good men and bad, being things which make us neither better nor worse. Therefore they are neither good nor evil.

Marcus Aurelius, *Meditations*

CHAPTER XI

THIS GREAT STAGE

CONCLUSION

WITH THE final enrichment of the materials by the religion pattern, the dramatic structure begins to stand out in all its comprehensiveness. In conflict we see two types of human conduct: on the one side, the traditional and the religious; on the other, the rationalistic, the individualistic, the opportunistic, seeking freedom from the kinds of restraint to which the former are subject. The religion pattern, which we have examined last, really pulls together all the other patterns which, taken as a whole, are Shakespeare's technique for giving the utmost fullness of expression to the complexities of human experience, and hence the means by which his play makes the impression of universality to which critic after critic testifies. All these inner organisms of image and symbol contribute to the total statement of the play; each of them, insofar as it incorporates its truth in a paradox, is a restatement of the central theme on a reduced scale—a restatement which never merely repeats, but amplifies, enriches, supports, and gives a new perspective to the central theme. For each paradox poses the problem of The World. The religion pattern, through which we see not only an age that is technically pagan but also a play that is pervaded by Christian influences,[1] exhibits the kind of belief which makes

277

it possible to assert the lesser importance of the world. That
is, there is a realm of eternal law and justice, of enduring
reality which demands the loyalty of mortals, and through
that loyalty they achieve their humanity. This achievement is
the ultimate one, no matter what men's fate in the world. This
is not to say that men ought to fail in the world: it is apparent,
at the end, that Edgar and Albany have arrived at some competence in the world. But they, it is true, have been through
a special kind of fire. The great in the world do not often go
through that fire, or do not survive it; the poor and the outcast in the world, whose life itself is a kind of tempering fire,
are the likeliest to earn the realm of spirit. To be great in the
world is to see well, to be well dressed, to be the lion and
the fox, to reason lucidly—and yet somehow to lose the
longer vision, and the world as well. The players on this
great stage are fools when, with so large a humanity to come
to ripeness, they yet seek so little with it, and even deny it.
Hence we must cry when we come here. But on the same
stage are the Fools—and the mad—who redeem mortality.

King Lear is universal in that its problem is an eternal
one. Yet Shakespeare sees that problem in a particularly
bright light because he catches it at the moment in time at
which the conflict in man comes to the surface in its most
complete and uncompromising form. The conflict is in man,
and that Shakespeare makes clear; but by making it also a
conflict between generations, he gives it a historical formulation. The conflict is eternal; but it has also temporal form.

THE HISTORICAL CRISIS

At an extraordinarily early time Shakespeare got hold of
the modern problem, got hold of it when the Renaissance

had, so to speak, barely started it on its way. Lear, in one sense, represents the old order, and the play becomes the tragedy of that order.[2] Lear represents the confusions and distractions to which an old order is liable—arrogance, hasty and indiscriminate action, a complacency and loss of equilibrium which encourage the lust for self-aggrandizement and novelty that are always latently present, and even a susceptibility to the errors which become the heart of the new order. In Gloucester, the passive man, we see especially the laziness of the old order, the tendency to lose sight of the ancient sanctions and to fall in with the spirit of the times, with the secularism that is always striving for autonomy. Thus, careless, too fond of ease, quick to draw conclusions, ready to evade political and moral responsibilities, the representatives of the old order are the first easy victims for a new order which is coolly calculating, on the make, quick to take advantage of flaws which sharp minds detect in the old men whose roots are in the past. In tracing the sufferings of Lear and the contortions into which a society is thrown by the emergence of his tragic flaw in action which has public consequences, and in choosing the particular ramifications of theme which we have observed, Shakespeare presents a conflict which must suggest a type of historical convulsion.

Now it is of importance to observe that any historical study which dramatizes the passing of the old order is in danger of becoming a sentimental lament; and to mourn the old as old is to fall into a lachrymose antiquarianism. Not that that which has become old may not have acquired, in the process of aging, as a kind of symbol of its success against time, a dignity of tone which can exact a measure of aesthetic regard. But it is the business of the tragedian, not to record the chance graces that years may bestow, but to deal with the essential strength by means of which a once-young order attains to ripeness, to get hold of the validating insights the shutting off of which is one of the premises of the new order (as well as the inner darkening which is a stimulus to try a new kind of light). The study of the old order at the level of its intuitions of truth is precisely the method of *King Lear;* and the time of the study is the moment of the dimming of the old creative intuitions, the dimming which gives access to a lower order of insight, lower but none the less grounded in the nature of man.

Given this clash of forces whose ramifications extend deep into the nature of man (Goneril, the representative of the new order, is of the flesh and blood of Lear, the representative of the old), Shakespeare outlines, in intense dramatic compactness, the overwhelming problems which beset both the individual and the age at the historical crisis. When shrewd minds lose the religious sense, break free from counterbalancing forces, upset "the plague of custom," and rationalize primitive drives (mind plus animal), the new world of power, of *de facto* sanctions, is going to inflict bitter injuries. Age must suffer—because of its own weaknesses, because it cannot be accommodated in a rational order, because, finally, it symbolizes what is being overthrown. Old age is the old age of an age.[3] Images of disease and injury and torture point the suffering of a world distracted by ripping out of old foundations. While some men are powerless and naked, others are overdressed, both in their hypocrisy and in their grasp of nine points of the law; as a sequence of images makes clear, clothes may protect, but they may also conceal; they signify the constant confusion of appearance and reality when standards are in flux. While some men in anguish seek justice, others identify it with their whims; trial scenes range from apparently legal brutalities to maniacal justice. Values which had long been accepted are overturned, and with a host of images men seek to identify and lay hands upon that which will endure. But some in their confusion get hold of tragically mistaken principles of evaluation; others are governed by the interests of the moment. Human nature seems to have abdicated, and human forms seem dominated by animal-like beings in whom sexuality, reckless ambition, and total indifference to all restraints are paramount. Hence man's fate approaches that of the animal. Not only in outright destructive characters, but even in those who represent conserving forces is the animal heredity visibly at work. Nature herself appears shaken and drawn into the vortex; her own convulsions beat physically upon the unprotected, and symbolize the moral storm afflicting a chaotic world. The rationalist claims her sponsorship; but at the same time the injured and distraught call upon her to redress violations of order. If for a time they appear to call futilely, the latter do not lose hope.

MODES OF UNDERSTANDING

The confusion and horror of distorted life give pre-eminence to the problem of understanding, and philosophic or quasi-philosophic struggles interpenetrate the battles for physical and moral survival. Goneril and Regan never waver in their concept of the world as a pliable entity that can be manipulated to advantage—even when experience forcefully demonstrates that they are not wholly "free"; in their concept of reality as amenable to their powers of calculation;

in their hatred for their father—for his age—as a symbol of the restraints upon the personal appetite in which they find their motivation. Edmund is akin to them in his enthroning of appetite ("Nature") and in his attitude to the old order; they coolly evaluate their father's defects and he attacks his father's astrological determinism. Edmund asserts the importance of the will that Gloucester wants irresponsibly to deny. But he inconsistently moves toward his own kind of determinism when he says "I should have been that I am"(I.ii, 143) and uses such a phrase as "despite of mine own nature" (V.iii, 244)—a naturalistic determinism, one is tempted to say, of a modern sort. He is illegitimate and he has a grievance: heredity and environment determine and justify his quality and his conduct. Now this position is in illuminating antithesis with the supernaturalistic determinism of Gloucester (just as Regan's psychological view of the lesson of experience is the antithesis of Edgar's moral and theological view). Edmund's skepticism is intellectually more respectable than Gloucester's credulity; yet the skepticism, as is symbolized by Edmund's incomplete fidelity to his new credo, is never a guide to moral values, whereas the credulity only temporarily interferes with the coming into action of an essentially uncorrupted view of things. The superstitious man becomes the religious man; his salvation is that he finds valid sustaining forces; he at least believes in the superhuman. There is a remarkable consistency in the portrayal of Gloucester. On one level, Gloucester's what-will-be-will-be attitude is what retards his recognition of evil in the usurper; on another, it is the sin of despair—precisely the sin that appears more openly when he wants to commit suicide. His spiritual darkness is perfectly symbolized by his blindness. But Gloucester is not alone in the difficulty of seeing: in the racked world which the play presents with dramatic fullness, the problem of understanding is always a crushing one, and the recurrent imagery of sight constantly underscores the failure to see, or the kind of seeing, by which the characters are in part defined. Darkness and light, eyes that glare or squint or even shed tears of pity— here are further variations upon the theme of blindness and perception.

The ultimate failure to find order in the world is madness, and the madness theme in the play is the most profound indication of the world in convulsions. A mad world drives men to madness, either as a pathological state or as a consciously sought refuge imposing humiliations that only desperation could accept. But if madness is asylum, it is also, paradoxically, the beginning of illumination; the feigned madman who, in part the victim of his own inertness and gullibility, had to seek safety as a lunatic, gains a new practical and moral insight and acts energetically in accordance with both; the Fool, who gained immunity by means of discordancies and irrelevancies which appeared to the unknowing to represent the innocuousness of essential disorganization, outlines the way of the world with relentless insight; the mad Lear, utterly baffled by the dissolution of a world to whose centrifugal movement he had given great impetus, yet finds in his mania a kind of order, an imaginative grasp of a disintegrating universe, a firmer sense of evil, of the ills of humanity which he had ignored, and of his own complicity in the breakdown of society. With regard to the central problem of understanding, wisdom, insight, there are other groups of characters. For Cordelia and Kent, the problem hardly exists; come what may, they act in accordance with their "bond"; duty is knowledge, and catastrophe irrelevant. Albany comes late into a recognition of the issues—and here he is related to Gloucester and Edgar. Gloucester and his two sons are related in their common speculative tendency, their groping, if incomplete, toward the formulae which define experience. But structurally the most significant of the groups is the Goneril-Regan-Edmund trio: to Lear's reason-in-madness there is opposed their tainted reason, a self-confident, unshackled sharpness of mind, shrewd and penetrating as far as it goes, but incapable, ultimately, of detecting its own frailty and limitations, of formulating a workable pattern of existence, and of bringing to them the saving insights of men of imagination. It is these devotees of the analytical mind, finally, who—with such exception as must be made for Edmund's partial defection—are less perceptive than Edgar, less understanding than the Fool, more mad than Lear; and who, to fill out the pattern, are more deluded and less free than their victims, are less "successful" than those who had stuck to a waning cause, to symbols apparently outmoded. It is they, too, and their followers, who do not call upon the gods, as Edgar and Albany and Kent do, and—more markedly—Gloucester and Lear, although, even to these devout, the gods may appear inscrutable.

THE MODES OF EXPERIENCE

Shakespeare builds into all the thematic patterns the dualistic structure by which he organizes experience for the play. In the background there is the metaphysical dualism of good and evil, with the definition of which he is ultimately concerned. Since the drama does not deal immediately with metaphysics, however, but with actual complex human beings who do not always fall simply into categories of good and evil, the dualism which impinges most directly upon our consciousness is that of the world of experience. Empirically we do not find ideal choices: but we do find alternatives which by mutual qualification define the problem. On one hand we have the naked philosopher; on the other, the well-dressed man of opportunity. The naked man is defenseless, but also innocent; the well-dressed man is protected against immediate blows, but "sophisticated." On one hand we have age, bumbling and bamboozled but able, through suffering, to achieve insight; on the other, active and direct youth, not fooled by present facts or by other men, but ultimately fooled by themselves. We have those who to their own apparent loss aid and defend age; those who to their apparent profit betray it. The well-meaning are taken in; the shrewd and wide-awake deceive. On one hand there is madness which can yet accommodate a sense of justice; on the other, sanity that makes a travesty of judicial procedure. Here there are the blind who eventually come to see; there, the sharp-sighted who, confronted by the whole of life, evince a fatal myopia. Here is the madness with which a fine understanding is yet compatible; and, on the other side, a close-packed reasonableness which misses the major point. Here is the imagination apparently out of hand; there, the reason, the practical good sense, which stifles the imagination. Here is the reliance upon gods who seem not to hear; there, the secular self-sufficiency which cannot hear the gods.

There are those who do what they want and call it "Nature"; there are those to whom right and justice, even though they are not apparent in the facts of the present, are "Nature." To see, to be sane, is to be in accord with nature. But there is such a thing as seeing too well, being too sane; "nature" may develop a constrictive hardness. The convulsion of nature is extraordinary, violent, and destructive; but again it is the safety valve, the break in the hardened pattern, the means of escape from the inflexible, factual, commonplace enclosure; it may break and overwhelm, but it is also an awakening force. Man is bound to earth, but he need not always lie on earth; to the animal he is always kin, in deed and status, but the ties of kinship need not determine his whole fate. If he will, the gods may inherit beyond the girdle.

Shakespeare does not finally, then, offer us merely a set of horrifyingly defective alternatives, though he indicates that at the level of experience life may often seem to fall into such a pattern. Nor does he bitterly claim pre-eminent value for nakedness, disease, suffering age, injury, blindness, and madness because these states here coincide with higher spiritual perception. The unmodified horror of the blinding scene, and of the madness as clinical fact, should guard against the view that Shakespeare is sardonically glorifying states which terrify mankind. Clothes and youth and wholeness and sight and sanity can be and should be goods: but they do not guarantee moral and spiritual insight. If the mad reason, the sane may rave. Shakespeare does not choose sides in any obvious sense; nor does he say that the sides, though characteristic of experience, exhaust experience. For, throughout the verbal and dramatic patterns of the play, throughout the structural dualities, there is a consistent and continual intimation: in the cosmos there is a justice (whatever the injustice in fact), there is an order (whatever the chaos in fact), there is an underlying reality (whatever the deceptiveness of appearance) ; in man there is a sight (whatever the blindness in fact) and an imaginative understanding (whatever the rationalistic obtuseness that may periodically dominate him) by which he may seize upon the realities necessary to his survival. These are the implications of the key words in the play. What is explicit is the distance by which—at certain phases in their history—men, because they are so caught in the world, fall short of the needful spiritual insight, and the anguish with which they attain or cling to it.

THE TONE OF KING LEAR

To us, in our world, *Lear* should not be too difficult or seem too bitter. We are familiar enough with the revolt against sanctions, with the cult of success, and, above all, with the rejection of all the claims that are not consistent with the belief that our sole destiny is mastery of the immediate, tangible world. We have moved far enough in history so that we would hardly find it necessary to use the parenthesis which Bradley inserts in a sentence on Goneril. Bradley calls her a "most hideous human being"; then he adds "(if she is one). . . ."[4] For we have seen many Gonerils—not always at a melodramatic distance—and become aware of the Goneril element in humanity. We can see a world in solution, an exacerbated sense of circumstance, a preoccupation with the here and now, a mastery of practical psychology and of the manipulation of the human mind, an unprecedentedly skillful awareness of things and objects—and a despair of the longer vision. We should have no trouble in seeing that Shakespeare has caught a world *in extremis,* when the quality of man's reasoning about reality is the main problem; in seeing that he has caught metaphysical evil in a particular historical formulation. We should easily understand the rightness of his picture. When the old order changeth, it is far less likely that wild bells ring in the new than that utter human anguish precedes and accompanies the enlargement, if so it be, of the old insight, or the recovery of an old insight which in the context seems new. All that anguish Shakespeare has infused into the play. What is remarkable is the imaginative leap by which he has got hold of human character at a relatively late stage, has caught it after it has moved a vast distance along the road which Faustus had opened. Lear and the Faustus of Shakespeare's contemporary, Marlowe, make comparable tragic errors in the realm of value judgments; but Faustus is a private figure, Lear a public; so the latter's astigmatism is attended by a wider reverberation of evil consequence. But Lear wants ease, Faustus power; and the implications of the latter's experiment are carried further by Lear's elder daughters. Faustus worked by means of the principle of evil and only halfheartedly attempted to deny its reality; for Goneril and Regan, no such principle exists; they need never think about it; they have no problem of conscience. All is tactics. Thus Shakespeare presents the human being as he looks when he has sloughed off all restraints, all disciplinary concepts, and the vital imaginative function, and when he moves in terms of reason and appetite. Faustus at least has imaginative grandeur; Goneril and Regan only desire and calculate. With such a vision Shakespeare might well be bitter. But the striking fact is the balance of the picture, the absence of cynicism. Shakespeare is able to imagine humanity having discarded all its essential humanizing influences, to see evil at work and to analyze that evil in fundamental terms, that is, as the product of rootless intellect. At the same time he can imagine some human beings clinging to the insights, to the imaginative integrity, through which their personal honor is secured.

But he is not sentimental: he spares no character the suffering that, when evil is loose in the world, must come both to tragic protagonist and to the bystander who, because no one is isolated, is enmeshed in the general human situation. The real sentimentality would be to consider the play cynical and "pessimistic" and unendurable. This sentimentality, which is not unfamiliar today, is that of finding evil too unpleasant to face. To the sentimentalist who prefers to see reality in some more comforting guise, Shakespeare may seem "bitter" or "morbid." Behind this error in emotional response lies a general error of understanding accompanied by a specific error in the reading of *Lear*. This error in reading is a failure to see the play as a *contrast in the quality of lives*. What saves the play from cynicism is not that some "good" characters do escape the heavy doom of most, but that Shakespeare can imagine characters who in the quality of their living resist entirely all the influences to evil that surround them and do not, even under threat of grossest torture and cruelty, capitulate to the enemy or yield any jot of honor, and that he can present them firmly and unsentimentally. He can imagine, too, not only the depraved characters, but also those who repent and to whom suffering is meaningful. He can imagine, above all, not only characters who retain their insight when the world argues compellingly for blindness, but also those who, partially stricken with blindness, can regain their lost intuition of truth. Lear and

Gloucester do not persist in error, as a cynic might make them do; rather they come to distinguish, one from another, their two kinds of children, and thus, at last, to distinguish, and make a right choice between, the kinds of moral capacity in themselves which are externalized in their children; for the children, by being children instead of unrelated persons of the same moral composition, become, on one plane, symbols of the clash within the protagonists. It is looking within that demands the finest visual equipment. That the saving perspective, which brings evil into focus, is possible to man even after he has made serious mistakes, is the play's ultimate assertion.

Pessimism does not consist in seeing evil injure good; it is instead the inability to see good; or it is to conclude only that evil is mistaken for good; or to discover total depravity, but no grace. To find the play painful or shocking is to be unable to grasp quality as quality, and to substitute success for quality; it is to think in terms of the naïve expectation that longevity, as well as invulnerability to mortal ills, is the reward of virtue.[5] This is the error of Lear at the beginning of the play—the introduction of irrelevant quantitative standards. Quantity of life or quantity of immunity to suffering has, alas, no relationship to moral integrity, or to quality of life which evokes admiration and which is the irreducible residuum after everything else is gone. To assume or seek such relationship is to substitute reward for merit, accident for substance; it is to move from tragedy to melodrama. Shakespeare stays firmly at the tragic level in his dramatic analysis of evil and of the fate of characters whom evil touches, of their ways of saving themselves even though subjected to deprivation and torture and death. In several of his patterns of meaning he poses the problem of the nature of security against outrageous fortune; in terms of the play, the answer is that there is none. Or at least there is none in a worldly sense. Man may achieve ripeness—that fulfillment of his humanity by which he may come to inner security. Thus he need not yield to fortune, nor need he be hood-winked by it. In his ripeness he may see beyond fortune. Shakespeare holds firmly to final value of imaginative insight,[6] and the play argues its persistence in a world of alien values. But Shakespeare makes no concessions to the sentimental. Nor does he despair.[7]

NOTES

NOTES FOR CHAPTER I

PRELIMINARIES

[1] Translated from J. W. Goethe, *Shakespeare und Kein Ende, Werke* (Stuttgart, 1867), XXXI, 302.

[2] Robert Penn Warren, "A Poem of Pure Imagination: An Experiment in Reading," in Samuel Taylor Coleridge, *The Rime of the Ancient Mariner* (New York, 1946), p. 117.

[3] Milton S. Mayer, "Socrates Crosses the Delaware," *Harpers Magazine,* CLXXIX (1939), 71. Mr. Mayer goes on to list, as another mark of the great book, that it "must be a work of fine art—it must have an immediate intelligibility and style which will excite and discipline the ordinary mind by its form alone." This statement raises a number of issues that need careful questioning. One thing is clear at first glance: multiple significances and "immediate intelligibility" are entirely incompatible. A family of diverse but reconcilable meanings do not become clear immediately; in fact, it is doubtful whether, in Mr. Warren's terms, we can ever become totally ready to deal with this aspect of greatness.

[4] In *The Well Wrought Urn* (New York, 1947) Cleanth Brooks has assembled diverse poems from three different centuries to show that they are susceptible of analysis by the same general method, a method which he had already applied to rather wide literary areas in *Modern Poetry and the Tradition* (Chapel Hill, 1939).

[5] John Crowe Ransom, "On Shakespeare's Language," *Sewanee Review,* LV (1947), 181–98.

[6] Montgomery Belgion, "Heterodoxy on *Moby Dick,*" *Sewanee Review,* LV (1947), 124. Cf. Hudson on *King Lear:* "Certainly, in none of his plays do we more feel the presence and power of that wonderful diction, not to say language, which he gradually wrought out and built up as the fitting and necessary organ of his thought" (Rev. Henry N. Hudson, *Shakespeare's Tragedy of King Lear* [Boston, 1891], p. 13).

[7] As Mr. Warren says, ". . . the analysis cannot render the poem, the discursive activity cannot render the symbolical" (*op. cit.,* p. 116).

[8] Caroline F. E. Spurgeon, *Shakespeare's Imagery and What It Tells Us* (New York and Cambridge, 1936). Cf. Harley Granville-Barker, *Prefaces to Shakespeare* (Princeton, 1946), I, 281–83. Granville-Barker notes various examples of striking repetition of words within a scene.

[9] Spurgeon, *op. cit.,* p. 5.

[10] Miss Spurgeon is as much concerned with relating imagery to the mind of the playwright as she is with relating it to the total effect of a play. The images "reveal to us the man himself" (p. 11). "There are certain things there can be no question Shakespeare himself fears and hates, . . ." (p. 75). ". . . we can obtain quite clear glimpses into some of the deeper thoughts of Shakespeare's mind through this oblique method, . . ." (p. 146). And so on. If this procedure is not to get out of hand, rather severe qualifications need to be set up as to the type of conclusions which may be drawn about the dramatist's mind by a study of his imagery. What one can do, of course, is to state, at a descriptive level, that such-and-such a dramatist tends regularly to present such-and-such a concept by means of such-and-such an image. But to leap from his poetic practice to assumptions about personality and philosophy is to come near to the old fallacy of reading dramatic lines as if they were statements of the writer's opinion. The completed work of art is a considerable clue to the type of mind which the artist possesses; but generalizations about that mind can follow only upon an understanding of the work as a structural whole. Such an understanding presumably must follow—at least in the case of a work mature enough to be interesting—careful analysis and resynthesis. At any rate, hypotheses about the artist can hardly be based on an element or two, however important these are, among all those that together constitute the whole.

[11] *Ibid.*, p. 213.

[12] *Ibid.*, p. 216.

[13] *Ibid.*, p. 335.

[14] It is possible that Miss Spurgeon's stopping short of the theoretical position toward which her materials and method point is in part due to the ironic circumstance that, for all of her immense assemblage of data on Shakespeare's language, she has not always read her plays meticulously enough. She finds, for instance, that in *Lear* the images which have primacy in the creation of tone—aside from the animal images which of course were observed long ago—are those of bodily tension, strife, and injury (pp. 338 ff.). That these images are present and do work in the way she describes is of course true. But they are still not the most important images in the play, as I hope to show later. Had Miss Spurgeon observed other important recurrences, she would have been driven, I think, toward some revision of her theoretical position; but since she has not observed them, she concludes that "it might be possible to know *King Lear* or *Macbeth* very well without realising the dominating symbolic motives in these plays" (p. 349). I doubt it.

[15] The problem of the nature of awareness lies outside the proper boundaries of the present study. But it is clear that awareness may range from the rationally formulated which occurs in the expository essay to an "immediate and intuitive" (Warren, *op. cit.*, p. 116) grasp of poetic elements whose impact is felt even though they may not be formally distinguished.

[16] This is of course the assumption of many individual critical acts. A relatively recent example is Mr. Warren's in his analysis of *The Ancient Mariner* (*op. cit.*, p. 94). Other critical analyses which proceed upon the same assumption are Leo Kirschbaum, "Shakspere's Cleopatra," *The Shakespeare Association Bulletin*, XIX (1944), 161–71, and Robert B. Heilman, "The Tragedy of Knowledge," *Quarterly Review of Literature*, II (1946), 316–32. Paul V. Kreider's *Repetition in Shakespeare's Plays* (Princeton, 1941) is principally concerned with repetition of plot situations, but Professor Kreider does deal with a number of cases of repetition of key words and images. He does not theorize much about the function of repetition. See pp. vii–viii, 159, 194, 214. The latest Shakespearian study based on iterative imagery is Richard D. Altick's "Symphonic Imagery in Richard II," *PMLA*, LXII (1947), 339–65. This article contains some theoretical discussion of repetition. Early intimations of the importance of repetition appear in the chapter "Some Notes on a Feature in Shakspere's Style" in E. E. Kellett's *Suggestions: Literary Essays* (Cambridge, 1923), pp. 57–78, and in Elizabeth Holmes's *Aspects of Elizabethan Imagery* (Oxford, 1929). Miss Holmes's main interest is in showing that metaphysical imagery is used by the Elizabethan dramatists. At one place she virtually identifies recurrency as a fact of Shakespearian imagery (p. 40).

[17] *The Well Wrought Urn*, pp. 29–30. In "Symbolism in Shakespeare," *Modern Language Review*, XLII (1947), 9–23, Elmer E. Stoll challenges Mr. Brooks's conclusions and attacks generally the methods of "present-day high-brow criticism" (p. 13). He asserts that the symbolism, irony, and paradox often detected in Shakespeare by the "new" critics simply are not there. But he does not provide a satisfactory alternative way of dealing with the problems of poetic language which manifestly are there.

[18] *The Well Wrought Urn*, pp. 45–46. Cf. G. Wilson Knight, *The Christian Renaissance* (Toronto, 1933), Chapters I to III.

[19] Miss Spurgeon comments upon the way in which, in Shakespearian practice, a cluster of related images tends to be called up together (*op. cit.*, pp. 186–87).

[20] *Op. cit.*, p. 300.

[21] *The Well Wrought Urn*, p. 37.

[22] The use of this assumption in interpretation is important in the various books of G. Wilson Knight, several of which I shall refer to in detail. At the moment I want to call attention to T. S. Eliot's approving comment on Knight's method in his Introduction to Knight's *The Wheel of Fire* (Oxford, 1930), pp. xvii ff. In *Seven Types of Ambiguity* (London, 1930), William Empson has a very interesting section on the relationship of one part of the dramatic poem to another by means of dramatic irony (pp. 58 ff.), by which, he says, the reader "can be reminded of the rest of the play while he is reading a single part of it." The work of genius, he says, has a "style" which "carries

its personality into every part of it" (p. 58). I suspect that A. C. Bradley has in mind the complexity of intraorganic relationships when he calls *Lear* "one of the world's greatest poems" (*Shakespearean Tragedy*, 2d ed. [London, 1918], p. 277), says that it appeals "not so much to dramatic perception as to a rarer and more strictly poetic kind of imagination," and decides that it is a great poem but an imperfect drama (p. 248). See also his remarks on p. 259. It is hardly necessary to remark that the distinction between poem and drama raises more difficulties than it settles.

Cf. Roy W. Battenhouse, "*Measure for Measure* and the Christian Doctrine of Atonement," *PMLA*, LXI (1946), 1029–59. According to Professor Battenhouse, the meaning of *Measure for Measure* finds expression both in the plot elements and in the imagery. See especially p. 1044.

[23] The quotations from *Oedipus the King* are from the translation by R. C. Jebb. I have checked the quoted passages with the Greek text. That the technique here described, which does appear in at least this one play by Sophocles, was a familiar practice with Aeschylus is indicated by W. B. Stanford, *Aeschylus in His Style* (Dublin, 1942), pp. 96 ff. With regard to the *Oedipus*: the sight pattern is considerably amplified by the frequent references to Apollo throughout the play.

[24] There is a more elaborate and more precise statement of the theme of *Oedipus* in Cleanth Brooks and Robert B. Heilman, *Understanding Drama: Twelve Plays* (New York, 1948).

[25] Mark Van Doren calls Lear "a great poet" and makes his poetic gift the chief basis of a contrast between him and Gloucester, "a plain man" of prose (*Shakespeare* [New York, 1939], pp. 239 ff.).

[26] Knight lays a great deal of stress on the ennoblement of humanity through suffering (*The Wheel of Fire*, pp. 214 ff.). His purgatorial view of tragedy keeps recurring throughout his works.

[27] *The Nation*, CLXIV (1947), 309. Mr. Blackmur is describing *The Ancient Mariner* as it is seen through Mr. Warren's analysis.

[28] The task of proving that Shakespeare's two plots are properly unified has been undertaken by editors and commentators at least as far back as Schlegel. Much has been said of the way in which the plots are intertwined, of the increase in intensity which comes from the use of a secondary plot, of the contribution to a sense of universality made by the double plot, and, finally, of the ironic effects made possible by comparable parental errors and the relationships between the Lear and Gloucester families. It is worth noting that the Gloucester plot is initiated only after the Lear plot is well under way and is effectually ended when Lear has still much left to do—a very useful chronological discipline of the materials. But the most subtle and successful means of subordinating Gloucester—insofar as subordination, rather than thematic elaboration, is the means of organizing the various plot elements— appears in IV.vi, in which Gloucester appears finally as a part of the materials

upon which Lear's mind works in its appraisal of the world. This is the climactic scene in which Lear's madness actually encompasses a very penetrating insight, so that the gnomic Edgar can summarize paradoxically, "Reason in madness" (IV.vi, 179). In Lear's synthesis are such lines as these on Gloucester, "Your eyes are in a heavy case, your purse in a light. You see how the world goes. . . . A man may see how the world goes with no eyes" (150–54). Insofar as the subject of the play is Lear's mind, Gloucester has become part of that subject. But his dramatic usefulness is demonstrable on grounds that eliminate the need of proving him mechanically absorbed into the main stream of action.

Bradley manages to have the matter of unity both ways. He devotes several pages to pointing out that the two protagonists and the numerous characters are never brought into proper dramatic unity (*op. cit.*, pp. 255–56) and several more pages to cataloguing the aesthetic advantages of this multiplicity of characters and actions (pp. 261–62). He is very lukewarm about Gloucester—the sketch of whose character is the only one, I think, in which he does not take full advantage of all the available evidence (pp. 294–95).

29 For further notes on the dramatic relationship between Lear and Gloucester, see G. Wilson Knight, *The Wheel of Fire*, pp. 185 ff., 190. R. W. Chambers, in *King Lear* (Glasgow, 1940), says that we cannot justify the ways of God to particular men, and, citing John S. Smart in his support, points a strongly admonishing finger at those who think Lear and Gloucester deserve their fate. It is, however, unhappily impossible to measure out a quantity of suffering appropriate to a given error; and to assume that some such relationship can be established is to risk falling into the mental habits of Lear's daughters, who felt that some rational system of determining the number of their fathers' retainers could be arrived at. The most we can hope to do is to see how a train of consequences, great or small, is set in motion by a certain kind of conduct. That consequences, in any given case, appear excessive may result from a failure to see how much is involved in the originating conduct. Or, as Ulrici said, "it is the nature of evil to spring up to an incalculable magnitude." (H. H. Furness, ed., *King Lear*, New Variorum Edition, 10th ed. [Philadelphia, 1880], p. 456. In subsequent notes I shall refer to this volume simply as "Furness.")

30 Cf. Bradley's hypothesis that the major evil characters in the play represent "the tendency of the imagination to analyse and abstract, to decompose human nature into its constituent factors, and then to construct beings in whom one or more of these factors is absent or atrophied or only incipient" (*op. cit.*, p. 264).

31 Thomas Middleton Raysor, ed., *Coleridge's Shakespearean Criticism* (Cambridge, Mass., 1930), I, 60. Cf. Hudson, *op. cit.*, p. 38. Granville-Barker notes that Cordelia's pride is exactly Lear's pride. His comment on the relationship between them is good; in fact, his whole discussion of her shows

299

great insight (*Prefaces*, I, 303 ff.). This is as good a time as any to say that Granville-Barker's analysis of *Lear* is excellent. Yet I do not see it much referred to, although it has been available in the English edition since 1927. Bradley's discussion of Cordelia is also first-rate; it is thorough and relatively unsentimental (*op. cit.*, pp. 318–21).

[32] R. W. Chambers makes an interesting use of sources in arguing that Cordelia had to die because in the source stories, which were widely familiar, she commits suicide. He contends that while Shakespeare therefore had to have Cordelia die, he was not content to have her despair, and so made her a victim of Edmund's machination (*King Lear*, pp. 15 ff.). He might have gone still further and argued that Shakespeare placed her directly in the stream of tragic consequences by making her bear an ancillary responsibility for the career of Goneril and Regan.

[33] Robert Penn Warren comments, in a personal letter, "Cordelia's problem is the old one of action and contamination vs. passivity and innocence. She is a kind of Brutus, one of the long series of Brutus-figures. . . . In fact, I think that a very fruitful paper could be written on the subject of action and contamination in Shakespeare. It appears over and over again, in different guises, a constant theme." It may be observed, parenthetically, that Mr. Warren has been especially concerned, in his own novels, with the problem of action-vs.-withdrawal.

Other theories of Cordelia's flaw, some rather eccentric, are recorded by Furness, pp. 16–17, 422, 430, 434, 459. Oechelhaeuser (1871) comes close to the withdrawal theory (Furness, p. 464), as does Ulrici (Furness, p. 456). Whatever their conclusions, many critics clearly feel uncomfortable about Cordelia; they sense that there is something to be explained. One of the most recent, however, rejects the theory that Cordelia has a flaw (Alfred Harbage, *As They Liked It* [New York, 1947], pp. 56, 142–43).

The theory of Lear's flaw as a failure in responsibility was implied by Franz Horn in 1823 (Furness, p. 451) and Ulrici in 1839 (Furness, pp. 9, 454). A comparable theory is implied in the discussion by Theodore Spencer in *Shakespeare and the Nature of Man* (New York, 1942), p. 145. In *Shakespeare's Tragic Heroes: Slaves of Passion* (Cambridge, 1930), Lily B. Campbell points out that Lear, in withdrawing from the kingship, exhibits what in Holland's translation of Plutarch's *Moralia* is called "sloth and want of courage" (pp. 182–83). Miss Campbell's main thesis, however, is that *Lear* is a tragedy of wrath in old age (pp. 181–207). The usefulness of this theory is considerably impaired by its failure to account for many very important elements in the play—e.g., the nature of evil as it appears in Goneril and Regan. Elmer E. Stoll, in *Shakespeare and Other Masters* (Cambridge, Mass., 1940), p. 37, denies the existence of a tragic flaw in Lear. Subsequently he argues against various flaws that have been attributed to Lear (pp. 74–75).

[34] Shakespeare's mastery of his materials is demonstrated by the fact that

PRELIMINARIES

King Lear did not come out a melodrama, for it makes use of at least two
types of action which Aristotle specifically says are not suitable for tragedy:
the bad individual passing from misery to happiness—Edmund, and, less
conspicuously, Goneril and Regan; and, on the other hand, the bad individual
brought from happiness to misery—again, Edmund and the sisters. If it seems
that the second of these should cancel out the first, it may be argued, perhaps,
that, even though it is technically of less duration than the little life remaining, the "success" of the villains still inflicts such suffering on other characters
and through their agony and death has such quasi-permanence of effect that
the "success" has a kind of paradoxical co-existence with the villains' downfall. They have inflicted such evil on others that the memory of it is one of
the major evocations of the play. What is presently clear, at any rate, is that
we have some interesting problems of structure: the first type of action (rise
of the evil trio) might easily become "shocking" or "odious," and the second
might too easily "satisfy the moral sense" (Butcher) or "arouse human feeling" (Bywater) and thus fall into the psychological patterns of melodrama.
But the fact is that the events of the play do not impinge upon the discrimi-
nating reader in this fashion.

For some readers, too, Cordelia has presented a problem in that she has
seemed to be the good individual who passes from happiness to misery—a
type of action which Aristotle calls shocking. A more suitable reading of the
role, however, appears to be that which I have proposed in the text. Whatever
the interpretation which satisfies the individual reader, we should recall that,
seen in proportion, Cordelia cannot have too large influence on the tone of
the play. She speaks in only four (I.i, IV.iv, vii, V.iii) of the twenty-six scenes
and has only about one hundred lines in a long play. What happens to Cordelia is not a central effect of the play; rather it is meaningful as it amplifies
the tragic experience of Lear. We see her always in her impact on him. This
does not mean, of course, that we are to be indifferent to her; it does mean
that the feelings she evokes should not be abstracted from the pattern and
enlarged—like a detail of a heroic sculpture—but should be subordinated to
the experience of the whole play centered in Lear. In interpreting Cordelia,
and in estimating her relationship to the total meaning, we ought to keep it
clear, also, that her fate can be considered merely "shocking" or ultimately
"shocking" only if we make physical survival, as well as immunity to suffering, the chief criterion in our response to or feeling about a character.
To use such a criterion is to substitute a rationalistic for a tragic view of life.

To return to Edmund, Goneril, and Regan: they offer special problems in
that tragedy rarely presents such embodiments of unmitigated evil and allows
them such vast scope as they have in *King Lear*. There is aesthetic danger at
every step. That their downfall does not call forth the true tragic emotion is
put in virtually Aristotelian terms in Albany's lines at the death of Goneril
and Regan: "This judgment of the heavens, that makes us tremble,/ Touches

301

us not with pity" (V.iii, 231–32). Almost as if illustrating a theory, Shakespeare has subordinated the untragic spectacle—of bad men brought to misery —to the sufferings of his protagonists: any isolated rejoicing in the downfall and death of villains, such as would characterize melodrama, is cut off immediately by the return of Lear to a central position which he holds, in his final desperate grief, until the end. In him we see that the evil which men do lives after them. What, then, of the passing to "happiness" of Edmund, Goneril, and Regan, who strike such blows at the lives and spirits of others that their deeds can never be undone? That we do not have, in the evil they do to others, a mere "shock," the product of a cynical view of experience, is evident if, once again, we see things in their structural relationships. For no more than Cordelia, the woman of integrity who goes down, are Edmund, Goneril, and Regan, the opportunists who in their temporarily effective machinations inflict outrageous suffering and death on others, the chief figures of the play. The ultimate impact of the play is not the damage which they do. For they are agents, servants of destiny, incarnations of an evil which their actions specifically define; they are, as it were, nemesis, means of bringing Lear and Gloucester face to face with reality, scourges analogous to the Eumenides; but, although we must be vitally concerned with them as influences, as symbols, as constituents and voices of the moral cosmos which Shakespeare is picturing, we must seek their meaning not in their impact upon us, but in their impact upon the consciousness of Gloucester and Lear. In their sensibility are focused the implications of the evildoers' actions. This should not be taken as a minimization of the evil which Edmund and the sisters do (cf. Denton J. Snider, as quoted in Furness, p. 430). The evil is real; Shakespeare is marked by his constant assertions of the reality of evil. The Eumenides cannot be laughed off as phantasms. But they must not be taken out of context, not regarded as autonomous, irrational reality. A dramatic statement that evil is real should not be read as the logical equivalent of "Evil always conquers."

There is a possible risk in the use of Kent and Edgar, "good men" who after suffering rise to happiness—a type frequent in melodrama. But Kent, though he sees the villains discomfited, has also seen Lear shattered and is himself crushed by what he has been through; and Edgar, who, if the sole problem were the succession to Gloucester, might be the conquering hero of Act V, has a coming to "happiness" so diluted by antecedent experience—his own suffering, what he has been through with Gloucester, his feeling partially responsible for Gloucester's death—and so qualified by the somberness of the post-Lear world that he is anything but the successful hero of melodrama. Whatever the fortunes of Kent and Edgar, too, both are only flying buttresses to the main structure, and neither has more than an allotted share of influence upon the tone. In the study of the problem of evil Kent's role suggests the impossibility, in an actual world, of combating evil without getting hurt; Kent chooses participation, with its dangers, rather than withdrawal and its immunity. It is possible to regard Edgar as an innocent victim, who, as long as he does not become a central character and therefore a source of pathos, usefully amplifies a presentation of the tragic world: when evil is set loose, others besides those morally responsible are bound to get hurt. But is not Edgar, after all, a good man with a flaw, and therefore, like Cordelia, a minor tragic figure? It is hardly necessary that Edgar be so gullible as he is in I.ii and II.i; he need not so credulously accept all that Edmund says; he fails in a responsibility to verify what is told him and to act in terms of a total situation. By taking the easiest rather than the most inclusive protective steps—which are perhaps obligatory—he contributes to the seizure of the world by the evil characters. In his physical withdrawal he has something in common with the other characters who make their own kinds of withdrawal—Lear, Gloucester, and Cordelia. They concede the world to the enemy, and they all must learn. Edgar's learning process changes him from a passive accepter to a man of resourceful activity.

The point is that all those elements in the play which, if not skillfully handled, might work against tragic effects, are carefully controlled, made to subserve the central tragedy as we see it through the consciousness of Gloucester and Lear.

NOTES FOR CHAPTER II

I STUMBLED WHEN I SAW

[1] There is an excellent analysis of Gloucester in Granville-Barker's *Prefaces*, I, 313 ff.

[2] The line numbers are the standard ones which appear in the Globe, Arden, Kittredge, and other editions. Except for the passages which are not in the folios, I am using the folio readings almost entirely. My authority is Leo Kirschbaum, *The True Text of King Lear* (Baltimore, 1945).

[3] There is an early comment upon the relationship among various sight passages in G. G. Gervinus, *Shakespeare Commentaries*, tr. F. E. Bunnett (London and New York, 1892), p. 633. Bradley says that the play "purges the soul's sight by blinding that of the eyes" (*op. cit.*, p. 327). In *The Fool: His Social and Literary History* (London, 1935), Enid Welsford suggests that the sight pattern has a structural relationship to the play as a whole (pp. 263–64). Paul Kreider gives an encyclopedic record of all the uses of words of seeing and allied terms in the play (*Repetition in Shakespeare's Plays*, pp. 194–214). J. I. M. Stewart, in "The Blinding of Gloucester," *Review of English Studies*, XXI (1945), 264–70, defends the blinding of Gloucester upon the stage as the culmination of the sight symbolism in the play. After all this, Charles Olson, in *Call Me Ishmael* (New York, 1947), expresses surprise that the sight

symbolism has not been observed. Although Olson's perception of the blindness paradox is not new, he adds new details in relating it to the language of the play (pp. 49–50).

Professor Kreider's account, which I discovered long after my own analysis was finished, does both a service and a disservice to this kind of criticism. The service is its heroic completeness; it is well, in an analysis of language patterns, to collect every possible example of contributory words. But it is very important to eliminate words that do not have a fairly demonstrable function, and I feel that Professor Kreider has somewhat neglected this side of his critical process. As for his interpretation: he believes that the function of the sight words is merely to unify the Gloucester and Lear plots; but it is questionable whether the words could have this effect without having a symbolic function. I think that Professor Kreider senses the existence of such a function, for he speaks twice of Lear's "spiritual blindness" (pp. 195, 196), once of his "faulty moral vision" (p. 212), and again of "situations demonstrative of both moral and physical sight or blindness" (p. 213), but these phrases, I believe, exhaust his analysis of meaning. He seems unaware of the irony and paradox which are the heart of the pattern.

⁴ *Coleridge's Shakespearean Criticism,* I, 57.

⁵ The echoes from one part of the play to another, which, as we shall see, are extraordinarily frequent, are illustrated by the fact that these last two speeches of Gloucester are reminders of the imaginary sins of which Edgar, as Tom, has given so full an account. Though a servingman, Tom appears to have been well off materially ("superfluous"); he "serv'd the lust of my mistress' heart" ("lust-dieted") and "did the act of darkness with her"; and he swore oaths "in the sweet face of heaven" (III.iv, 87–92).

⁶ Cf. Edmund's way of reassuring Edgar: "You have now the good advantage of the night" (24).

⁷ Some commentators are extraordinarily unwilling to see any sort of moral continuity in the play. Typical of these is George Brandes, who regards the opening scene as a lazy borrowing, full of incredible actions. Hence he can describe the "ruin of the moral world" as consisting in all the disasters to people of noble character. In Gloucester's experience all he sees is that "he who is merciful . . . , taking the suffering and injured under his roof, has the loss of his eyes for his reward" (*William Shakespeare: A Critical Study,* tr. by Archer and others [New York, 1898], II, 141). The ruin of the moral world comes about, however, not through the efficacy of evil, against innocent victim or tragic hero with *hamartia,* but through a general acquiescence in or rationalization of evil.

⁸ Others are measured, also, by the way in which they look at him. Albany becomes a more clearly outlined character because of the shock with which he receives the news of the blinding of Gloucester (IV.ii, 72 ff.). Regan, on whose hard practical view of things more remains to be said, regards the blind-

ness merely as an unfortunate source of popular indignation (IV.v, 8–10), and suggests to Oswald that it may be profitable to cut off "that blind traitor" (IV.v, 37–38). Hence to Oswald "that eyeless head" is only a possible source of advancement (IV.vi, 231–32). Oswald also belongs to the blind.

⁹ See Chapter I, p. 34. Later Edmund looks at Lear in the same hard, pragmatic way. He has sequestered Lear, he tells Albany, lest the aged king "pluck the common bosom on his side/ And turn our impress'd lances in our eyes" (V.iii, 49–50). *Pluck* and *eyes* recall the blinding scene; we remember, also, that at the blinding scene the "common bosom," in the form of the Servant, revolted against Cornwall. Edmund's realism here makes it highly unlikely that we are to take literally Regan's statement that Edmund has gone to dispatch his father "in pity of his misery." Harbage does take it literally (*op. cit.*, p. 66), but Bradley calls it a "lie" (*op. cit.*, p. 299).

¹⁰ The sight pattern is used specifically to exhibit the once-gullible Edgar as the possessor of a new resourcefulness. After he has killed Oswald, he says, "Let's see his pockets; . . . Let us see" (IV.vi, 261–63)—the very words Gloucester used in I.ii just before reading the forged letter signed "Edgar." Then Edgar finds and reads the letter in which Goneril encourages Edmund to kill Albany; with this knowledge Edgar goes on to plot successfully the overthrow of Edmund. First he plans to "strike the sight/ Of the death-practis'd Duke" (283–84) with Goneril's letter.

¹¹ In the experience of Lear there is of course no such event as the blinding of Gloucester to focus the sight pattern, and it is possible simply to read the language of sight in a literal and restricted sense. But the sight symbolism in the presentation of Gloucester, where it is explicit, can hardly be kept from transferring itself also to the passages by or concerning Lear. As Robert Penn Warren says, "Once the symbolic import of an image is established for our minds, that image cannot in its workings upon us elsewhere in the poem be disencumbered of that import, whether or not we are consciously defining it. The criterion for such full rather than restricted interpretation is consistency with the central symbolic import and, insofar as it is possible to establish the fact, with the poet's basic views as drawn from external sources" (*op. cit.*, pp. 89–90). We cannot establish Shakespeare's views from external sources, but the sight symbolism, as it appears in the Lear passages, is exactly consistent with "the central symbolic import." Besides, there is in the Lear passages the fact of recurrency which draws our attention to the existence of a sight pattern.

¹² Bradley, Granville-Barker, and Chambers agree that Lear dies in the ecstasy of thinking that Cordelia is alive (see Chambers, *op. cit.*, pp. 44–45). Chambers has observed the relationship between the first-act and fifth-act episodes which I am here discussing (p. 43).

¹³ The sight pattern suggests that at the end the search for understanding animates even the supporting characters. "O, see, see!" cries Albany (V.iii,

304) as Lear stoops over Cordelia's body, just before his dying speech. Edgar, who earlier describes Lear as a "side-piercing sight" (IV.vi, 85; this is in direct contrast with Edmund's attitude to Lear), asks, when Lear has demanded a looking glass to determine whether Cordelia is breathing, "[Is this an] image of that horror?" (V.iii, 264). In his search for understanding he sees the episode as a likeness to the end of the world. His final words addressed to Lear, it may be worth noting, echo his words to Gloucester just after Gloucester's imaginary leap from Dover cliff. His words to Lear are, "Look up"; but Lear is dead. His words to Gloucester are, "Do but look up" (IV.vi, 59); Gloucester replies, "Alack, I have no eyes!" (60). The request to Gloucester has of course a quite literal meaning in the context: look at the height from which you have fallen. But the symbolic overtones are audible: see better what the moral situation is. And Gloucester, though he must mention his blindness, is seeing better. Perhaps, in speaking similarly to Lear at the end, Edgar, who is characteristically hopeful and encouraging, has some idea that Lear may be "brought around."

[14] Dr. Carl Hense wrote, in 1856, ". . . the point is, that the light of the moral world has now ceased to shine, and the darkness incessantly increases" (Furness, p. 460).

[15] Cf. Gloucester's later remark on what Lear "in hell-black night endur'd" (III.vii, 60).

[16] The chief of these are II.i, II.iv, III.i, ii, iii, iv, v, vi. It is possible, also, that the action of II.ii, in which Oswald is "in the dark," takes place before daybreak.

[17] Perhaps, after the continued stress upon darkness, it is not wholly fantastic to suggest that Lear's phrase in his second speech in the play—"our darker purpose" (I.i, 37)—can be read as containing, besides its literal meaning, a mild anticipation of things to come.

[18] In the second sentence, the *not* is from the Qq. Some editors stress the change in prose in the last twenty-five lines of I.i as a symbolic accompaniment of the change to the sisters' dispassionate calculations.

[19] Oswald's insolence creeps into his facial expression. Lear exclaims, "Do you bandy looks with me, you rascal?" (I.iv, 91).

[20] Thus there is an unaccented lightning pattern, which really is an elaboration of the darkness-and-light pattern. In the storm Lear cries:

> You sulph'rous and thought-executing fires,
> Vaunt-couriers of oak-cleaving thunderbolts,
> Singe my white head! And thou, all-shaking thunder,
> Strike flat. . . .   (III.ii, 4–7)

Again, "Rumble thy bellyful! Spit, fire! spout, rain!" (III.ii, 14). If the storm symbolizes Lear's emotional suffering, the lightning is also excess of light—the new knowledge which is a part of the anguish he undergoes. The pattern is also used to help define the quality of the tragic protagonist, to indicate the apparent disproportion of nemesis to deed which characterizes tragedy. Cordelia asks, after the storm,

> Was this a face
> . . . .
> To stand against the deep dread-bolted thunder?
> In the most terrible and nimble stroke
> Of quick cross lightning? (IV.vii, 31–35)

Before this, Gloucester, in his first partisan lines, extended the lightning pattern to characterize Goneril and Regan and suggest their future. It is after commenting on "such a storm as his bare head/ In hell-black night endur'd" (III.vii, 59–60) that he assures the sisters, "But I shall see/ The winged vengeance overtake such children" (III.vii, 65–66). Thunder and lightning are the agents of divine justice.

21 This expression of relationship between manner of looking (seeing) and feeling prepares for Gloucester's subsequent line, which I have already discussed, on the man "that will not see/ Because he does not feel" (IV.i, 69–70).

22 It may be pushing the evidence too far to suggest that, after the bodies of Goneril and Regan are brought out on the stage, Albany's words, "Cover their faces" (V.iii, 242) are, besides a command for the usual mantling of the dead, a reminder of what these faces especially contained—frowns, dark looks, scornful glances, lustful expressions. It is only twenty lines later that Lear begins studying Cordelia's face for signs of life, and fifty lines after this first calling for a glass that he dies, all his attention focused on Cordelia's face.

23 This interpretation is made by W. L. Phelps in his edition of *King Lear* (the Yale Shakespeare [New Haven, 1917], p. 131).

24 Weeping becomes not only necessary but obligatory after the death of Cordelia. Lear cries:

> Howl, howl, howl, howl! O, you are men of stone.
> Had I your tongues and eyes, I'ld use them so
> That heaven's vault should crack. (V.iii, 257–59)

He wants them to show grief, of course; but what is also implied is that they should show insight into what Cordelia stood for.

25 The lines quoted in the text and in this note are spoken by Kent after he has been put into the stocks by Regan and Cornwall. Kent comments drily, "Nothing almost sees miracles/ But misery" (II.ii, 172–73). The passage as a whole contains some effective implied irony. Kent uses the sun as a metaphor for Lear's suffering (167–69), then prays to it as a bringer of light by which he may read Cordelia's letter (170–72), and then, with day coming on, calls for the darkness of sleep: "Take vantage, heavy eyes, not to behold/ This shameful lodging" (178–79). The darkness prayed for is different from the darkness of some of the other characters: It is desired because of a courageous unwillingness to dwell upon immediate ills.

26 Mr. Ransom's article on Shakespeare's use of Latinate English (see

Chapter I, note 5) encourages me in the suspicion that Shakespeare has embedded a number of bilingual puns in the lines which accompany Burgundy's rejection and France's acceptance of Cordelia. Just after Cordelia speaks of a "still-soliciting eye" France says,

Love's not love
When it is mingled with *regards* that stands
Aloof from th'entire point. (I.i, 241–43)

Cordelia says of Burgundy that "*respects* of fortune are his love" (251), and France, addressing Cordelia as "most lov'd *despis'd*" (254), comments that neglect has strangely kindled his love to "inflam'd *respect*" (258). The words which I have italicized are all derived from words of seeing, which the educated would certainly recognize.

[27] It is perhaps well to add a final assurance that there are many uses of words of seeing and of allied terms in *King Lear* which have no symbolic overtones but are restricted to their immediate literal meaning. There is an example at IV.iii, 19.

[28] This is one of the points at which the smell pattern and the sight pattern work together. We shall come to many more examples of such collaborations.

NOTES FOR CHAPTER III

POOR NAKED WRETCHES AND PROUD ARRAY

[1] The painful doubts which are among the early factors in Lear's mental downfall are parodied in the scene in which Kent, as Lear's messenger, runs into Oswald, Goneril's messenger, before Gloucester's castle, and denounces and beats him.

Osw. Why dost thou use me thus? I know thee not.
Kent. Fellow, I know thee.
Osw. What dost thou know me for? (II.ii, 12–14)

Kent then launches into his famous series of vituperative terms for Oswald, who comments, "Why, what a monstrous fellow art thou, thus to rail on one that's neither known of thee nor knows thee!" (28–29) For Oswald, the problem of identity remains at the level of introductions, and his questions are a comic version of Lear's anguished inquiries. There are other comments on the problem of identity in Mark Van Doren's *Shakespeare*, pp. 245, 249.

[2] Note how the courteous vocative adds to the incisiveness of the irony. Lear's tense incredulity is balanced by Goneril's matter-of-fact assurance,

This admiration, sir, is much o' th' savour
Of other your new pranks. I do beseech you
To understand my purposes aright. (I.iv, 258–60)

308

[3] In a later scene, waiting for Cornwall outside Gloucester's castle, Lear makes a tremendous effort to control his growing rage and comments,

> We are not ourselves
> When nature, being oppress'd, commands the mind
> To suffer with the body. (II.iv, 108–10)

[4] Cf. Lear's statement that his *"frank* heart gave all" (III.iv, 20).

[5] Harbage has a chapter on Paradoxes (*op. cit.*, pp. 73 ff.) but makes no mention of those in this play. He does point out how misery enlarges the sympathies in *Lear* (pp. 175–76). The paradoxes of clothing and nakedness in *Lear* are similar to those in *Macbeth* which Cleanth Brooks has pointed out (*op. cit.*, pp. 42 ff.). A point made by Miss Spurgeon is relevant to the present discussion: "Another aspect of evil which specially interested Shakespeare, and seemed to him its most dangerous feature, was its power of disguising itself as good—. . . . This quality is pictured by him chiefly in terms of clothing and painting, and is especially frequent in his early work" (*op. cit.*, p. 164).

[6] A sentence in Sidney's *Arcadia* comes very close to describing Lear's present situation. The king of Paphlagonia tells how he gradually lost his function to a bastard son, ". . . so that ere I was aware, I had left my selfe nothing but the name of a King" (quoted, Furness, p. 388).

[7] Cf. Chapter I, pp. 35–36.

[8] The problem which Lear faces suggests different metaphors to different readers. One critic has said, in a conversation, "Lear needs to be re-educated. The plot of the play is his re-education. When he learns what the images are saying, his education is complete." Another: "Lear is living in a melodrama. He has to learn to live in a tragedy." That is, he must progress from a simple blame of villains to an awareness of his own responsibility for disaster.

[9] Kittredge's note (*King Lear* [Boston, 1940], p. 182). Cf. G. Wilson Knight's discussion of this passage in *The Wheel of Fire*, p. 201, and the connection he makes between the clothes symbolism and the nature theme.

[10] For an elaborate discussion of these points see Furness, pp. 257 ff.

[11] To G. Wilson Knight this meaning is central to the interpretation of *Lear* and of the tragedies generally. See *Principles of Shakespearian Production* (New York, 1936), pp. 83, 222 ff. Knight argues that each tragic hero is a "miniature Christ" (p. 231) and that the "ritualistic concept of sacrifice" dominates the tragedies. The heroes give up earthly kingship and undergo spiritual initiation. The clothes pattern which I am tracing in this chapter takes us very close to such a conclusion. Granville-Barker speaks of Lear's taking upon himself the burden of the whole world's sorrow, of his "transition from malediction to martyrdom" (*op. cit.*, p. 289).

[12] Chambers, who makes *King Lear* a play about love (*op. cit.*, pp. 49 ff.), stresses the fact that Gloucester and Lear both die in a happy knowledge of

the recovery of their children's love. It may be said that Cordelia and Edgar are equally happy to recover parental love. If, as Knight and Chambers, among others, argue, Lear and Gloucester travel through Purgatory, perhaps the same interpretation may be made of Edgar's naked wandering. This view is coherent with my earlier suggestion (see Chapter I, note 34) that at the beginning of the play, in so unquestioningly allowing himself to be put upon by Edmund, Edgar is guilty of an error comparable to the tragic flaws of the major characters who are equally deceived. Since Edgar's mistake leads him to commit no wrong and has no direct effect upon another's destiny, his purgation is comparably mild. It is, too, purgation at a nonsacramental level; he becomes less the man of spiritual than the man of practical vision.

[13] See pp. 67–68.

[14] The clothes symbolism also makes a skeletal commentary upon Kent's change of fortune. Kent is forced into disguise, and shortly thereafter he is placed in the stocks—"cruel garters," as the Fool calls them (II.iv, 7) (he puns on *crewel*, worsted, as all editors point out), ironically treating the materials of punishment as if they were an adornment. Later Kent tells a Gentleman that "Some dear cause/ Will in concealment wrap me up awhile" (IV.iii, 53–54). Then, when things seem to be going better, Cordelia urges Kent,

> Be better suited.
> These weeds are memories of those worser hours.
> I prithee put them off. (IV.vii, 6–8)

Clothes are directly made into a symbol of condition. But the irony of it is that conditions only seem to be better. Like Edgar, Kent does not appear as himself until the final scene in the play; but his struggles, and the emotional impact of his experiences, have exhausted him, and it is clear that he will not live long (V.iii, 321–22).

[15] Earlier, Kent sneers at Oswald, ". . . a tailor made thee" (II.ii, 59–60). Oswald's naïve incomprehension permits Kent to expand on his joke. Oswald's particular kind of obtuseness is given further expression in another scene when he reports to Goneril how Albany had received from him the news "Of Gloucester's treachery/ And of the loyal service of his son": Albany "told me I had turn'd the wrong side out" (IV.ii, 6–9). Oswald has missed the point again. But at the same time his lines have almost a choral value, for, as the clothes pattern makes clear, many characters have turned the wrong side out.

[16] Kent, though he is disguised, has his own kind of nakedness in the world. The Fool makes this point when he says that Kent should take his coxcomb. He explains, "Why? For taking one's part that's out of favour. Nay, an thou canst not smile as the wind sits, thou'lt catch cold shortly. There, take my coxcomb!" (I.iv, 111–13) The irony of Kent's being liable to "catch cold" is that his situation is his own choice, and it is obviously different from what Lear expected it to be. In exiling Kent, Lear said, "Five days we do allot

thee for provision/ To *shield* thee from diseases of the world" (I.i, 176–77).
Kent disguised himself against Lear but could not disguise the honesty which
gets him into trouble with Cornwall. In passing, we may note the possibility
of a pun in *provision*. Kent did not "see for" himself in the way Lear assumed
that he would. But he does see for himself morally.

Lear's grant of five days in which Kent may prepare to "shield" himself prepares an effective irony in that Kent not only shields himself but spends most
of his time shielding Lear—to the extent that either can be shielded; the reversal of their roles is comparable to that in the relations of Gloucester and
Edgar. *Shield*, with a rather general meaning abstracted from the original
metaphor, is a convenient link between the dramatic use of clothes and that
of shelter, which plays a considerable part in the drama, not only in a literal
way but also at the level of implication and overtone. Lear gives up one castle,
is virtually forced out of two others (cf. II.iv, 179–80, 206 ff., 291 ff.), faces a
storm in the open, and finds shelter in hovel, farmhouse, and tent. His problem is pointed by the continued witticisms of the Fool on the subject of shelter (I.v, 30 ff.; II.iv, 52–53, 81–82; III.ii, 25 ff.). Edgar, Gloucester, and Kent
have similar experiences. What we have is a series of symbolic statements,
comparable to those made in terms of dress, about man's defenses against the
world, and about what man has done to man. Yet the main problem is never
the one of finding or recovering shelter: that approach belongs to the problem
play. For the ambivalence which such a word as *shield* may have, see Albany's
line to Goneril, "A woman's shape doth shield thee" (IV.ii, 67). Man must be
shielded; but a shield may also protect evil.

We enter a special wing of the shelter problem, so to speak, in the matter
of Lear's retinue and its reduction: how does one distinguish luxury from necessity? Shakespeare clearly perceives the psychological basis of the problem.
But the answer made by the play—if *answer* be not taken as a simple statement of sums and quotients—comes properly under the theme of rationality
and irrationality, with which we shall deal in Chapters VIII and IX.

[17] Cf. Cordelia's asking Lear for his benediction and telling him he must
not kneel (IV.vii, 57–59). Later he is still planning to kneel and ask her forgiveness (V.iii, 10–11). Humility in exile is the reverse of the original pride
in prosperity—in both characters.

[18] Earlier in the same scene Regan uses a word which seems a deliberate
choice. She speaks of Edmund as "In my rights/ By me *invested*" (V.iii, 68–69)
—thus echoing Lear's own word in Act I, "I do invest you jointly with my
power" (I.i, 132), and repeating his process of trying to make the succession
in political power conform to the emotions of the moment. But both investi-
tures fail to achieve their end—a failure intimated immediately by means of
another language pattern which the play uses, that of disease and medicine:
Regan soon cries "Sick, O, sick!" (V.iii, 95), just as in the first scene Kent
speaks of Lear's "foul disease" (I.i, 167).

311

¹⁹ Miss Spurgeon comments that Shakespeare's interest in the human face and his use of it in indicating emotions have never been adequately noticed (*op. cit.*, p. 58).

NOTES FOR CHAPTER IV

THE BREACH IN NATURE

¹ The fullest discussion of the storm is that of G. Wilson Knight in *The Shakespearian Tempest* (Oxford, 1932), pp. 194 ff. Knight expressly elaborates upon the fact that the storm is both realistic and symbolic. He shows how the storm is part of Lear's purgatorial experience and how at the same time Lear's endurance of the storm is an anodyne for the pain caused by the conduct of his daughters. He notes the functional relationship between the storm and the animal imagery of the play, and he likewise connects the storm with storm imagery elsewhere in the play. His discussion, of course, makes comparisons between the storm in *King Lear* and the storms in other plays. He finds in *Lear*, as in other plays, an opposition between the storm and music (as in IV.vii, 16, 25). But in *Lear* the use of music is so slight that it can hardly be felt as a structural counterpoise to the storm.

On the general importance of the storm, and its ambivalence, see also Granville-Barker, *op. cit.*, I, 265 ff.; Bradley, *op. cit.*, p. 315; and Edward Dowden, *Shakespeare: A Critical Study of His Mind and Art*, 3d ed. (New York and Oxford, n.d.), p. 229.

While the present volume was in proof, I came upon Professor Moody Prior's recent *The Language of Tragedy* (New York, 1947), which contains an examination of some of the poetic language of *King Lear* (pp. 74–93). Professor Prior is especially concerned with what I have called the nature pattern, which he and I interpret in approximately the same way; in this connection he deals with the animal imagery as I do, and he also comments on some of the clothes imagery. His critical method and mine have a good deal in common.

² *Op. cit.*, p. 66. Cf. Stoll, *Shakespeare and Other Masters*, p. 41.

³ Miss Spurgeon comments on the collaboration of the storm and the animal imagery in giving a picture of the moral failure of man (*op. cit.*, p. 342). Cf. Bradley, *op. cit.*, pp. 265–68.

⁴ An anonymous *Blackwoods* critic made approximately this point in 1819: "Throughout all the play is there not a sublimity felt amidst the continual presence of all kinds of disorder and confusion in the natural and moral world,—a continual consciousness of eternal order, law, and good?" (Furness, p. 425). Cf. Hudson, *op. cit.*, p. 51.

⁵ There is a similar view of *Lear* in Theodore Spencer's *Shakespeare and*

the Nature of Man, pp. 141 ff. Spencer also notes the ambivalence of the storm (p. 136), the thematic importance of the treatment of sex (pp. 143–45) which I shall discuss shortly (see pp. 98–105), and Shakespeare's awareness of the problem of appearance and reality (p. 149), with which my Chapter III is in part concerned.

[6] The animal imagery has been observed by nearly all commentators. Miss Spurgeon notes the use of such imagery in other tragedies as well—in *Macbeth* (p. 334) and *Othello* (pp. 335–36).

[7] Cf. Wyndham Lewis, who in *The Lion and the Fox* (London, 1927) asserts that in Shakespeare the lion and the fox were "imperfectly combined: for his was not an emancipated and scientific mind, like that of the great Italian in question" (p. 11). Indeed, as we shall see, Shakespeare attacks the "emancipated and scientific mind." For a more elaborate discussion of this point, see Chapter IX, Madness in Reason.

[8] Spencer lists a number of passages that contribute to this effect (*op. cit.,* p. 143).

[9] Quoted, Furness, p. 424.

[10] Oswald is rather thoroughly described by the animal imagery, especially by the dog imagery which we have seen applied to Goneril and Regan. Lear calls him "mongrel" (I.iv, 54) and "whoreson dog" and "cur" (I.iv, 88–89); and Kent climaxes his denunciation of Oswald with "son and heir of a mongrel bitch" (II.ii, 25). Later Kent calls him "goose" (89) and compares him to "rats" (80) and "dogs" (86). Edgar describes Edmund as "most toad-spotted traitor" (V.iii, 138).

[11] Cf. Hudson: ". . . to bring out their characters truly, it had to be shown that the same principle which unites them against their father will, on the turning of occasion, divide them against each other" (*op. cit.,* p. 17).

[12] France says it is strange that Cordelia could

> . . . in this trice of time
> So many folds of favour. Sure her offence
> Commit a thing so monstrous to dismantle
> Must be of such unnatural degree
> That monsters it. (I.i, 219–23)

Kent's full speech is:

> A sovereign shame so elbows him; his own unkindness,
> That stripp'd her from his benediction, turn'd her
> To foreign casualties, gave her dear rights
> To his dog-hearted daughters—these things sting
> His mind so venomously, that burning shame
> Detains him from Cordelia. (IV.iii, 44–49)

[13] It is difficult not to connect the epithet *cowish* with two other terms of contempt which Goneril applies to Albany. Only a few lines after the remark to Oswald she apostrophizes Albany directly, "Milk-liver'd man!" (IV.ii, 50)

It is interesting that even before they clashed openly her opinion of him was much the same; in Act I she complains of his "milky gentleness" (I.iv, 364). But the man she thinks of as meek and cowardly turns out to be of the forces that *nourish* society.

14 At the beginning of Act I Gloucester refers jauntily to adultery; in I.ii Edmund elaborates his justification of bastardy. They prepare for Goneril's expression of outraged virtue: at first glance she seems a person who, at least in sexual matters, has sharp moral sensibilities. But we have already seen her moral sensibilities in action in other ways, so that her hypocrisy is immediately apparent. Her hypocrisy is further evident in the remedy which she proposes—"to disquantity your train" (I.iv, 270). If her allegations are correct, the solution is not a reduction of men, but discipline of the offenders or a replacement of the badly behaved men by others.

15 Edmund's metaphor involves a reversal of the usual relationship of terms which often appear in Renaissance word play. Here, the fact of death is denoted by the term *marry;* usually, the consummation of the sexual act is denoted by the term *die.* This conventional pun appears at least twice in *King Lear.* It is only a short time after the famous reason-in-madness speech that Lear exclaims, "I will die bravely, like a smug bridegroom" (IV.vi, 202). Several scenes earlier there is an interchange between Goneril and Edmund which contains several kinds of sexual innuendo:

> *Gon.*   This kiss, if it durst speak,
> Would stretch thy spirits up into the air.
> Conceive, and fare thee well.
> *Edm.*   Yours in the ranks of death! (IV.ii, 22–25)

For other word play of the same kind in Shakespeare and elsewhere see Leo Kirschbaum, "Shakespeare's Cleopatra," *The Shakespeare Association Bulletin,* XIX (1944), 165 and note 13, and Cleanth Brooks, *Modern Poetry and the Tradition,* pp. 27–28. Cf. G. Wilson Knight, *The Wheel of Fire,* p. 189 and note. Cf. note 16, *infra.* Stoll opposes such readings ("Symbolism in Shakespeare," pp. 16 ff.).

16 Edmund puns on tumescence; thus his prayer becomes phallic ritual.

17 It need hardly be said that, whereas the language and other elements of the play which we are observing in this chapter are used specifically to identify the animal in man, the definition of man-as-human is the function of the play as a whole: the human being as such may be saved by devotion, discipline, sacrifice. But there are also several passages which comment directly on the nature of man. Kent, disguised after his exile, tells Lear that he is "A man" (I.iv, 11)—the same term by which Edgar refers to him in V.iii, 208; he can obey "authority" (I.iv, 32) and serve it vigorously, as appears in his treatment of Oswald. In contrast: ". . . a tailor made thee" (II.ii, 59–60), Oswald is told by Kent. Another aspect of manliness is suggested by Edgar's reply to Gloucester's "A man may rot even here"; Edgar says, "Men must endure/

Their going hence . . ." (V.ii, 8–10). Such lines as these are in effective contrast with a speech of the Captain to whom Edmund gives written orders, not yet disclosed, to kill Cordelia. The Captain says, "I cannot draw a cart, nor eat dried oats;/ If it be man's work, I'll do't" (V.iii, 38–39). How well this amplifies the animal pattern. The Captain will not do animal's work or eat like an animal—but he will murder Cordelia. The episode makes a fine ironic comment on manliness. Furthermore, we should connect it with the scene in which Goneril speaks of Albany as "cowish" (see note 13, *supra*) : in the same passage she both calls him "Milk-liver'd man!" (IV.ii, 50) and sneers contemptuously, "Marry, your manhood mew!" (68) Clearly her view of manliness, like the Captain's, allows no room for moral or spiritual quality.

Two references should be made at this point. First, Goneril's and Regan's conception of manliness is remarkably like that of Lady Macbeth, which is discussed in Chapter II of Mr. Brooks's *The Well Wrought Urn.* Second, Goneril's attitude to Albany shows how completely she has missed his quality: though he can call her, "self-cover'd thing" (IV.ii, 62; clothes pattern), she can toss at him the insults I have quoted above and can say, also, that he "hast not in thy brows an eye discerning/ Thine honour from thy suffering" (52–53). She, who thinks he is blind, is really the one who does not see. This failure to appreciate Albany and its fatal results for the evil characters, as well as the general importance of Albany in the play, are excellently discussed by J. W. Mackail, *The Approach to Shakespeare* (Oxford, 1930), pp. 78 ff.

[18] Animal imagery is occasionally used to qualify particular situations, especially to represent stupidity. ". . . thou bor'st thine ass on thy back o'er the dirt," the Fool tells Lear (I.iv, 177–78) ; and says ironically of himself, "May not an ass know when the cart draws the horse?" (244) In the next scene he tells Lear the fable I have already quoted—that the snail knows enough not to give his house away to his daughters (I.v, 30 ff.). Later he invents another ironic fable for Kent: "We'll set thee to school to an ant, to teach thee there's no labouring i' th' winter" (II.iv, 68–69). He has already used *winter* as a metaphor for hard times or decline of fortune: "Winter's not gone yet, if the wild geese fly that way" (II.iv, 46–47).

[19] We should also note how the word *necessity* anticipates the use of *need* by both Regan and Lear later in the scene (II.iv, 266, 267, 274). For a full discussion of this matter see the next section, The Condition of Man: Chorus, p. 107, and Chapter VII, *infra.*

[20] Various critics, including Granville-Barker (*op. cit.,* p. 286), speak of Lear's hundred retainers as being a burden, and there is an occasional critical willingness to accept Goneril's description of their behavior as literally accurate. Perhaps from one point of view it is perfectly sound to conceive of the retainers thus; yet such a conception should not get out of hand. At most, it illustrates the complexity with which Shakespeare is presenting the situation—giving it two sides instead of oversimplifying it. But the most important

315

point is the sisters' absolute failure to comprehend, or unwillingness to admit, the scale of values by which the retainers are justified. Perhaps the fact that the retainers are a nuisance, if they are a nuisance, has not so much the effect of justifying Goneril and Regan in their objections—as it seems to do for some critics—as of underscoring their false system of values: only the immediate, local, physical, material convenience has meaning for them. To understand a symbol when there are concrete discomforts attendant upon the presence of the symbol is the real duty of the authorities upon whom a society depends—and, for that matter, of private individuals.

The Holinshed account itself gives a clue as to how the retainers were to be understood. When Lear escapes to France, Cordelia sends him money to buy clothes "and to reteine a certein number of seruants that might attende vpon him in honorable wise, as apperteined to the estate which he had borne: . . ." (Furness, p. 385).

21 *Op. cit.*, pp. 26 ff. We should also recall, in this connection, Chambers' demonstration that Shakespeare changed the traditional Cordelia story in order *not* to have her die by despair; Shakespeare seems bent upon denying, in every way, the validity of despair. We shall come to other evidence later. See also Gervinus, pp. 633–34.

22 G. Wilson Knight remarks that in *Lear* "the suffering of mankind is sublimated into a noble, stoic destiny." He argues that it is a mistake to regard the play "as in essence pessimistic" because "humanity is shown as intrinsically grand" and "there is purpose and a noble destiny." Again, "High tragedy and cynicism are incompatible." These remarks appear in *Myth and Miracle: An Essay on the Mystic Symbolism of Shakespeare* (London, 1929), pp. 7–8.

NOTES FOR CHAPTER V

HEAR, NATURE, HEAR

1 Professor Eric Voegelin has pointed out to me that the conceptual split in the treatment of nature is comparable to the distinction between *nomos* and *physis* which appears first among the pre-Socratics. Lear's Nature, as well as Gloucester's, is comparable to *nomos*, law, that is, the law of the whole; Edmund calls simply upon *physis* and wants to throw out *nomos* as the "plague of custom." I am indebted, in my development of the chapter, to Professor Voegelin's elucidation of this point.

Different critics comment on Shakespeare's use of nature. Gervinus says, loosely, "Special weight is laid upon the fact that it is a heathen time; nature is the goddess of Lear as well as of Edmund; chance reigns above, power and force below" (*op. cit.*, p. 619). G. Wilson Knight notices the large part which nature has in the scenes and language of the drama, and he connects the nature theme with the animal imagery (*The Wheel of Fire*, pp. 147 ff.). He makes the interesting point that man is turned back to nature in his purgatorial experience (p. 198). But he seems to me to overstress the point that the play is "naturalistic"; and he sees in it "movement from civilization" (p. 220) that I do not believe the evidence will sustain. This I hope my coming discussion will make clear; we quote virtually the same series of passages, but my stress is quite different from his.

[2] Edmund speaks of Edgar's "nature" (I.ii, 196) and uses the phrase "despite of mine own nature" (V.iii, 244). Cf. also II.i, 117 (Cornwall on Edmund), II.ii, 82 (Kent on lords), II.ii, 104 (Cornwall on Kent), and I.i, 238 (France on Cordelia).

[3] Regan says to Lear, ". . . you are old!/ Nature in you stands on the very verge/ Of her confine" (II.iv, 148–50). Cf. IV.vi, 39 (Gloucester on himself), and IV.iv, 12 (the Doctor on Lear).

[4] There is excellent irony in the way in which Edmund's use of the term is repeated in Gloucester's exhortation just after he has been blinded, "Edmund, enkindle all the sparks of nature/ To quit this horrid act" (III.vii, 86–87). But this is not Edmund's real view of Nature, as we shall see.

[5] II.iv, 109 (Lear) and III.vi, 103 (Kent on Lear).

[6] This is the first suggestion of the endurance theme. A little later Lear says, "Pour on; I will endure" (III.iv, 18); and then there are Gloucester's resolve, "I'll bear/ Affliction" (IV.vi, 75–76) and Edgar's aphorism, "Men must endure/ Their going hence" (V.ii, 9–10). But in the development of this theme the words are relatively few and therefore carry less weight than the actions of characters themselves—characters who do endure what their choices have brought upon them and are not permitted to compromise, sell out, or despair. As we have said in Chapter IV, the presentation of man's capacity to endure is one of Shakespeare's ways of contrasting the humanity of man with the animality of man.

[7] It has been suggested to me that Lear means his "natural kindness." Possibly so. But the phrase still is consistent with the other quotations in this section: they all show, or suggest, some sort of departure from a "natural" condition of things.

[8] Miss Spurgeon speaks of Shakespeare's fear of the "disruption of the social order, for the frame of human society . . . seems to him . . . to have a mystical significance, to be one with a higher law, and to partake of the same nature as the mysterious agency by which the order of the heavens, the stars, planets and the sun himself is determined" (*op. cit.*, pp. 75–76). Knight says that the tragedies are "addressed to a minute analysis of disorder in all its forms" (*The Shakespearian Tempest*, p. 267), and says that in Lear evil is regarded as "a defacing of 'nature'" (*The Wheel of Fire*, p. 202). Spencer has a good section on the play's stress upon violation of natural law and of the

order of nature (*op. cit.*, pp. 142 ff.). That King Lear, in its constant implications of the existence of a cosmic order, was in harmony with its times is
indicated by E. M. W. Tillyard's *The Elizabethan World Picture* (New York,
1944), which is devoted largely to a definition of the terms in which that order
was realized. Tillyard devotes his second chapter (pp. 7 ff.) to a discussion of
the fact that order was taken for granted in Shakespeare's day. In the drama,
therefore, the conception is rarely given direct expression, but is always implied. What Tillyard says of the general situation is exactly borne out by
King Lear. See also Tillyard's *Shakespeare's History Plays* (New York,
1946) pp. 7–20. Cf. Lily B. Campbell's statement that Shakespeare "had a
definite, fundamental conception of universal law" (*Shakespeare's Histories*
[Huntington Library, 1947], p .7).

Dowden says, "We feel throughout the play that evil is abnormal; a curse
which brings down destruction upon itself; that it is without any long career;
that evil-doer is at variance with evil-doer" (*op. cit.*, p. 239). Cf. Spencer,
Chapter I, "Man in Nature: the Optimistic Theory," and Chapter II, "Man
in Nature: the Renaissance Conflict."

[9] *Op. cit.*, pp. 338 ff. "This rest might yet have balm'd thy broken sinews,"
Kent says to Lear later (III.vi, 104). Again at Lear's death it is Kent who
says, "He hates him/ That would upon the rack of this tough world/ Stretch
him out longer" (V.iii, 313–15). Albany, who earlier threatens to Goneril "to
dislocate and tear/ Thy flesh and bones" (IV.ii, 65–66), speaks at the end
about "the gor'd state" (V.iii, 320). An unusual number of passages refer to
the breaking of hearts. Early in the play Gloucester says, ". . . my old heart
is crack'd, it's crack'd" (II.i, 92), and Lear insists that before he will weep,
his heart "Shall break into a hundred thousand flaws" (II.iv, 288). Act V is
full of broken hearts. Albany swears to Edgar, "Let sorrow split my heart if
ever I/ Did hate thee, . . ." (V.iii, 177–78). Edgar exclaims, "O that my
heart would burst!" (182) He describes Gloucester's death, "But his flaw'd
heart/ . . . / Burst smilingly" (196–99), and says of Kent, ". . . the strings
of life/ Began to crack" (216–17). At Lear's death Kent cries, "Break, heart;
I prithee break" (312). In this world of actual and imaged injury, the first
suggestion of a physical hurt is Edmund's self-inflicted stab wound when he
is persuading Edgar to run away from Gloucester (II.i, 36). How ironic is
the contrast between this false injury and the real ones which are to follow.
Cf. note 11, *infra.*

[10] *Natural* is a pun of course: "illegitimate" and "acting according to the
order of things." There is an ironic echo of Gloucester's phrase a little later
when Edmund, referring to his betrayal of the Gloucester who has so praised
him, pretends to some misgiving about his "nature" giving way to his "loyalty"
(III.v, 4–5, 23). It is even more ironic, perhaps, that Gloucester seems to be
praising Edmund for illegitimacy as if it were morally sustaining, whereas,

it will become clear, the begetting of an illegitimate son is to be understood as one of the moral causes of Gloucester's later disasters.

11 Miss Spurgeon comments several times on Shakespeare's use of the imagery of disease (*op. cit.*, pp. 129 ff., 160).

Throughout the play there is a slight but persistent pattern of disease imagery which collaborates with the nature-passages and the injury pattern in suggesting a violation of the fundamental order of things. Disease—including madness, naturally—is an "oppression of nature"; yet, with ironic appropriateness, something to which nature is liable. The passage just quoted in the text ("thou art . . . a disease . . . in my flesh") is an echo of a line by Kent in Act I; in fact, in this later passage Lear gives further substance to Kent's ironic exclamation, "Kill thy physician, and the fee bestow/ Upon the foul disease" (I.i, 166-67). Later, the thoughts suggested by the Fool's derisive words are a "pestilent gall" to Lear (I.iv, 127). When Cornwall and Regan at first refuse to see him, Lear exclaims ironically, "They are sick?" (II.iv, 89)—and the reader is aware of a greater sickness than Lear yet suspects. The irony of the situation is heightened when Lear pulls himself up and in the lines beginning "May be he is not well" (II.iv, 106) tries to excuse Cornwall's discourtesy. Lear's madness, which on one level is a symbol of a world out of order, is carefully identified with the disease pattern. "Let me have surgeons;/ I am cut to th' brains," says Lear (IV.vi, 196-97); in place of Kent, the "physician" whom he "killed" in Act I, there is an actual physician present (IV.vii); Cordelia hopes her lips will give him "medicine" (IV.vii, 27). The meaning pattern described here might also be approached, to a considerable extent, through the figures of medicine and medication which are found in the play in some number.

Related to the disease pattern, and contributing like it to the sense of violated nature, is a small but traceable poison pattern. Of the sisters who loved him, Edmund says that they are as jealous of each other "as the stung/ Are of the adder" (V.i, 56-57)—a simile which is a nice anticipation of the fact that one does away with the other ("Sick, oh, sick," says Regan, V.iii, 95) by poison instead of some other means. But what gives Goneril's use of poison greater significance, and indeed makes it into another symbol of the whole situation in Britain, is Lear's line to Cordelia after he has awakened from his restoring sleep: "If you have poison for me, I will drink it" (IV.vii, 72). What he has had, so to speak, from the sisters, and now half-expects from Cordelia, one of them will give to the other (here is a parallel to the tracing in the sight imagery of the turning of evil upon itself). The giving of poison, which produces sickness and death, betokens an especial kind of moral sickness—the sickness of the man who does harm by deliberation rather than by passion. The final perfection of the poisoning theme is Goneril's line, after Regan's "Sick, oh, sick"—"If not, I'll ne'er trust medicine" (V.iii, 96). Her use of *medicine* exactly parallels Edmund's use of *nature;* there is the same ironic ambivalence. Goneril uses *medicine,* which normally connotes curing, to describe a murder; Edmund uses *nature,* which to the other characters connotes the order of things, to describe his violation of that order.

[12] Of the philosophic ideas which lie behind the phrase "all germens spill" there is an excellent discussion by Walter Clyde Curry, *Shakespeare's Philosophic Patterns* (Baton Rouge, 1937), pp. 29–49.

[13] Cf. II.iv, 165–66, 167 ff.

[14] For Marlowe's development, in *Tamburlaine,* of a concept of Nature whose variance from the "normal doctrine" of the Renaissance is somewhat like the variance of Edmund's doctrine from Lear's, see Paul H. Kocher, *Christopher Marlowe* (Chapel Hill, 1946), pp. 189–90.

[15] Hudson remarks shrewdly that Edmund "takes only so much of nature as will serve his turn" (*op. cit.,* p. 22).

[16] Cf. Dowden: "His mind is destitute of dread of the Divine Nemesis. Like Iago, like Richard III, he finds the regulating force of the universe in the *ego*—in the individual will" (*op. cit.,* p. 237). Cf. Enid Welsford's remark that the Goneril-Regan-Edmund universe is the Hobbes universe where every man's hand is against everyone (*The Fool,* p. 258) and her statement that the play as a whole gives the sense of the evil conduct as something "abnormal and unnatural" (p. 261).

[17] Cf. Dowden: ". . . the recognition of a moral law forces itself painfully upon his consciousness, and he makes his bitter confession: 'The wheel is come full circle, I am here' " (*op. cit.,* p. 240). In the same passage Dowden makes a good comment on Gloucester as being, "after the manner of the self-indulgent, prone to superstition; . . ." (*ibid.*).

[18] This conclusion indicates the ground of my disagreement with Knight's insistence, in *The Wheel of Fire,* on the "naturalism" of the play. Although he does admit that in time Lear moves away from a naturalistic theology, Knight does not distinguish between Lear's Nature and Edmund's. For him, Lear's Nature is simply the physical world rather than the *lex naturalis,* with its implication of the order of the whole, of a retributive principle. Knight treats Edmund as a rebel against civilization—a fruitful suggestion; but in describing Edmund merely as a primitive he misses entirely the rationalistic element in Edmund, an element which comes out of a late period of civilization (this aspect of Edmund I shall discuss in Chapter IX). Knight tries too hard to schematize Edmund as barbarian past, Lear as a combination of barbarous and human, and Cordelia as the ideal future, human perfection. He ignores the complicating elements in both Edmund and Cordelia. Knight has a strange fondness for Edmund; I find Granville-Barker's description of him as an "ignoble scoundrel" (p. 317) much closer to the point. Stoll's description of Edmund is also good (*Shakespeare and Other Masters,* pp. 277–80).

There is an excellent treatment of the nature theme in Msgr. F. C. Kolbe's *Shakespeare's Way* (London, 1930), pp. 130 ff. Msgr. Kolbe's theory is that the central idea in the play is Pietas, "the reciprocal fulfilment of all obligations arising from the ties of Nature,—those between the Creator and His creatures, between the citizen and his country, between man and wife, between parent and child, between friend and friend, between feudal lord and vassal, between employer and employed" (p. 131). He shows how the relations between father and child, the storm and Gloucester's astrology are integrated by this concept. And he makes a very shrewd observation about what I call the *tone* of the play: "The sole consolation in the double tragedy comes from those who are faithful to their piety" (p. 132).

In analyzing the plays Msgr. Kolbe is seeking their "design," and he is especially concerned with what he calls "dramatic colouring." What he finds, it seems to me, is structural patterns of the sort which the present essay is concerned with.

On Edmund's Nature Bradley is also good (*op. cit.*, pp. 301–302).

NOTES FOR CHAPTER VI

IF YOU DO LOVE OLD MEN

[1] This is given further development in the parent-child theme, to which a number of lines throughout the play contribute. When Gloucester says to Lear during the stormy night, "Our flesh and blood is grown so vile, my lord,/ That it doth hate what gets it" (III.iv, 150–51), and when Cordelia calls Lear "this child-changed father" (IV.vii, 17)—changed, that is, to a child (Cleanth Brooks suggests that the phrase is a pun which also includes the meaning, "changed by his child")—we have further contributions to the system of paradoxes upon which the play depends. Cf. Edgar's comment on Lear: "He childed as I fathered!" (III.vi, 116) Lear makes a number of references to his daughters' conduct as being a reversal of all expectations: what he believes to be his kindness has begotten unkindness. Here is another expression of the violation of the principles of Nature to which nearly all the characters subscribe. The counterparadox is that his unkindness to Cordelia seems to have begot kindness; or at least it has not killed kindness—Nature persists despite man's attacks upon it. The parent-child paradoxes are especially apparent in the Gloucester plot: again, apparent kindness begets treachery, and harshness fails to kill filial devotion: but, more conspicuously, the father, blinded, is reduced to the status of a child and is cared for by his own child, Edgar. This outcome, as we have seen in the discussion of the sight pattern, is ironically identical with the parent-child relationship which Edmund,

speaking to Gloucester, accused Edgar of scheming to bring about.

2 Cf. "Singe my white head!" (III.ii, 6), and the Gentleman's "tears his white hair" (III.i, 7).

3 This view is put forward earlier in the play, albeit with a sharply qualifying difference of tone. In kindly, if blunt, correction Kent had spoken: ". . . Lear is mad. What wouldst thou do, old man?" (I.i, 148) Lear himself speaks to his "Old fond eyes" (I.iv, 323)—fond because by weeping they tell Goneril that she has "power to shake my manhood thus" (I.iv, 319). Cf. also IV.vi, 97 ff.

4 Cf. her saying, a little later, ". . . these white flakes/ Had challeng'd pity of them" (IV.vii, 30–31), i.e., Goneril and Regan.

5 A little earlier Regan says, referring to Gloucester's beard, "So white, and such a traitor" (III.vii, 37). To her, age is a means of scoring off an enemy.

6 The concern of *King Lear* with the subject of justice has been observed by various critics,—e.g., Chambers, Spencer, Harbage. Chambers' comments are very interesting (pp. 32–34). The fullest discussion of the treatment of justice in the play is that of Knight, *The Wheel of Fire*, pp. 209 ff. Knight says the justice which is executed in the play is "natural justice." The applicability of the term depends upon the definition of *natural*, which, to my mind, Knight uses rather loosely.

7 There is a short but excellent comment on this fact in Ronald Peacock's *The Poet in the Theatre* (New York, 1946), p. 155. The comment comes in a good section on the relation between tragedy and morality.

8 This impression is enhanced by two lines which most editors regard as a reference to Doomsday: Kent's "Is this the promis'd end?" and Edgar's, "Or image of that horror?" (V.iii, 263–64)

NOTES FOR CHAPTER VII

LARGEST BOUNTY AND TRUE NEED

1 We need not, of course, pay attention to those episodes in which money or other valuables are simply considerations for services, e. g., IV.i, 65, 77–78; IV.iv, 10; IV.vi, 28–29, or evidence of status, e. g., III.i, 44–46. In the last-named passage Kent identifies his position by the contents of his purse. Thus he is in contrast with the King, whose situation he had underscored by his description of himself to Lear, ". . . as poor as the King" (I.iv, 20).

2 Cf. V.iii, 184.

3 Granville-Barker advances the interesting hypothesis that Shakespeare originally intended to make the plot turn on a quarrel over the divided property (*op. cit.*, I, 273, note 6).

⁴ If Lear's condition is pathological, a new problem—the defense of the play—comes up. For then we have, actually, drama of the sort Rymer found in Shakespeare: not tragedy, but a sociological treatise with a moral, "Kings should give up the throne before they lose their mental faculties," or even, in Lear's own words, "Age is unnecessary." The merely clinical approach to Lear betrays, without the awareness of the critics who use it, a characteristic weakness of that kind of positivist criticism: it can make no case for Lear— either for him as an old man or for him as the lord of a hundred knights— except a sentimental one. It ignores the fact that Lear acts in a representatively human way, that his conduct is morally significant, that he himself comes to understand it as such, and that a tremendous problem of values is involved. It is probably unnecessary to say more on this. As far as I know, no modern critic shares the passion of certain nineteenth-century critics for clinical analysis of Shakespearian characters.

⁵ Cf. Hudson: ". . . he at once forgets the thousand little daily acts that have insensibly wrought in him to love Cordelia most, and to expect most love from her" (*op. cit.*, p. 30).

⁶ The significance of the language used by Goneril and Regan, as well as Lear's error in interpreting the language, has been noted by innumerable critics. For some interesting early comments by Horn and Ulrici, the reader may consult Furness, pp. 451, 454–55.

⁷ See Chapter I, pp. 35–36.

⁸ Lear's misinterpretation of *bond* is roughly paralleled by Gloucester's being taken in by the words attributed to Edgar in the note forged by Edmund: "I begin to find an idle and fond bondage in the oppression of aged tyranny, . . ." (I.ii, 50–52). It is, of course, really Edmund who chafes under bondage, and he and Goneril and Regan who are faithful to no bonds.

⁹ We should notice, too, how the Fool leads Lear on to an ironic repetition of his earlier words. When Lear demands that Cordelia speak, the dialogue goes thus:

> *Cordelia.* Nothing, my lord.
> *Lear.* Nothing?
> *Cordelia.* Nothing.
> *Lear.* Nothing will come of nothing. Speak again. (I.i, 89–92)

In the later scene, after the Fool has recited a jingle, the dialogue is this:

> *Kent.* This is nothing, Fool.
> *Fool.* Then 'tis like the breath of an unfee'd lawyer, you gave me nothing for't. Can you make no use of nothing, nuncle?
> *Lear.* Why, no, boy; nothing can be made out of nothing. (I.iv, 141–46)

There is possibly a pun involved in that a great many things have come from Cordelia's *nothing:* her *nothing* is the nonparticipation which in effect turns the world over to her sisters. In another sense, Lear has learned how nothing comes of nothing. His words to Cordelia meant, "No large assurances of love, no property"; what he has learned is, "No love, no respect and consideration and no keeping of word." He has learned something about the nature of nothing: that words cannot make nothing into something. There is a more elaborate discussion of the relationship between these passages in Empson, *Seven Types of Ambiguity*, pp. 59–60.

10 Cf. Kent's similar speech to Cornwall, II.ii, 134–39.

11 Kreider makes the interesting point that, in conformity with the practice of Shakespeare's villains generally, Goneril and Regan insist upon their legal rights and move within the letter of the law (*op. cit.*, pp. 105–106). For Kreider's view of the source of evil in Edmund and the sisters, see pp. 58–61.

12 There is no point in belaboring Tate's version of *Lear*, the bad taste of which is common knowledge. But for one example of Tate's extraordinary failure to see what the play is doing: he cut out the very important "Reason not the need" speech, with its synthesis of patterns and its indication of a new insight in Lear, and substituted for it this noisy nonsense:

> Bloud! Fire! here—Leprosies and bluest Plagues!
> Room, room, for Hell to belch her Horrors up
> And drench the *Circes* in a stream of Fire;
> Heark how th' Infernals eccho to my rage
> Their whips and Snakes.—

13 The relationship between Lear and his evil daughters is partly implied by a remark of Wyndham Lewis about Shakespeare's "colossi" to the effect that "they have always to be overcome by trivial opponents who substitute a poor and vulgar thing for the great and *whole* [italics mine] thing that they have destroyed" (*The Lion and the Fox*, p. 188).

NOTES FOR CHAPTER VIII

REASON IN MADNESS

1 In a sense Lear's madness may be said to expiate a defect of understanding, just as Gloucester's blindness expiates a defect of sight. Yet the expiation is paradoxical, for Lear comes to better understanding, and Gloucester to better insight, than he had before. To put the matter in another way: Lear and Gloucester have too little grasp of the "practical understanding," whereas their ambitious children have too much; but the parents prove, so to speak, their tragic quality by expiatory experiences which never come to the children. The parents repent; the children—except for faint traces of death-bed repentance in Edmund—do not. Various critics, notably Knight and Chambers, have spoken of the purgatorial quality of the experiences of Lear and Gloucester.

2 For other such examples of interplay and balance among characters in

Lear, see Stoll, *op. cit.*, pp. 42–43; for possible sources for all three types of mental abnormality which Shakespeare uses in this group, see Roland M. Smith, "King Lear and the Merlin Tradition," *MLQ*, VII (1946), 153–74.

³ Hudson speaks of "the effect and progress of his [Lear's] passion in redeveloping his intellect" (*op. cit.*, p. 31), of Lear's "whirling tumult and anarchy of thoughts, which, till imagination has time to work, chokes down his utterance." Hudson continues, "Then comes the inward, tugging conflict, deep as life, which gradually works up his imaginative forces, and kindles them to a preternatural resplendence. . . . Thus his terrible energy of thought and speech, as soon as imagination rallies to his aid, grows naturally from the struggle of his feelings—" (p. 32). Wyndham Lewis generalizes that in Elizabethan tragedy, when a man "becomes *mad*, he shows a strange tendency to become what we usually call a philosopher" (*The Lion and the Fox*, p. 249). In *English Pastoral Poetry* (New York, 1938), William Empson remarks, in discussing the Elizabethan attitude to lunatics, "they had some positive extra-human quality; they might say things profoundly true" (p. 49).

⁴ Cf. Empson: ". . . the Fool acts as a sort of divided personality externalized from the king" (*Seven Types of Ambiguity*, p. 60).

⁵ Cf. Lear's later remark, "I am even/ The natural fool of fortune" (IV.vi, 194–95).

⁶ The ablest discussion of the role of the Fool which I know is in Miss Welsford's *The Fool*, pp. 253–70. Her analysis of Lear, which I did not come upon until I had finished my own, sketches some of the paradoxes which I am treating in detail in this essay. If one extreme in the commentaries upon the play has been the dismissal of the Fool with extravagant praise but without much perception of his functional value, Miss Welsford restores the balance by making the Fool the functional center of the play. I feel, however, that the structural paradoxes would be clear even if there were no Fool, though the absence of the Fool would certainly weaken the system of paradoxes upon which the play relies. The paradoxes developed or suggested by the sight, clothing, nature, and justice patterns, although various lines of the Fool may aid in their development (this is especially true of the sight pattern), all are worked out without overt reliance upon the concepts of folly that appear in the play; and, too, the Fool disappears when there are still more than two acts to be developed, and when very significant aspects of the plot are still to be resolved. But this statement of disagreement is largely concerned with the matter of stress, for Miss Welsford's grasp of the role of the Fool and of the general direction of the play is brilliant. Her knowledge of the fool tradition is especially valuable in her discussion of the King-Fool counterpoint, and it seems to me that, in bringing to bear upon her interpretation the relationship of the Fool to the Christian tradition, she sheds real light upon the play. Her answer to Wyndham Lewis' reading of the play is effective. And while she thinks—and in this I concur—that the play does finally suggest solutions to human

325

enigmas, she is immensely right in her statement that "Shakespeare provokes questions and reveals ambiguities" (p. 257).

⁷ Miss Welsford has a very interesting analysis of the passage (*op. cit.*, pp. 255–56). For a different interpretation see Bradley, *op. cit.*, p. 460. Granville-Barker objects to a Fool "etherealized by the higher criticism" (*op. cit.*, p. 311).

⁸ Several times the Fool comments upon the fate of fools with respect to the weather. "He that has and a little tiny wit" must be resigned to the worst, he says, "For the rain it raineth every day" (III, ii, 74–77). The storm is more than a storm: it is also "the rainy day" to which fools are especially liable because they invite bad fortune. Cf. Chapter IV, note 18.

⁹ The word *fool* is given still another meaning in the passage in which the Fool describes the folly of "lords and great men," who do not let him be "altogether fool." He adds, "If I had a monopoly out, they would have part on't. And ladies too, they will not let me have all the fool to myself; they'll be snatching" (I.iv, 165–70). Aside from the sexual innuendo in the second sentence (which anticipates the concluding lines of Act I—I.v, 54–55—often considered of doubtful authenticity), the Fool is here commenting not on the problem of getting on in the world but simply on the folly or triviality of great people generally. For once the word is used in a common acceptation.

¹⁰ Cf. Stoll, *op. cit.*, p. 43.

¹¹ Bradley makes the point that the sacrifice upon which gods throw incense (V.iii, 20–21)—that is, Lear's renunciation of the world and decision to seek truth quietly with Cordelia—might "never have been offered but for the knowledge that came to Lear in his madness" (*op. cit.*, p. 290).

¹² Innumerable comments have been made upon the insight which Lear shows in his madness. Miss Welsford says he learns that there is no poetic justice (*op. cit.*, p. 265). Knight says Lear shows a "penetrating insight into man's nature" (*The Wheel of Fire*, p. 211). Van Doren's comment is apposite (*op. cit.*, 245). Granville-Barker's comment, lengthier than most, is perhaps the best of all (*op. cit.*, pp. 293–98). He recognizes that the mad scenes "belong to a larger synthesis" (p. 293). He points out specifically how Lear's remarks on justice (IV.vi, 160 ff.) echo the mock-trial scene in III.vi (p. 297). For earlier comments on Lear's madness, see Furness, pp. 425, 428 (Hallam), 421 (Lamb).

¹³ IV.vi, 83–93. Lear's disjointed remarks refer to counterfeiting, the nature-art controversy, conscription, archery, catching mice, challenges, falconry.

¹⁴ See Furness, p. 281.

¹⁵ The suggestion of secret evil which runs through the passage is reminiscent of another speech of Lear's, that in which he thinks of the storm as carrying a special threat to those who conceal guilt (III.ii, 49 ff.).

¹⁶ Cf. Kent to Lear: ". . . where is the patience now/ That you so oft have boasted to retain?" (III.vi, 61–62) ; Albany to Lear: "Pray, sir, be patient"

(I.iv, 283); Edgar to Gloucester, "Bear free and patient thoughts" (IV.vi, 79). This list is not exhaustive.

17 In minor characters we see thematic echoes of the major lines of action. Just as Oswald is a rather pale imitation of his superiors, so the First Servant, who fatally wounds Cornwall, acts precisely as do Kent and Cordelia—with an immediate, instinctive opposition to the brutal injustices which he sees his superiors doing to Gloucester (III.vii. 72 ff.). Like them, he leaps to action in a cause which he knows cannot be "successful," at least in any terms which might include him. Unlike them, of course, he does not have even a fighting chance. But the tradition in which he has been nurtured holds none the less strongly for him.

18 Cf. Bradley, *op. cit.,* p. 308. Kent acknowledges that he had "more man than wit about me" (II.iv, 42).

19 Cf. Willard Farnham in *The Medieval Heritage of Elizabethan Tragedy* (Berkeley, 1936): "But spiritually Lear rises through the course of his anguish to a wisdom which he has never before approached, including a sympathetic appreciation of suffering among the world's unfortunates and a full realization of Cordelia's love" (p. 451). Cf. pp. 442–43.

20 To their fellows in the world which the play represents, their unlikeliness must have seemed a great deal more irreparable than it does in retrospect. The conventions are much less strong and unbreakable when one is on the outside looking in. To be in the Goneril-Regan world must have meant being under tremendous pressure to accept it and its values—values which it is easy to condemn from a distance. It was a very shrewd piece of playwriting to present men like Gloucester and Albany as slow in seeing the truth.

21 In contrast with the world of direct action of Kent and Cordelia, whose wisdom is a relatively unformulated wisdom of deed.

NOTES FOR CHAPTER IX

MADNESS IN REASON

1 This is not to say, of course, that they do not think. But they do not think about action, for their responses are automatic; nor do they think much about the results of action, for their values are sure, and with them the act is the thing. They may reflect, and Kent does have some reflective capacity. But his reflections have rather the manner of asides than of formal evaluations of experience, like those of Lear and Edgar, or of imaginative leaps into major truths like those of the Fool. This judgment of him is sustained, I believe, by the three speeches of his which have a somewhat philosophic cast: II.ii, 167 ff.; III.ii, 42 ff.; IV.iii, 34 ff. Always he is conspicuously engaged in action.

2 See pp. 60 and 96.

[3] Cleanth Brooks has quoted Robert Penn Warren as saying that "all of Shakespeare's villains are rationalists" (*The Well Wrought Urn,* p. 40). In a personal letter, Mr. Warren has amplified his statement thus: ". . . evil in Shakespeare is always a manifestation of the special combination of the view of man-as-nature (man-as-animal, appetite as all) plus the pragmatic intelligence (pride-in-the-non-animal)." As my discussion shows, I am much indebted to his theory.

[4] It is possible that this relationship between father and daughters is implied in a speech of Albany to Goneril which I have already quoted in another connection:

> That nature which contemns its origin
> Cannot be bordered certain in itself.
> She that herself will sliver and disbranch
> From her material sap, perforce must wither
> And come to deadly use. (IV.ii, 32–36)

In general, of course, what is involved is the idea of unnaturalness, of the fatal result of being separated from nature. Jennens' annotation, however, suggests the possibility of an additional meaning: ". . . it is separated from a communication with that which supplies it with the very identical matter by which it (the branch) lives, and of which it is composed" (Furness, p. 241). Goneril is "slivered" from her father: she derives what she is from him, but there is much in him that she does not have. That is the cause of her downfall. She has his "reason," not his imagination.

[5] Hudson says of Goneril and Regan: "Whatever of soul these beings possess is all in the head: they have no heart to guide or inspire their understanding, and but enough of understanding to seize occasion, and frame excuses for their heartlessness" (*op. cit.,* p. 16). Granville-Barker speaks of their "passionless appraisement of evil" and of their being "level-headed and worldly-wise" (*op. cit.,* pp. 301, 302).

[6] They state as a general characteristic, in terms of which they must act, the quality which Kent regards as an aberration that he must fight against. He has said to Lear: "And in thy best consideration check/ This hideous rashness" (I.i, 152–53).

[7] In the scenes in which they deprive Lear of his followers. See Chapter VII, p. 170.

[8] See Chapter V, pp. 123 ff.

[9] Hudson has a good paragraph on Edmund. He describes Edmund as "so discerning of error in what he does not like; in which case the subtilties of the understanding lead to the rankest unwisdom" (*op. cit.,* p. 23). Dowden says much the same and quotes an apposite phrase from *Romola:* "the hard bold scrutiny of imperfect thought into obligations which can never be proved to have any sanctity in the absence of feeling" (*op. cit.,* p. 237).

[10] In a personal letter Leo Kirschbaum suggests that Edmund, dying in

the midst of the good people, "takes on a protective coloration." I am indebted
to this suggestion, which seems to me to define exactly the sentimental element in the latter-day Edmund.

NOTES FOR CHAPTER X

THE GODS ARE JUST

[1] Various critics have commented upon the treatment of the gods in *Lear*.
Spencer has noted that the "good" characters in the play invoke the gods and
that the others do not (*op. cit.*, pp. 146–48). But he accepts Gloucester's "As
flies to wanton boys" speech as a final statement of man's relation to the
gods. This interpretation is refuted by Chambers (*op. cit.*, pp. 26 ff.). Knight
is at first inclined to belittle the importance of the various invocations of the
gods and to argue that whatever religion does appear in the play is naturalistic. But he sees a change occurring in the course of the play: Lear, he
says, achieves a "less naturalistic theology" (*The Wheel of Fire*, pp. 204–208).
Bradley makes the point that religious references are more frequent in *Lear*
than is usual in the tragedies (*op. cit.*, pp. 271 ff.) and shows how the sense
of justice held by the characters of the play is dependent upon their belief
in divine agencies. Wyndham Lewis keeps calling Shakespeare a "nihilist"
(e.g., *The Lion and the Fox*, pp. 179–80). In this passage on Shakespeare's
view of the gods, Lewis takes issue with Bradley, but even if seen only
through Lewis' quotation of him, Bradley has the better insight into Shakespeare. There are, however, many good things in Lewis' book.

[2] Kent's addition of "By Juno" to Lear's "By Jupiter" also echoes an exchange of theirs a few lines previously, when Kent first adds a female element
to a remark of Lear's:

> *Lear.* What's he that hath so much thy place mistook
> To set thee here?
> *Kent.*   It is both he and she—
> Your son and daughter.   (II.iv, 12–14)

[3] Bradley somewhat diffidently questions the religiousness of Kent and
says that he "refers" to the gods "less often than to fortune or the stars" (*op.
cit.*, p. 310). Unless *refers* be taken in the narrowest possible sense, this statement is inaccurate. Kent makes three references to fortune (II.ii, 164, 180;
V.iii, 280), none of them inconsistent with his belief in the gods, and one to
the stars (IV.iii, 34–37), which is a method of expressing incredulity rather
than belief. To the record of Kent's religiousness we might add his exclamation when Lear enters carrying the dead Cordelia. "Is this the promis'd end?"
(V.iii, 263)—evidently a reference to the Day of Judgment.

[4] These pointed comments on the death of evil characters can be read as

giving especial reassurance of divine justice, since the deaths come almost as the fulfillment of prophecies. After the blinding of Gloucester there are these speeches:

> 2. *Serv.* I'll never care what wickedness I do,
> If this man come to good.
> 3. *Serv.*   If she live long,
> And in the end meet the old course of death,
> Women will all turn monsters.   (III.vii, 99–102)

The expectation of justice implied in these words of the humble is another detail in the development of the theme of The World.

[5] Bradley says he is the most religious person in the play (*op. cit.*, p. 296). Granville-Barker quotes Edgar's "let's exchange charity" and calls him "a very Christian gentleman" (*op. cit.*, p. 321). Edgar also refers to fortune (cf. note 3), as does Albany (V.i, 46; V.iii, 41). A small point, but a significant one, is the implication of Edgar's third speech at the beginning of the play. He says to Edmund, "How long have you been a sectary astronomical?" (I.ii, 164) Edgar too scorns astrology, but unlike Edmund, he retains his piety.

[6] Bradley notes his superstitiousness (p. 295). So far as I know, only Hudson has pointed out that superstitiousness is evidence of a religious temperament (*op. cit.*, p. 23).

[7] It may be worth noting that Shakespeare's use of a non-Christian theological framework permitted a venturesome sympathetic exploring—as distinguished from an acceptance—of possible heretical attitudes that might have been prohibitively difficult in a Christian framework. Cf. Dowden, *op. cit.*, p. 240.

[8] Evidently he feels that the oath is binding, for later he says to Burgundy, "Nothing! I have sworn; I am firm" (I.i, 248). It is possible that his oath holds him to a course which even now he would be willing to abjure. Just twelve lines earlier he has said to Cordelia, "Better thou/ Hadst not been born than not t'have pleas'd me better" (236–37). *Pleas'd me* takes the problem into the realm of personal accommodation and out of the realm of high principle.

[9] *Op. cit.*, p. 292.

[10] Cf. "There's such divinity doth hedge a king."

[11] This remark fits into the context very successfully. Edmund also uses *unnatural* hypocritically (52) and suggests to Gloucester that Edgar has been "conjuring the moon" (41)—an appeal to Gloucester's astrological habit of mind. The thunder as punishment anticipates Lear's speech at III.ii, 49 ff.

[12] Edmund, of course, is not compelled to be the detector. Ironically, in saying what "good form" demands on this occasion, Edmund comes very close to using the same kind of deterministic thought which he scorned in attacking Gloucester's astrology. Cf. Chapter XI, Modes of Understanding.

NOTES FOR CHAPTER XI

THIS GREAT STAGE

[1] Christian ideas, traditions, attitudes, or practices are implied by the constant questioning of the values of this world, the belief in divine justice (justice pattern), the expiatory suffering of Lear and Gloucester, the rejection of Gloucester's despair (IV.vi), the dualistic theory of man which is developed by the nature pattern and directly expressed by Lear (IV.vi, 126 ff.), the nature pattern generally and its hint of the *lex naturalis*, the possible defense of free will in Edmund's attack on astrology (I.ii), the presentation of the repentant spirit in Gloucester (III.vii ff.) and Lear (IV.iii, 43 ff.), the humility of Lear and Gloucester and their compassion for the poor (III.iv; IV.i), the attribution of insight and wisdom to the miserable and outcast (the madness pattern; cf. also V.iii, 15 ff.), the specific renunciation of the world (V.iii, 20–21), the continual stress on patience (e.g., IV.vi, 182), the resemblance of Gloucester's attempted suicide to the temptation of Christ (IV.vi), the resemblance of Lear's crown of nettles and weeds to Christ's crown of thorns (IV.vi), the reflections of the Ten Commandments and the Seven Deadly Sins (III.iv), Edgar's charity (V.iii, 166), the references to Doomsday (V.iii, 263–64; cf. I.ii, 192; cf. Bradley, *op. cit.*, p. 328, note 1), Lear's use of the principle of "Let him who is without blame cast the first stone" (IV.vi, 164 ff.). Cf. the Gentleman's description of Cordelia: "There she shook/ The holy water from her heavenly eyes" (IV.iii, 31–32). Miss Welsford stresses the Christian quality of fool literature, and in her discussion of the Fool in *Lear* she constantly refers to Christianity (*op. cit.*, pp. 241, 254, 263, 268–70). In *Shakespeare's Biblical Knowledge* (London, 1935), Richmond Noble lists fifteen passages in *Lear* which are possibly of Biblical origin (pp. 229–322). Willard Farnham points out how the play is reminiscent of medieval tragedy (*op. cit.*, pp. 451–52).

In this connection the reader should consult especially S. L. Bethell's excellent study, *Shakespeare and the Popular Dramatic Tradition* (London, 1944), pp. 52–61, as well as the shorter passages dealing with *King Lear*. Bethell establishes the relationship between the treatment of nature, the treatment of the problem of evil, and the religious atmosphere of the play.

[2] For some very interesting comments on Shakespeare himself as caught

between two ages (chivalry and commerce; chivalry and positivist nature) see Wyndham Lewis, *The Lion and the Fox*, pp. 11, 22–23, 284–85. Miss Welsford has a shrewd comment to the effect that the popularity of the Fool in the Renaissance was itself evidence of a crumbling world (*op. cit.*, p. 241). For brief comments on the sense of the passing of an era which possessed the tragic dramatists of the first few years of the seventeenth century, see Una M. Ellis-Fermor, *The Jacobean Drama: An Interpretation* (London, 1936), Chapter I (especially pp. 1–4 and note, and pp. 20 ff.), and pp. 258–59.

[3] Something like this is implied by Edgar's concluding lines, ". . . we that are young/ Shall never see so much, nor live so long" (V.iii, 325–26). Two speeches early in the play possibly fit in with this interpretation. Gloucester, worried about the breakup of Lear's kingdom, remarks, "We have seen the best of our time" (I.ii, 121–22). And when Goneril is talking about the instability of her father, may her words not also reflect a kind of sense of superiority to a passing epoch? She says, "The best and soundest of his time hath been but rash; . . ." (I.i, 298). The new era intends to exclude rashness.

[4] *Op. cit.*, p. 300.

[5] Cf. Bradley, *op. cit.*, pp. 279, 304 (". . . the world . . . *is* convulsed by evil, and rejects it"), 325–27; and Dowden, *op. cit.*, pp. 202–203. Dowden makes the very good point that "a less robust spirit [than Shakespeare] would have permitted the dominant tone of the play to become an eager or pathetic wistfulness . . ." (p. 230). Harbage, who refers rather disparagingly to Bradley (*As They Liked It*, p. 120), seems to me to mistake Bradley's intention.

[6] It may be observed that, at the end, the most vividly imaginative characters do not survive: in a civilizational crisis, though humanity may retain or regain the capacity for achieving a high quality of life, the most highly organized sensibilities are likely to succumb to the racking stresses. Although Edgar and Albany have come to see things straight, they have neither the incisiveness of the Fool nor the comprehensive vision of Lear. They are best described, perhaps, as men of character and moralists, practical political moralists—the especial need of "the gor'd state."

[7] Cf. J. Dover Wilson, *The Essential Shakespeare* (Cambridge, 1942), pp. 124–27. In *Art and Artifice in Shakespeare* (Cambridge, 1934), Elmer E. Stoll points out that evil has not triumphed (p. 165). But he questions the judgment of Dowden and Bradley on the tone of the play (p. 164).

332

INDEX OF PASSAGES
REFERRED TO

The entries are arranged according to act, scene, and line numbers within each scene. Page numbers are in italics. Page numbers of fuller or more important discussions are in boldface.

INDEX OF SUBJECTS
AND NAMES

336